ONE SIGNAL PUBLISHERS

ATRIA

Also by Ann Larson

Can't Pay, Won't Pay:
The Case for Economic Disobedience and Debt Abolition

CLEANUP ON AISLE FIVE

Essential Work, Poverty Wages, and the View from Behind the Supermarket Register

ANN LARSON

ONE SIGNAL PUBLISHERS

ATRIA

New York Amsterdam/Antwerp London
Toronto Sydney/Melbourne New Delhi

ATRIA

An Imprint of Simon & Schuster, LLC
1230 Avenue of the Americas
New York, NY 10020

First One Signal Publishers/Atria Books hardcover edition June 2026

ONE SIGNAL PUBLISHERS/ATRIA BOOKS and colophon are registered trademarks of Simon & Schuster, LLC

Simon & Schuster strongly believes in freedom of expression and stands against censorship in all its forms. For more information, visit BooksBelong.com.

For information about special discounts for bulk purchases, please contact Simon & Schuster Special Sales at 1-866-506-1949 or business@simonandschuster.com.

The Simon & Schuster Speakers Bureau can bring authors to your live event. For more information or to book an event, contact the Simon & Schuster Speakers Bureau at 1-866-248-3049 or visit our website at www.simonspeakers.com.

Interior design by Davina Mock-Maniscalco

Manufactured in the United States of America

1 3 5 7 9 10 8 6 4 2

Library of Congress Control Number: 2026933576

ISBN 978-1-6680-9450-1
ISBN 978-1-6680-9452-5 (ebook)

Scan here to get book recommendations, exclusive offers, and more delivered to your inbox.

For the cashiers

Contents

CLEANUP
ON
AISLE FIVE

Cast of Colleagues

The following is a list of employee roles at the supermarket featured in this book in order of highest to lowest status.

The Executives worked out of the corporate office and were only rarely in the store.

Top Bosses worked out of offices on the upper level of the supermarket.

The Bankers collected cash and receipts each day and kept the store's accounts.

Managers were responsible for a single department, such as the deli or the produce section.

Stockers unloaded trucks and stocked shelves.

Security Guards were responsible for preventing shoplifting and keeping workers safe.

Supervisors had authority over cashiers, baggers, and cart collectors.

Department Employees worked in the bakery, produce, dairy, deli, or other areas.

Cashiers operated the registers and performed customer service.

INTRODUCTION

Welcome to Your Neighborhood Supermarket!

At the end of each opening shift at the Grocery Store (TGS) supermarket, I walked six blocks home on legs that felt like jelly after standing, walking, bending, and lifting for eight hours. I curled into a fetal position on the sofa in my studio apartment overlooking the park. By the time I woke up from a fitful sleep, and sometimes a nightmare where I was drowning in groceries, it was almost time for dinner. I might throw some black beans and cheese into a tortilla and watch whatever the Netflix algorithm recommended. I didn't have the energy to do more. An 11:00 p.m. bedtime was critical if I was opening the store again the next morning at 7:00.

On the nights I worked the late shift, I got home just before 11:00 and inhaled a peanut butter sandwich before collapsing into bed. By the end of my year of employment at TGS, I was a walking peanut butter sandwich. Being perpetually too tired to cook was one of the ironies of working at the supermarket. Another was that exhaustion made me less afraid of the pandemic that was sickening and killing people across the country at the time. Even in a store crowded with people, I thought about little else but getting to the end of my shift.

The day a man dropped his pants and took a shit on the floor was a turning point. I heard the news when I arrived at work one afternoon and ran into a colleague at the time clock. "Did you hear?" she asked and pointed to the floor outside the public restroom. "A guy took a dump right there." She was just sharing information, like any report an employee might give to a coworker. "We're short one cashier; there's a sale on lunch meat; a guy took a shit on the floor."

Based on the location of the offending shit, we both knew what had happened. The code to access the public restroom was printed on the bottom of every receipt and given out only to paying customers. It was common for people who weren't shoppers to wait outside the door so they could grab it when someone exited. But this time, no one had opened the door quickly enough.

When I got to my register, colleagues were discussing the incident. Some saw what happened as an unfortunate consequence of circumstances outside of the man's control. One said, "He was probably homeless and in an emergency situation." Others were furious that a customer had defiled our workplace. It felt like a personal affront. George, a security guard, asked which side of the split I was on.

"Everyone has to shit somewhere," I said, shrugging. It was my way of defending the man.

George was in the other camp. "A janitor had to clean it up," he snapped.

George had a point. He was saying that employees had to stay on guard because we never knew what unsavory task might be assigned next. We were employed in a nonunion store in Utah, a "right-to-work" state where legal barriers made worker organizing difficult. Without clear rules around roles and obligations, the next time, it could be any one of us bleaching the floors.

My response to the shitting incident was partly a result of the fact that I was new to the job and learning to navigate the store's culture. I had landed at TGS in the fall of 2020 after finding myself unemployed. Raised in a small town in Idaho, I had attended college in Utah. Later, I moved to New York City to attend graduate school in English at the City University.

After I graduated in 2009, I spent time looking for an academic job. In the meantime, I taught college courses part-time and sometimes worked as an office temp. After two years of rejections from colleges and universities, I had to face the reality that I was one of many educated people with virtually no chance of a future in their field.

In 2015, I cofounded an organization called the Debt Collective. My colleagues and I lobbied the federal government to cancel the student loans of borrowers who had attended scam for-profit colleges, eventually winning billions in loan relief.

Philanthropic support for the Debt Collective allowed me to earn a decent salary for a couple of years. But eventually funds for organizer salaries became harder to come by. Almost twenty years after arriving in New York, I was out of work. In the spring of 2020, I moved back to Utah to make a new start in middle age.

I moved into a downtown neighborhood that some called "transitional." A few years earlier, it had been the site of a homeless shelter and a drug market. But the shelter had recently been torn down to make room for new apartments. The area was now a mix of residents who lived in the run-down, low-rent buildings that had been there for decades and a few middle-class people who occupied the newer apartments. I paid $1,350 per month for a studio in one of the new buildings. While the weekly farmers market in the park below my apartment was a sign of gentrification, at night, the drug activity continued. A couple of blocks away, people were sleeping on the street. The good news was that I could walk to TGS to shop, a necessity since I could not afford a car.

Then the pandemic hit and the world stopped. I applied for jobs but received few responses from employers, rarely even a "thanks but no thanks." I felt luckier than others. Members of my family were reeling. My sister-in-law, a bookkeeper, was laid off with no promise of getting her position back. (Indeed, she was not rehired when the pandemic subsided and spent almost a year in unemployment limbo.) My brother, a bartender, also lost his income when his workplace closed. For a reason that had to do with missed paperwork, which I still don't understand, he was unable to get unemployment benefits.

The virus was frightening, but I was even more unnerved by the uneven effects of the policy response. While professionals worked from home, others were laid off. Stimulus checks, unemployment, and other benefits did not alleviate the anxiety of not knowing when or if anyone would get their jobs and lives back. Still another group, including warehouse employees, health care workers, and grocery staffers, was still on the job, worried about getting sick.

Doing my grocery shopping at TGS was a pleasant experience, as if the store existed in another world. I was grateful (and a little guilty) that employees were coming to work every day to ensure that the rest of us could buy food.

One day, I lingered at the cheese counter reviewing the options. An employee approached wearing a name tag that listed her time on the job: "Two Years of Serving You." She asked how she could help in the friendly manner that I had come to expect. I said that I was craving a grilled cheese sandwich. The employee's eyes lit up. "*You* want the good stuff." She offered a local cheddar that had been soaked, she explained, in beer. "That's why it's got that deep, rich color and unique flavor." She promised that the cheese made "the best grilled cheese you'll ever have" and recommended a store-made brioche. I bought both products.

The encounter impressed me. The employee had treated me like an individual whose cravings mattered. She had even appeared to take pleasure in serving me. I started to think about getting a job at the store. I was going crazy from being isolated at home. Working at a supermarket seemed like a way to serve my community during the pandemic. At TGS, I could earn money while treating people like the cheese counter employee had treated me.

In October 2020, I uploaded my résumé to the store's website. A couple of weeks later, I was hired as a cashier and supervisor in a department called the *Front End*. The day after the interview, I arrived at the store at 7:00 a.m. for my first shift, becoming one of almost four million people who work as retail salespeople, one of the most common jobs in the country.

During my first weeks on the TGS Front End, supermarkets became a subject of media attention. A genre of writing emerged, let's call it the *COVID explainer*, that offered advice for how to shop for groceries safely. Most articles recommended going to the grocery store during nonpeak hours, wearing a good mask, frequent hand sanitizing, and getting in and out quickly.

The explainers offered some good advice. But all I could think about while reading them was: What about those of us who worked at the supermarket? We couldn't avoid stores when they were crowded or get in and out quickly. If we didn't show up to our jobs, no one would be able to buy groceries, and we wouldn't earn a paycheck.

The media was missing an important part of the story. I started thinking about trying to publish an article about what it was like to work in a store during the pandemic. But the physical and mental demands of spending forty hours a week behind the register made writing seem impossible.

The shitting incident forced me to reconsider. Maybe this story was bigger than just the pandemic. I was perplexed by my colleagues' reactions. Why had some denounced the man, while others had been sympathetic? A professional studying working conditions in the retail industry might use those questions as a starting point for research. A journalist might conduct worker interviews, while an academic might distribute a survey to better understand and compare employees' opinions.

But I was not a journalist or a sociologist. Researching the job and doing the job felt like contradictory activities. One demanded plenty of time to read and analyze, while the other required serving shoppers in a sixty-five-thousand-square-foot space with nineteen registers on two levels. Even if I had the energy to occasionally slip into the role of academic or journalist, I couldn't imagine asking my exhausted colleagues to sit for an interview just to satisfy my curiosity.

Instead, I started taking notes. I forced myself to delay my after-work collapse long enough to open my laptop and summarize the shift. I wrote about incidents and conversations that seemed unusual or noteworthy and recorded conflicts between shoppers and customers and between workers and bosses. I documented the gestures and movements required to sell thousands of grocery items each day, the everyday life of one supermarket that was like all the others.

Sometimes, during a shift, I jotted down a few words about an incident or a conversation. I wanted to get the details right. Occasionally, I noted something about a colleague's background or a detail that they had shared about their personal life. The writing energized me. I started doing research, reading about the history of the retail industry and the supermarket's role in our society.

If you envision a city, you visualize houses, schools, hospitals, and supermarkets. These places are incorporated into our language and imaginations. In the pages of language textbooks, we are encouraged to ask about *el supermercado* or *le supermarché*. Game shows from *The Price Is Right* to *Supermarket Sweep* are a testament to the stores' central place in our culture. The comfort of a grocery store is its banality, the fact that you don't have to think about how it operates.

On the job, I developed a different view. Grocery stores may all seem the same. But the supermarket as an institution is anything but ordinary or one-dimensional. Take the shitting incident. For some colleagues, the man who dropped his pants was a sympathetic figure even as the mess he made added to our labor and stress.

The two sides of the grocery store are visible in our culture. A character in Don DeLillo's *White Noise* believed that unraveling the secrets of the supermarket could lead to a higher state of consciousness. Annie Ernaux described the supermarket as a place that reminds us that we all have "human bodies and human needs." Zombie movies and TV series feature the supermarket as a refuge as well as a danger.

After I left TGS, I reviewed my notes with the intention of writing about what I had observed and experienced behind the register. The pages were filled with discrete events featuring people whose names and faces I was already starting to forget doing a job whose routines were now lost to me. At TGS, as many as one hundred people might be working during a single shift. I knew many of them only by sight or via occasional, fleeting interactions.

High employee turnover meant that developing relationships was difficult and probably a waste of time. When I first started the job, most colleagues ignored me, rarely saying hello or acknowledging my presence. They were saving energy and effort in a workplace where I might not be around for long. The few elements I had captured in my notes about some colleagues' lives outside the store were fragments that often posed more questions than they answered.

My notes read as limited because I was in a position of relative privilege from which to judge them. By then, I was working as a freelance journalist and part-time teacher. Both vantage points were essential. It was only as a grocery insider that I had been able to see what grocery work actually entailed and what it does to people. And it was as an outsider that I saw how the supermarket as an institution is a window into larger social divisions and injustices.

To write the book in your hands, I combined research with memoir and used journalism to fill in the gaps caused by work, exhaustion, and precarity. Each chapter shows how traditions like customer service, community, and convenience disguise a reality that shoppers don't see. If you are confused by the number of employees in this book, including a few who appear rarely or only during a key moment that features them, you know what it was like for me as an employee. I have changed the names of all of my coworkers and managers along with some identifying details, and in certain instances I have created composites.

Finally, I have tried to be honest about my thoughts and behaviors at TGS, even if I was not always proud of them. While working in a factory in 1930s France to study the lives of industrial workers, the philosopher Simone Weil found that the repetitive labor and submission to authority prompted inhuman behavior. "It is next to impossible not to become as indifferent or brutal as the system in which one is caught," she wrote. My experience on the job confirmed this assessment. But it's not the whole story. At the supermarket, I found a microcosm of society: a place of brutality and violence as well as solidarity and the promise of change.

CHAPTER 1

Customer Service

My first days as a supermarket cashier were like being thrown out of a plane without a parachute. I was overwhelmed by the basics of operating the scanner at what employees called "the checkstand." *This frozen pizza is $6.99. But it scans at $8.99. What do I do? How do I price this box of Oreos that doesn't have a barcode? Does TGS accept checks? Google Pay?*

One shopper wanted to buy a small cup of soup from the buffet. Since there was no barcode on the container, I couldn't scan it. I flipped aimlessly through an employee manual. "My soup is getting cold," the customer complained. I left my post to interrupt the colleague at the next checkstand. "Can you help me ring up some soup?" By the time we got back to my lane, the shopper was gone. The lukewarm soup was still on the counter.

The sight of fresh fruits and vegetables filled me with dread. Cashiers had to enter a four-digit price lookup code, or PLU, for each variety. Sometimes the sticker with the code was missing or damaged. *What is the PLU for Gala apples again? Or are those Honeycrisp? Are lemons sold by the pound or by number? Is that a regular or an organic avocado?*

Even if I knew the PLU, a split-second loss of concentration could result in a customer being charged the wrong price.

Once, when I entered the code for hothouse tomatoes, the digital screen read "Onions." I realized that I had been entering the wrong code for weeks, giving countless customers a discount. Since I didn't know how to fix the error, I ignored it and kept scanning. Another time, I charged a shopper for freeze-dried strawberries at $28 per pound instead of the fresh fruit they were purchasing, priced at $3.99. That time, I admitted the mistake. While customers in line waited, a manager deleted the item so I could reenter it correctly. A few days later, I failed to correctly process a customer's credit card and had to chase him to the exit.

I was deeply intimidated by the prospect of supervisor training. Watching coworkers in the role, I wished I had declined that part of the position, asked to just be a cashier. Supervisors managed the whole Front End, even the whole store at times. If lines were too long, a supervisor made an employee wait to take her break. If there were no carts in the lobby, she sent someone to fetch them. (Like Sisyphus's rock rolling downhill, the carts disappeared almost the moment they were returned to the lobby.) If a shopper could not find the sun-dried tomatoes or the nine-volt batteries, a supervisor walked him to the shelf. If a customer had a complaint, a supervisor was responsible for smoothing things over. Virtually every step she took and every word she spoke was aimed at customer satisfaction: Supervisors were a vector of others' wants and desires.

Part of being a supervisor was wielding a power as intimidating as it was enviable. By swiping a card called an *override* over a scanner, supervisors could perform tasks unavailable to cashiers, such as changing prices or deleting items from an order. I had been given the override before I knew how to use it. Cashiers who knew I had the card sometimes asked me to fix an error. I wanted to help. But I had to first tell the register what I wanted it to do. Most of the time, I had no idea which buttons to push.

One night when I was working as a cashier, a supervisor announced that she was taking her lunch break. "Ann is in charge," she said as she disappeared into the elevator. *What if something happens that I don't know how to handle?* The instant that terrible thought crossed my mind, a customer stepped up to a checkstand with four empty milk bottles. "I need to get a refund on these," she said. *Bottle refunds?* No one had taught me how to do that. The cashier called out to me. "Can you help me?"

I entered the number of bottles and then pressed a button that said "Bottle Return" because it seemed like the logical choice. That was my first mistake. The register made a clanging noise and displayed an error message that read "Check sequence." The checkstand was saying, "You've pushed the right buttons but in the wrong order. Try again. I'll wait."

Trying to fix the error compounded it. Every time I tried to perform what colleagues called a *void*, the machine inexplicably added an additional two dollars. Now I had to do the bottle return *and* remove four dollars from the customer's order. The line at the register was growing. Customers sighed and looked at their watches. I felt embarrassed and incompetent.

I made a mayday call on the radio. Moments later, the supervisor who had gone to lunch emerged from the elevator still chewing on the last bite of her meal and no doubt regretting that she had left a dunce like me in charge. She expertly pressed buttons almost without looking, swiped her override card, and BOOM, it was done. The bottle refunds had been granted, the mysterious four dollars had been removed from the total, and the customer was on her way. I was mortified, convinced that I would never master the machines.

Learning to cashier might have been easier had I been able to focus on the keys in front of me. But I had to pay attention to social cues. Some shoppers hardly acknowledged me, while others wanted to chat. A few watched me scan every item, as if they expected to be overcharged. Once, a shopper brought his receipt back to my register. "This says I was charged fourteen dollars for eclairs. But I did not buy any eclairs." The customer seemed to think that I would remember him. He was saying, "Surely you recall that I did not have eclairs when I came through your line an hour ago."

It was entirely possible that I had charged him in error. In fact, it was likely. But I had served so many customers in the meantime that an hour might as well have been a year. I did not remember the shopper or what he had bought. I made another mayday call (it was becoming a habit). A manager arrived and took the customer to another register. I did not know what was happening. Had I charged the man for eclairs he did not buy or not? How could the manager tell? I was completely lost.

Customer service was supposed to be the easy part—the store was designed for that purpose. TGS had every kind of food and household item that I could imagine under one roof. Clear signage, cheerful music, and appealing displays made buying groceries fun. Banners advertised "Good Food for Good People," as if the store were up to date on shoppers' morality and ethics.

The store sent weekly emails and texts that congratulated shoppers for being "fabulous food lovers" and offered discounts and free gifts. "Every tenth loaf of artisan bread you buy is on us!" On weekdays, customers received a text about the lunch special. Favored shoppers could get a dollar off. All they had to do was swipe their frequent shopper's card at checkout and the discount would be applied. From the moment they walked in the door, and even while they were not in the aisles, TGS shoppers were treated like special individuals with unique needs.

When a cashier scanned a frequent shopper's card, a name popped up on the screen, which allowed for a personalized greeting. "Did you find everything you were looking for today, Mr. Smith?" I followed the lead of other cashiers by complimenting shoppers' selections. "Looks like you're making lasagna tonight. I see you've chosen TGS's house-made tomato sauce! Good choice!" I also reminded customers about the loyalty program. "Two more loaves of bread, and you'll get your free loaf!" The supermarket was more than a place to buy groceries; it offered attention and affirmation.

Customer service was not a one-way street. A seventy-nine-year-old named Cindy had been bagging groceries for nine years when I met her. After we had worked together for a few weeks, I asked her why she was still punching a clock well past retirement age. She seemed surprised by the question. "What would I do at home? Stare at the wall? I like working here." Cindy derived satisfaction, self-worth, and identity from her job. She distributed candy and stickers to children, and everyone marveled at her ability to lift pumpkins and bags of kitty litter into carts.

Cindy regaled workers and shoppers alike with stories about her time as a high school majorette. "I marched at football games and twirled a baton—a baton that was on *fire*!" A great-grandmother, Cindy had not lost her flair for the dramatic. She wore colorful eye shadow and adorned her uniform with beaded necklaces and brooches more suitable for a Mardi Gras parade than a supermarket.

The pandemic briefly turned grocery staffers like Cindy into heroes. Some shoppers thanked my colleagues and me for coming to work. "What would we do without you?" A few called me by name and treated me like an old friend. "It's nice to see you!" One woman stopped me in the aisle and inquired about my well-being. "How are you holding up?" When customers addressed me as an individual, I became a person with an identity. "I love working here," I replied and meant it.

Once, a shopper in my checkout line told me that he couldn't find the baked vegetable crisps. "I'm supposed to get them for free," he said. The customer was referring to a product that TGS gifted people who signed up for a frequent shopper's card.

"I'll be happy to get them for you," I said. I hurried to the salad bar, where the boxes were displayed. Back at the checkstand, I put the item in the shopper's bag, saying, "You can't skip the free stuff."

He was touched that I would go out of my way. "What do you do with them?" he asked. I suggested serving the crisps with tomato soup. "I'll try that for lunch tomorrow," he said.

Before I worked at TGS, I wouldn't have believed that I could bond with a stranger over vegetable crisps or that doing so would be a pleasure.

One customer stopped me in the aisle to ask which brand of granola to get from the dozen on display. I could have pointed to a package and kept walking. Instead, I whispered, like I was sharing a secret. "You don't want any of these brands. Follow me." At the bakery, I handed him a box of TGS's house-made granola. "This is the good stuff," I said.

The shopper whispered back to me, sharing in the secret, "Thanks for the tip."

We laughed like old friends.

"Do you have any cupcake mix here?" another shopper asked. This was a strange question in a supermarket. But I wanted to help.

"Let's go find it," I said. I left the man's items piled up on the counter and walked him to aisle number two, where there were three rows of cake mixes.

The shopper was perplexed. "That says 'cake mix,'" he said, "I'm making cupcakes."

I laughed with, not at, the customer. "Sir," I said, "it's the same mix; you just put it in cupcake tins instead of a cake pan."

His eyes lit up like a great mystery had just been solved. "I see!" he said.

The culture of service at TGS was genuine and satisfying. Sure, I was still struggling to operate the register, but I had found a way to feel useful during the pandemic while earning an income. I even felt, at times, valued and appreciated.

My first paycheck was a sign that everything was not as it appeared. Of course, I knew that my wage was $15.80 an hour. Since I had been hired as a supervisor, the figure was a couple of dollars higher than what regular cashiers earned. But I had not done the math to calculate my weekly pay. When my paycheck was about $500, reality set in. More than half of my monthly income would go to rent. My take-home pay would be even less three months later, after insurance payments kicked in at $40 per week, giving me a wage of about $1,840 per month.

The retail industry is notorious for low pay. During the year that I was on the job, grocery staffers around the country earned under $15 on average. Since then, wage increases have not kept up with rising prices. It wasn't always as bad as it is today. Grocery work used to be considered a skilled occupation. At some stores, as late as the early 1990s, unionized employees earned middle-class wages. But pay fell off a cliff along with unionization rates. These days, only about 4 percent of retail workers are unionized. Even as profits spiked during the pandemic, employers did not pass the benefits to workers.

Staffers who work behind checkstands are among the worst off. Disproportionately women, cashiers earn the lowest wages in the retail industry. Sexist ideas about women's place in society are a big reason for the gender imbalance. Since women are considered more nurturing and caring, they are more likely to be assigned customer service roles. But when jobs are staffed mostly by women, the work is considered less important and less skilled, and wages fall.

One day, at TGS, a deli department employee came into my line with a basket. She watched carefully as I scanned her items. When the total, after her employee discount, appeared, she said, "I don't have enough." She asked me to take two items off the order. "I'll have to go on a diet this week," she said. "And find a second job fast." As a deli employee, her paycheck was smaller than mine.

Paula, the Front End manager, and my boss, had also struggled to make ends meet. She told me that, about a year before I met her, she had been the manager of the meat department in another chain across town. After her husband got laid off from a manufacturing plant, the couple and three children were struggling to keep food on the table. Paula was finishing her shift one day when she spied a package of ground beef with an expired sell-by date. "After three days, meat is considered rotten," she told me. "But you can still eat it." She marked down the price to ten cents per pound and bought the meat. A colleague informed on her, and Paula was terminated for shoplifting. Her family relied on food banks and help from friends until she got the job at TGS. At the job interview, she admitted to managers what had happened and promised never to do anything like that again.

When Paula told me the story, she dropped the deferential tone. "I was loyal to that store for twenty years," she said, her eyes flashing with anger. "And they fired me over some old meat."

Over time, I observed that Cindy's lunch was a two-dollar child's chicken fingers meal or a small cup of soup for about the same price. With her employee discount, the meals cost even less. She told me that it was all she could afford. To keep her energy up, the elderly woman kept a bottle of Diet Coke under a checkstand and sipped on it throughout her shift. "It's the only drug I've ever been addicted to," she told me. Colleagues teased her about the lukewarm beverage. But Cindy didn't see the point of buying a fresh, cold bottle. "It's still got caffeine, doesn't it?"

My fellow cashier, Charles, had originally been hired in the deli department. A few years before I met him, however, he had been hit by a car while crossing the street. The accident left the fifty-five-year-old with a bad leg and a limp. Deli employees had to move quickly between the hot buffet, the salad bar, and the counter, where customers ordered cooked dishes by the pound. After the accident, it was impossible for Charles to keep up. So he was transferred to the

Front End. One day, on his lunch break, he tried to purchase a burrito while I was supervising. His credit card was declined. "I guess I can't have lunch today," he said, shrugging. The cashier and I split the cost of the five-dollar meal so Charles could eat.

Many grocery workers are food insecure. A 2022 report by the Economic Roundtable showed that about three-quarters of workers at Kroger, the second-largest grocery company in the country, struggled to afford regular meals. Kroger could not claim that it didn't know. Years earlier, an internal company report showed that hundreds of thousands of its employees relied on food aid and other public benefits. It's not surprising perhaps that federal food aid programs are acting as a subsidy to low-wage employers. The nation's largest retailer, Walmart, for example, took in more than $26 billion in its customers' food aid in 2024 alone.

At TGS, some colleagues qualified for the Supplemental Nutrition Assistance Program, or SNAP. A federal program that provides limited food aid to low-income people, twenty-three million adults used SNAP in 2023. Forty percent of beneficiaries were children. The program has regularly been targeted for cuts by both parties. President Ronald Reagan demanded reductions as part of the 1981 federal budget while, in the 1990s, Bill Clinton's welfare reform policies led to significant cuts. In 2025, Donald Trump further slashed the program. Today, the typical SNAP recipient is a woman who cooks for a family after coming home from work. And one program user may be serving another at the supermarket—around 23 percent of cashiers rely on SNAP.

One of them was my coworker Willow, who I saw using SNAP to pay for groceries. But the program does not cover the cost of all basic goods. One evening, she logged out of her checkstand and told a colleague that she was going home. "I got my period, and I don't have any money to buy pads." Because we cared about Willow, and because her absence would mean longer lines, my colleagues and I rallied to her rescue. A cashier told her to get a package of maxi pads off the shelf. "We'll take up a collection," she said. A few minutes later, Willow retook her place behind her register. "Don't worry," she announced. "I got the cheapest ones." Each cashier put a dollar in the till until we covered the cost of the pads.

It wasn't just food and sanitary supplies—some of my colleagues could barely even afford a roof. Bonnie relied on a Housing Choice Voucher, a federal program that assured that low-income tenants didn't pay more than 30 percent of their income on rent. The forty-year-old cashier praised the program and gave her coworkers tips about how to apply. "I'd be on the street without my housing voucher," she explained. Bonnie counted herself lucky. The waiting list could be years long.

A cashier we called "Darth" was not so fortunate. He had earned the nickname because he was tall, with a deep voice, and wore a black pandemic face mask that made him look like Darth Vader. Darth and I were neighbors. He lived two blocks from me on the side of the neighborhood that was rapidly gentrifying. A few weeks after I met him, the fifty-seven-year-old learned that his apartment building was slated to be demolished for a new condo development. He didn't have time to apply for a voucher and wait for approval. Afraid of ending up homeless, he moved across town, where apartments started at $950 per month, significantly more than he had been paying before. Darth didn't have much furniture. He slept on an air mattress on the floor. Coworkers pooled funds to buy him a coffeemaker as a housewarming gift.

Other TGS colleagues skimped on health care. "Did I tell you about my shot?" Lucia asked one day in between customers. "I just found out I have diabetes." She was talking about a blood sugar test. The fifty-five-year-old with a round face and a belly laugh that could be heard around the store was trying to be upbeat about the diagnosis. "It's okay," she said. "But no more bread, pasta, or cookies." I asked about her treatment plan. "I don't have insurance. But the clinic prescribed pills and told me what not to eat." She was referring to a low-cost clinic where people lined up for treatment for everything from cuts and broken bones to heart disease.

It was not the first time Lucia had visited the clinic for a serious condition. She had also gone there to get treated for arthritis. Now she was juggling medications and unsure about when to take them. "I can't take the diabetes pill at the same time as my arthritis medication," she said.

"So, if you treat your diabetes, your arthritis flares up?" I asked.

"Today I took the diabetes meds, but now I'm in pain. Tomorrow, I'll skip those and take the arthritis pill instead," she explained.

Lucia's lack of insurance made me wonder what coworkers thought of TGS's company health plans. I had taken the job in part for the health insurance, but I was shocked at the cost. I had selected an option that came with a $4,000 deductible. (Even after reaching that amount, my plan only covered about 80 percent of the cost of care—and that was only if I stayed "in network" for all treatments.) I was starting to wonder if I had made a good choice.

One day, I asked a cashier named Aurelie if she was insured. The thirty-five-year-old with a blond pixie cut had a reputation for workaholism and a sweet tooth. When business was slow, she swept up around her checkstand. During her breaks, she could be found in the candy aisle looking for deals on mini Twix and Junior Mints. She rolled her eyes at my question. "I'm not going to let an insurance company take money out of my paycheck," she said. "I might never even hit the deductible." Aurelie said the words *insurance company* like she was talking about a criminal organization. She told me that health insurance was a scam. "It's throwing money down the garbage disposal," she went on, "The cost keeps rising." She was right. Over the prior decade, premiums had outpaced inflation, and deductibles had more than doubled.

Willow, the cashier who couldn't afford pads, suffered from a severe case of eczema. The skin around her nose and eyes was red and flaky, her knuckles and fingers white and blotchy. Skin flaked off onto her register as she worked. The thirty-year-old had trouble sleeping because letting her skin touch anything—even the sheets of her bed—was painful. "Is there a treatment?" I asked.

Willow used an ointment, she said, but it didn't always help. "There is a shot that would clear it up, but it costs four thousand dollars, and I can't afford insurance." I asked about Medicaid, the federal insurance program for low-income people. Willow said that she earned just over the income limit to qualify. "I would have to reduce my hours to get it," she explained. "But then I would have less money for food."

Critics of welfare often accuse recipients of fraud and abuse. The complaint is bipartisan and rooted in racist and sexist assumptions about low-wage workers. In the 1980s, Ronald Reagan stoked the myth of the "welfare queen" by regaling audiences at his campaign rallies with stories of a Black woman who used welfare money to buy steak. In the 1990s, President Bill Clinton's "welfare reform" kicked poor mothers off assistance if they did not get jobs. On the job at

TGS, workers still didn't earn enough to escape poverty and were forced to choose between food and health care, or between paying rent and putting gas in the car.

Another cashier suffered from a toothache so painful that she could barely eat. "I need a root canal," the twenty-five-year-old told me. Since she did not have dental insurance, she was waiting for a spot to open up at a dental school. "If you let the students practice on you, the treatment is free," she told me. A week later, I asked her if she had seen a dentist. She was still waiting for an appointment. "The good news is, I eat ice cream for dinner. It's the only food that doesn't hurt."

Since Medicaid doesn't cover the cost of dental care in most cases, low-income people suffer from tooth pain and related symptoms from self-consciousness to depression. A person's class status is often apparent from the moment they open their mouth. One-quarter of adults in the United States over the age of sixty-five are missing all of their teeth, and our country has one of the highest rates of toothlessness in the world. And since tooth pain is a common cause of absences from school, a lack of dental care can keep children from getting an education.

While I worked with her, Cindy began to lose her hearing. She could no longer chat with customers or ask children how they were doing in school. Like tooth pain and missing teeth, hearing loss is associated with economic hardship. Low-income adults are more likely to lose their hearing than others. One reason may be that they work in high-noise environments like construction sites. Or, like Cindy, because they cannot afford adequate health care. Impaired hearing is not just about physical disability. It can lead to social isolation and even dementia.

Cindy's daughter submitted her name to a local television news show that featured local people who needed financial help. One day, a colleague reported that Cindy had been selected to appear on the program. A reporter would interview the longtime bagger on-air and then make a "surprise announcement" that a corporate sponsor was donating $3,000 for hearing aids. Cindy knew about the donation in advance, but she was supposed to feign surprise.

The morning after the program aired, business was slow on the Front End. I found the segment online. My colleagues and I gathered around my phone to watch Cindy's star turn. She had joined the show remotely from her daughter's house. "Seventy-nine-year-old Cindy is still working as a bagger at TGS. Isn't that amazing?" said the host. My colleague beamed; her dark purple eye shadow matched a floral brooch that bloomed on her chest. "I love helping people! I love my job!" Cindy said. When the reporter announced the donation for hearing aids, she expressed Oscar-worthy astonishment. "You can't do that!" she exclaimed. "Thank you so much!"

Still, a onetime donation from a corporate sponsor could not solve my colleague's health problems. Cindy's weight dropped to ninety pounds. Once, she called the store to say she didn't know what day it was. "Do I work today?" she asked. Shortly afterward, her daughter called to report that Cindy had had a "minor stroke." Later, Cindy called from her hospital bed. "I want to come back to work," she said.

I told her that everyone at TGS was pulling for her. "You'll be back on the Front End in no time," I said. I hoped that I was right.

From seeking out alternative forms of care to pushing through pain, the workers I met at TGS were fighting individual battles daily to survive. I started to wonder if I should try to organize a union at the store. As the cofounder of the Debt Collective, I had experience with collective action. I knew that it was only by joining together that my colleagues and I could improve our lives.

But I hesitated. Most colleagues did not talk about our common problems in collective terms. And I had never heard the word *union* at the store. I thought I knew why. The prohibition was not explicit. No manager, to my knowledge, had ever warned us against organizing. They didn't have to. I sensed that if the news that workers were organizing got to management, everyone involved would be fired. Everyone even *rumored* to be involved would be shown the door. Even though I knew that this kind of retaliation is illegal, the bosses might fire people first and answer questions later. Fear, precarity, and poverty made collective struggle feel like an idea that belonged to a different, more privileged universe, one my colleagues and I didn't live and couldn't imagine visiting.

Scarlet had the tattoo of a rosebush and thorns from forearm to shoulder and was always within arm's reach of a thermos of iced coffee—no milk or sugar. "Black as my soul," she told me. The cashier studied online ads to find deals on groceries and shared her tips with the rest of us. Once, she told me that she had found a store across town that sold toilet paper for half the price of what TGS charged. I said it sounded too good to be true. "On our next day off, we should go buy toilet paper and then stop at a bar," she said. "We'll take up four seats, two for us and two more for our twelve-packs of toilet paper."

Like me, Scarlet was new to cashiering. Before the pandemic, she had worked in a high-end restaurant, where her income from tips made her feel "almost middle class," she told me. She had been able to care for her teenage daughter and three cats. But the restaurant had closed during the pandemic. It was like being dropped off an income cliff. "I need to bring in double my current pay to survive," she said. One day at TGS, she told me that she had applied for a second job at a gas station near her apartment. A few days later, she announced that she had declined the job after discovering that it only paid $7.50 an hour. "How do employers expect people to work for that? It's depressing." She sighed. "I can't afford groceries right now."

Most of us have heard that depression is caused by a chemical imbalance in the brain, one reason doctors prescribe medication to correct low serotonin levels. But new studies have questioned the relationship between serotonin and depression. Some researchers believe that psychological distress is a product of the struggle to earn a living. One national study found that poor mental health was a result of "the exploitation inherent in wage labor." It turns out that earning a paycheck that was just enough (if we were lucky) to enable us to come back to work the next day was a recipe for depression. A union would have helped my colleagues and me to think collectively, to see each other as allies in the fight for better jobs.

The decline in Scarlet's income and her depression made her a distracted, acerbic employee. She rarely said hello or "have a nice day," or asked about frequent shopper cards. She didn't bother with personalized greetings. Cashiers were supposed to stand in front of their registers to greet customers. But Scarlet stood behind the counter looking glumly at her phone. When a manager caught her scrolling job ads, he warned, "I'm keeping an eye on you."

Surveillance didn't help. A former restaurant employee,

Scarlet knew how to perform customer service. But as her situation became desperate, she lost all motivation and took her frustration out on shoppers. Once, a customer bought grapes at her checkstand and returned minutes later for a refund. Scarlet didn't ask why. Instead, she offered snark. "Changed your mind in the last five minutes, did ya?" To a customer buying three cases of beer, she said, "I hope your next stop is Alcoholics Anonymous!" It was like she was trying to get fired. She may have felt too hopeless to care that she would not qualify for unemployment benefits that way. A few days after a manager reprimanded her for phone usage, Scarlet stopped showing up to work.

In some cases, the connection between employees' financial anxiety and customer service was more direct. Employees groaned about the discomfort of pandemic face masks. (By the end of a shift, red lines marked our faces where the fasteners had dug into skin.) But not Lucia. The cashier who suffered from diabetes and arthritis wore a mask long after the store no longer required them. "I like masking because no one can see that I'm missing teeth," she said. Lucia told me that she was saving money for dentures and would only remove her face mask once she had them.

One day, she announced that she had finally done it. By putting aside $20 a week from her paychecks for a year, and with help from family, Lucia had saved $1,500 for dentures. She arrived on the Front End after a visit to a clinic where a dentist had taken a mold of her mouth. A local anesthetic explained her slurred speech. Minutes later, I was bagging at her lane when a customer asked about his frequent shopper's card. "Did my phone number go through?" Lucia ignored him. He asked again. She replied softly, "What's the number?" The customer didn't hear. "Sorry?" Lucia asked again, annoyed this time. "YOUR NUMBER?" She typed it in.

As the man was gathering his bags to leave, he said to me, "She was rude for no reason." I knew the reason. Since talking was difficult, Lucia had whispered. But the customer didn't know about her long-standing dental issues. To him, Lucia was just a surly cashier. Lurking below the surface of every friendly greeting and welcoming smile was the possibility of a breakdown in norms. Given workers' wages and living conditions, a bedrock value of the supermarket—customer service—was hanging by a thread.

The attentive treatment we expect at the supermarket is a relatively recent invention. In the early twentieth century, shoppers lined up behind their neighbors in small mom-and-pop stores where shopping was hard labor and a socially awkward, even humiliating, experience. Since prices were not posted, each shopper had to negotiate with the clerk. Tight quarters meant that everyone knew what everyone else was having for dinner as well as their financial status. Clerks might extend a line of credit to one customer while refusing another. Favored customers might receive the freshest merchandise while others were offered day-old goods, or nothing at all.

Women suffered the most from the indignities, because they did most grocery shopping and were judged by how well they performed at the counter. The pressures to negotiate well and spend wisely were so intense that housewives who could afford to send servants still did their own shopping to demonstrate that they cared about what their families ate. But the risks were highest for those on a budget.

The power dynamics played out with greater severity along racial lines. Black shoppers who had migrated north to escape Jim Crow in the 1920s found that grocery stores were much like their Southern counterparts. A clerk might tape a silver dollar to the bottom of a scale or attach a piece of gum to inflate the price. In the 1930s, the African American newspaper *The Chicago Defender* reported that "chickens dying from various diseases were not discarded but sold" to Black shoppers. Once they had been cheated, shoppers' options were limited. Customers who could not trust officers to side with them over clerks did not call the police.

For today's shoppers, the supermarket is a major improvement. Customers are often praised and flattered, their whims and desires celebrated and revered. Though it still exists in stores of all kinds, racial discrimination is illegal. No one wants to go back to the bad old days. But the power shift has come at a cost. Paradoxically, a union that helped guarantee better working conditions would have benefited TGS in terms of happier, healthier employees and consistently better customer service. But that argument wouldn't convince our bosses to let us organize. Food retailers are in the business of selling basic goods, not caring for workers and shoppers. The difference matters. Retailers have transferred the suffering that produces profit from customers to employees who now pay the price of customer service.

One evening, a manager pulled me aside to tell me that a customer had called to complain about a cashier named Irene. Earlier that day, the woman had come through Irene's line. The customer had said, "How are you?" But Irene did not respond. The sixty-year-old had grimaced and grunted but did not speak. "Her mind was elsewhere, and I was invisible," the shopper reported.

The manager wanted to know if I knew why Irene had ignored the customer. I said that I would try to find out. The manager couldn't wait. "We can't have shoppers calling to complain about rude employees," she said. "If Irene can't perform customer service, then she can't work on the Front End." A few days later, my colleague was moved to a job in the lobby distributing masks to shoppers.

The next time I saw her at the store, I asked Irene about the incident. She told me that she had been struggling with the physical demands of cashiering. Standing for long periods had aggravated a back injury that she had incurred at a prior job caring for elderly and disabled patients in a nursing home. "I hurt my back moving residents in and out of their beds," she explained. "Now I'm the one who needs help." Irene sometimes forgot to smile and say hello because she was focused on working through her pain. All that mattered was getting to the end of a shift and going home to sit down.

It didn't help that Irene had to walk to work since she did not live on a bus route and taxis refused to pick her up. "The ride costs four dollars," she said. "I offered the drivers a five-dollar bill. But they told me it wasn't worth the trip for such a small amount. I can't take Uber because that would cost nine dollars, nearly an hour of pay." By the time Irene got to TGS, she was already in pain. She was reluctant to quit, because she didn't know how long it would take to find another job. Irene had more than her own economic situation to think about—she was helping to support her daughter, who had been laid off and was being threatened with eviction.

Irene's poverty made her a less-than-friendly cashier. But caring for shoppers was also a *cause* of her anguish. Like at many supermarkets, TGS cashiers worked from a standing position so they could bag groceries. The posture permitted easier swiveling and pivoting from the register to the bags. (In Europe and elsewhere where customers bag their own groceries, cashiers sit.) Bagging may not seem like heavy lifting. But it's the accumulation that counts. On average, supermarket cashiers handle as many as one thousand items per hour and lift as much as six thousand pounds during a shift. The combination of lifting, swiveling, and pivoting put pressure on Irene's back. Providing one form of service (bagging groceries) made her unable to perform another (smiling and saying hello).

Darth regularly stopped working in the middle of a shift. He would wait for a pause in customers in his line, turn off his checkstand light, and step back from his register. No light meant that his station looked closed, which sent shoppers to other lanes. The result was longer lines and frustrated customers and employees. One day, he stood behind his register for fifteen minutes without serving a single customer.

The next day, I overheard a colleague complain to Paula about Darth's behavior. "Darth turns his light off every shift!" Paula sighed and shook her head. She explained that he was in pain. The repetitive motion of cashiering had led to a stabbing sensation in his arm. Our coworker was suffering from a musculoskeletal injury, likely carpal tunnel, that is common among cashiers. By turning off his light, Darth could temporarily relieve the pain. Paula saw no solution except a different job. "I don't know how much longer he is going to be able to work here," she said. To shoppers, supermarket scanners speed up the checkout process. But the technology might eventually cost Darth his job.

In 1898, H. G. Wells published *The War of the Worlds*, a science fiction thriller about aliens who invade earth and destroy cities with a "heat ray" like "an invisible but intensely heated finger." The Cold War between the US and the Soviet Union prompted President Eisenhower to try to turn lasers, or light amplification by stimulated emission of radiation, into a reality. He created the Advanced Research

Projects Agency (ARPA, now DARPA) in part to develop the technology as a battlefield weapon. The military had high hopes. One official thought lasers might become "the biggest breakthrough in the weapons area since the atomic bomb."

Lasers flopped as an arm of war. The beams were not very good at killing people (at least not yet). But the Kroger grocery corporation had another idea. The company collaborated with the Radio Corporation of America (RCA) to find out if a "heat ray" could get customers out of grocery stores faster. RCA scientists eventually figured out that lasers could read barcodes. Since then, a unique barcode has been printed on individual grocery items, and a cashier's primary job is moving their arm across a scanner.

Lasers' transition from science fiction to military weapons to a common piece of grocery store infrastructure happened on June 26, 1974, when Sharon Buchanan arrived for her shift at a supermarket in Troy, Ohio. An executive handed her a pack of Wrigley's Juicy Fruit gum. She passed the product over a device installed at her register. *Beep*. The amount—sixty-seven cents—appeared on the screen. Buchanan was the first cashier to use a scanner, and the Juicy Fruit went on to be displayed in the Smithsonian Museum.

Since then, the lasers in supermarket scanners have become a threat to workers that even a science fiction writer couldn't have imagined. Shoppers may assume that the most dangerous job in a supermarket is sawing up sides of beef or stocking shelves. But cashiering is just as risky. Scanners have led to what one researcher called an "epidemic" of upper body injuries.

We might assume that federal Occupational Safety and Health Administration (OSHA) enforcers would step in and protect retail employees from harm. After all, it's the agency's job to keep American workers safe. But OSHA has been underfunded since its inception in the 1970s. Business leaders who objected to government oversight of the workplace attacked the agency. Under the George W. Bush administration, it virtually stopped enforcing safety standards. Today, OSHA is a toothless organization that struggles to do its job.

At TGS, cashiers were highly encouraged to scan fast. Once, I attended a supervisors meeting led by Paula. There was something different about the fifty-year-old that day. She was usually pacing around the Front End, her brown hair in a tight ponytail, like a volleyball player preparing to block an opposing team's spike across the net. But at the meeting, Paula's hair was down around her shoulders, and she seemed relaxed and unhurried. I got the impression that, for her, an hour away from the frenzy of the Front End was as much of a reprieve as a day at the spa.

Paula announced that lines were getting too long at the registers. "We need cashiers to scan faster so that customers don't get impatient." She wanted workers to scan at least twenty-one items per minute, or more than 1,200 per hour. One supervisor said that cashiers were already working as fast as they could. Paula disagreed and proposed an incentive. The store would run a contest, she said, and the cashiers with the fastest scan rates would receive a five-dollar deli gift card.

Until that day, I had not realized that supermarket registers recorded scan rates or that fast scanning was considered a form of customer service. But the push for speed is as old as the barcode and lasers that make it possible. In 1974, the vice president of Kroger told members of Congress that the purpose of checkstand scanners was to push employees to work faster. In the 1980s, Walmart celebrated cashiers who scanned at the breakneck pace of five hundred items per hour. These days, some stores advertise fast scanning as a fun experience for shoppers. The Aldi supermarket chain is famous for its workers' scanning speed. There, the checkout process is known as "thrill at the till."

Near the end of my first month on the job, I realized that customer service was far more complicated than it had first appeared. While workers' attentive treatment of shoppers was genuine, and employees also benefited from the mutual care and positive vibes, tensions and rudeness were products of larger injustices, including pain, low pay, a lack of health care, and even wage labor itself.

Store employees and customers didn't have to change; the supermarket as an institution did. And that would require organizing a union. Still, given the complexity of organizing in Utah, I tried not to think too much about trying to change the industry from the worker side of the checkstand. After all, I didn't plan on making a career at the supermarket. I was just passing through. But the dark side of customer service would soon implicate me in ways I couldn't yet imagine.

Although I had not yet been trained as a supervisor, on the Front End, colleagues kept treating me like one. Cashiers regularly asked me to delete items or change prices. With practice, I was able to help. But one kind of transaction was harder than the others. Processing refunds, or what employees called "doing a return," was so fraught with pitfalls that I felt a little sick every time I was asked to do it. For one thing, in addition to a receipt, I had to get a returner's phone number and see their ID, requirements intended to deter thieves from finding a receipt in the trash, taking the items off the shelf, and trying to return them. But these additional steps lengthened the process and understandably annoyed customers.

Most returners had bought the wrong item or were dissatisfied with a product. One woman returned a twenty-five-dollar fir-scented candle because she regretted buying it. I hit RETURN and then scanned the item. The machine instructed me to select, from a number of options, the reason for the return. I selected WRONG ITEM. That wasn't exactly right, but since BUYER'S REMORSE wasn't an option, I picked the next best. I scanned the override card to register the return, at which point the cash drawer was supposed to open.

This is where returns often went bad. The screen indicated a successful transaction, but the drawer didn't open. I pressed another sequence of keys that normally opened it. But in the case of a return, it rarely worked. It was as if the machine were saying, "I have calculated that TGS owes this customer twenty-five dollars, but I have no intention of allowing you to give it to them."

In the case of a credit card purchase, customers inserted their card into what employees called the "PIN pad." But I could not always get that option to work, either. Once, I canceled a return and advised the shopper to go to the office upstairs to get the refund. I knew that "the bankers" would hate me for it. (At TGS, the employees who kept the books were known as "the bankers.") But what was I supposed to do? Pry the drawer open with a screwdriver?

I started breaking the rules even when the process worked as expected. A man wanted to return some facial moisturizer. "I found this product for half the price on Amazon," he said. "Can you match that price?" I wasn't sure if

TGS offered refunds on items sold for less online. But there was a line at the checkstand, so I gave him eighteen dollars and wished him a good day.

Another time, a woman had been overcharged for a dozen eggs. She had paid $3.79. "But the sale price was $2.79," she protested. I didn't know if the eggs had ever been $2.79. But I didn't care. "The customer is always right," I told myself as I refunded her purchase. A man wanted to pay the correct price for two cantaloupes. He had been charged the wrong price per pound. But I was too tired to do the math to determine how much he really owed. I refunded the melons. "It's your lucky day!" A woman wanted to return some vitamins. I didn't ask why or get an ID. I was an expert at making regretful shoppers whole again. "You want the money back on your credit or debit card? Or would you prefer cash?"

Inevitably, I got caught. Paula told me that a banker named Dana had complained. "She said that the Front End is not doing returns correctly." Paula urged me to follow all the steps "or we'll never hear the end of it from her." Despondent at the prospect of spending more time on returns, I tried to reason with my boss. "Most returns are due to employee error," I said. "If a cashier charges someone for twenty-two avocados instead of two avocados, we are supposed to ask for an ID?"

Paula was unmoved. "Tell them that we are sorry, but we need the information," she said.

When word got around that rules for returns would be strictly enforced, cashiers grumbled that customer service would suffer. "Very stupid," one cashier said.

The dustup had another result. "You start supervisor training next week," Paula said. I tried to put a positive spin on it: I would finally get some formal instruction. Except that didn't turn out to be the case. When I saw the schedule, it was clear that "training" did not mean being tutored by an experienced supervisor but being left to manage the check-stands alone.

CHAPTER 2

Community

The Front End was in a frenzy. Coworkers were upset. A cashier was wiping away tears. "A customer was harassing Liam," George told me when I got to my checkstand. Minutes earlier, a shopper had mocked the cashier's appearance and made homophobic remarks. "Why do you have painted nails?" The man's tone had turned menacing as he began filming the twenty-one-year-old employee with his phone. "Are you a fag?" Someone called security. George rushed to Liam's checkstand followed by a manager. The shopper headed for the exit while screaming slurs.

Staffers got in a line to offer Liam pandemic hugs (fist bumps) and words of support. "That guy will never be allowed back in here," the manager said. (Later, a photo of the harasser captured on a security camera was posted with a note that said, "Alert security if you see this person in the store.") I got in the fist bump line but gave Liam a bear hug instead. The attack made me forget about the virus. This felt personal. A shopper had come after one of our own.

Before I got a job there, I saw that people looked out for one another at TGS. The store had instituted a face mask policy that applied to everyone. Posted signs encouraged shoppers to "protect our staff" by wearing masks and respecting social distancing rules. Like many stores, TGS affixed decals to the floor that instructed customers to move down the aisles in one direction and in single file, staying six feet apart. Hoarding was banned. Shoppers were limited to two packages of toilet paper at a time to preserve stock. At the checkstand, the store installed plexiglass barriers between cashiers and customers, and a handwashing station so employees could disinfect their hands.

A few weeks before the attack against Liam, a supervisor named Stewart had kicked a shopper out of the store for making a racist comment to a cashier. "I told the guy to get out if he was going to talk to an employee that way," Stewart told me. Since only managers and security guards had the authority to tell a shopper to leave, his decision was a breach of protocol. But Stewart was proud to have stood up for his coworker. The cashier was still telling colleagues about the incident the next day. "Stewart defended me," she told me.

I replied that Stewart had already shared the news. "It's the TGS way," I observed.

Another day, a customer started hitting on a cashier. "I wish you could take your mask off so I could see your smile, honey," he said. The employee stiffened and kept scanning. The shopper's tone became aggressive. "Why don't you remove your mask so I can see your face, honey? Why can't I see your pretty face?" A bagger spread the word. Two cashiers left their stations to gather at the checkstand. "It's time for you to go," one of them said. "We're not leaving until you do," said the other. The man picked up his bags and left.

Since many workers did not have cars, Stewart operated a "taxi service." Many nights, I squeezed in between coworkers in the back seat of his car. ("We're all getting

COVID tonight!" someone usually joked.) Once, when Stewart pulled up to an employee's house, her sister was on the front porch cradling a toddler—the employee's child—who was screaming into the night. "Work is over, and now parenting begins," she said and sighed. Next, Stewart dropped off a cashier who lived in a low-income housing complex, followed by a stocker who rented a studio apartment in a building squeezed between a Motel 6 and a gas station. Since I lived near the entrance to the freeway, I was the last to get dropped off before my "taxi" driver headed to the suburbs.

Before long, I saw that shoppers treated the store as a community as well. They didn't even have to buy groceries to benefit. Some logged in to the Wi-Fi network while waiting in line at the coffee bar, or they plugged their phones into outlets while using the restroom. Homeless people used the bathroom to freshen up. Customers left their bicycles on the Front End while they shopped knowing that employees would keep an eye out. Shoppers got cash at the ATM and exchanged ten-dollar bills for quarters for the laundry machine in their buildings. People moving out of their apartments asked for cardboard boxes. A Girl Scout troop sold cookies in the lobby, while charities posted calls for donations. TGS leaned into its status as a community center, offering a healthy eating newsletter and cooking classes.

My colleague, Gordon, loved antiques even if he couldn't afford to buy them. On his day off, the fifty-seven-year-old wore Wrangler jeans and cowboy boots while visiting estate sales on the hunt for collectibles to photograph. He once showed me a picture of a phone dialer from the nineteenth century. It looked like a handle with a ball on one end. "It was used by ladies who wanted to make calls without chipping their nails," he told me. Another time, he found a baby's sweater so small and moth-eaten that it fit inside a sandwich bag.

Gordon paid special attention to elderly shoppers who came in during the early morning to walk the aisles for exercise. They told him that they felt isolated at home. With fewer shoppers in the store at that hour, they could walk and talk while maintaining a safe distance. As the walkers passed his checkstand, Gordon sang songs from the 1950s and '60s and complimented them on their "marathon physiques." To a customer buying several single-serving containers of Ben and Jerry's ice cream, he teased, "How many of these will you eat tonight?" I once saw him come around his checkstand to wrap his arms around a gray-haired shopper who said she was having a bad day. The next person in line was so moved by the gesture that she burst into tears. "To most people, the elderly are invisible," she said to Gordon. "Not to me," he told her.

The dozen burly men who stocked shelves on the graveyard shift were not known for being friendly or warm. They arrived at 9:00 p.m. and worked silently with headphones on, downing energy drinks to stay awake. Some nights they were joined in the aisles by a young woman who was not employed at TGS. She usually spent an hour going up and down the aisles "facing shelves": pulling products to the front with labels facing out. When asked, she explained to the stockers that she had an anxiety disorder and found the work calming. They welcomed her as if she were a colleague.

One night, a man wearing a dirty face mask and rumpled clothes was slumped on the window ledge near checkstand nine. "He was caught stealing," the cashier told me. George arrived with a steaming cup of noodles and slipped two white pills into the man's hand. "He was putting candy bars in his pocket," the guard said. "I bought him some noodles that I heated up in my office. He also wanted Tylenol." As the customer headed toward the exit, I noticed that he was heading out into the early-winter day without shoes. A few months earlier, George had railed against a person who took a shit on the floor. This time, his response surprised and touched me. I thanked my colleague for caring for the man instead of calling the cops. "He's just a guy who is hungry and in pain," he said.

One customer stopped a staffer in the aisle. "Can I get your opinion?" He said that he had received text messages from a stranger who had been kidnapped in a foreign country. One message said, "If you mail a $500 Visa gift card to this address, my captors will let me go." The customer wanted to know if he should buy and mail the gift card to free the stranger. The employee explained that there was no kidnapping. "This is a common scam." Another staffer said that he had received similar messages. "Someone is trying to steal from you." The workers convinced the customer to stop responding and block the scammer.

Rebecca Solnit has chronicled how people come together to support one another during disasters from hurricanes to wildfires to earthquakes. In such moments, she wrote, our "neglected desires" to be part of a society become more pronounced. Normal barriers from competition to timidity fall away as we seek comfort even from strangers. The pandemic put the supermarket at the center of our social lives in a new way. But poverty is a constant state of emergency. For people who need food, attention, or even advice, the supermarket is a resource.

TGS was more than a grocery store; it was a public square. But there was more to the story of mutual care.

One morning, a shopper asked me for a custom flower arrangement for his wedding anniversary. There was no florist on duty. "We have many lovely premade options to choose from," I said. The refrigerated case in the floral department was full of colorful bouquets. The shopper insisted on individual service. Unable to come up with a solution, I stuttered, "You could try coming back later." As soon as the words came out of my mouth, I knew I would regret them. I did not know if a florist was scheduled that day.

An hour later, the shopper returned, but the florist hadn't yet arrived. "I've been shopping at TGS for years, and I've never been treated this way," the customer said. "And on my *wedding anniversary*!"

I pleaded for help on the radio. "There is an angry customer in floral."

A manager of the stocking crew arrived. Phil had always reminded me of a spinning top because he was short and slim, had a barreled chest, and was constantly on the move. When he arrived in the floral department, the shopper said, "*She* told me I would be served if I came back." He pointed like he was picking me out of a lineup.

Phil offered a discount on a premade bouquet to make up for my poor customer service. I was sure that I was about to be reprimanded. But after the shopper left, Phil spun away from the Front End without looking in my direction. It was as if he were saying, "I'm not going to validate that customer's rude behavior by mentioning it."

Another day, a shopper gestured to me with her index finger like I was a naughty child. *Come here.*

I followed the finger. "What can I do for you?" I asked.

She pointed to a checkstand conveyor belt. "This thing is

filthy. I'm not putting my groceries on *that*." As it happens, that cashier was famous for religiously disinfecting her station. A manager had once praised her for operating the cleanest checkstand in the store. "You could eat off that," she had said. But the customer kept pointing to dirt that wasn't there. A contented smile spread across her face as I wiped down the area with a rag.

Later, when I mentioned the incident to another colleague, he told me it wouldn't be the last time. "Some people are used to having servants," he said. "They treat us like their domestics."

Caring for one another as a form of self-defense didn't always work. A young man strolled up to my checkstand one day, eating a gelato. "I want cash back on my debit card." I explained that he had to make a purchase. He rolled his eyes. "Charge me a penny and then give me cash."

Offended that a customer would tell me how to operate my register, I stood my ground. "Sir, it's store policy that you have to buy something for cash back."

He cursed at me. "You're a dumbass!" I gave him the cash hoping that he would leave. Instead, he turned to the bagger. "What are you looking at, bitch?" The shopper tossed the soggy napkin from his gelato toward the bagging station.

Anyone who has worked in the service industry has had similar experiences. In 2022, scholar Christine Porath reported on a study of workplace "incivility," defined as "rudeness, disrespect, or insensitive behavior." From airline passengers who abuse flight attendants to rude behavior in stores, three-quarters of service workers reported regularly experiencing incivility on the job—a jump of about 15 percent from ten years earlier. Porath blamed the phenomenon partly on overwork. People on both sides of the checkstand are laboring harder and longer for what feels like little reward. Exploitation pushes us to take our frustrations out on others—and service employees are a convenient target.

Another evening at TGS, a woman wearing a long floral dress and beaded necklaces came into the store barefoot. "You aren't allowed in here without shoes," George said.

"I'll just be a minute," the shopper said.

The guard insisted. "It's against store policy. There could be glass on the floor."

The woman asked to speak to a manager. When the manager arrived, she said, "This employee just kicked me out of the store!" The shopper wanted the guard to be fired on the spot. "He should lose his job over this aggression!"

"I understand this was upsetting for you," the manager said. His servile tone made me anxious on my colleague's behalf. George's brother had recently died after contracting COVID, and he was helping to support two orphaned children, his nieces. But after the customer left, the manager's tone changed. "We're not firing anyone because a customer decided to come in without shoes," he clarified. "I was only trying to get rid of her." George and I were relieved.

George was on a streak of bad luck. At closing time a few nights later, he went to lock the side door that the last shoppers used to leave the building. When we met upstairs near the time clock, he looked like he had been punched in the face. "A customer thought he was locked in," he said. "He said that the exit was hard to see and called me a fucking retard." My coworker was distraught.

"That's awful," I said. "I'm sorry he said that."

George wanted to talk, but I was carrying heavy bags of cash and coins from the checkstands after a long shift. I wanted to drop them off and go home. Besides, I thought, there was nothing I could say that would erase what had happened to him. I headed for the vault. "A *fucking retard*," George repeated to himself, looking at his feet.

Once, a cashier told a man that she could not sell beer without proper identification. (During the pandemic, when face masks made it more difficult to determine age, employees were forbidden from selling alcohol without ID.) "Only stupid people who can't tell that I'm forty years old work at this supermarket!" the customer growled. He gestured around the Front End. "I own this place! You all work for me!"

Christopher left his checkstand to stand next to the cashier. Something of a Swiss Army knife at TGS, Christopher worked in multiple departments: on the Front End and as part of the custodial crew. The twenty-eight-year-old with dark hair and olive skin also sometimes helped out in i-grocery, the department that filled online orders. It was rare for workers to be trained in so many areas, a testament to Christopher's skills and reliability. On his days off, he told me that he kept himself busy writing a dystopian cyberpunk novel about a society ruled by three rival corporations.

On the day when the shopper complained to the cashier who asked for ID, Christopher added bodyguard to his list of job titles. The customer pointed at him with a long, bony finger. "You're a hoodlum! A *hoodlum*!" The shopper was trying to provoke Christopher into a confrontation. But he didn't react. The customer threw up his hands and left without his beer.

Another day, I heard shrieks and yelling coming from checkstand number seven. I turned around to see Lucia cowering behind her register. A customer was pacing in front of the counter. "I've been wandering around looking for Brillo pads for half an hour!" he said. "I have a pan to clean! What kind of supermarket doesn't have Brillo pads?"

I called security. "We need help at number seven!"

The shopper lunged forward to headbutt me. I ducked out of his way. By the time George arrived, the man was backtracking toward the exit and giving us the finger.

"One minute he was fine, and then he freaked out," Lucia said. "I don't know what happened."

George saw such events an inevitable consequence of working in a supermarket. "Anyone can come in here," he said. Looking out for each other couldn't protect us from everything.

The supermarket was a public resource because anyone and everyone could come inside. But being open to all put workers at risk of mistreatment or worse. Having to duck out of the way of a customer's headbutt before help arrived changed my view of community at TGS. There were two versions of community at work. In one version, shoppers and employees cared for one another. In the other, workers had to defend themselves from shoppers.

The grocery store's split identity goes back to the era when mom and pops were replaced by chains. By the 1920s, tens of thousands of the stores with names like Kroger and Safeway were operating from coast to coast. Chains improved on mom and pops by offering individual attention. The Kroger Grocery and Baking Company's Housewives' Advisory Service corresponded with customers and hosted conferences and cooking classes. Mom and pops were notoriously dirty and unsanitary. But Kroger cleaned up stores and added ventilation systems. Within a few years, corporate owners were painting chains in soft, pleasing colors and adding "kiddie corrals" with toys so that mothers could shop without having to hire a sitter.

Corporate ownership led to other efficiencies. Prices

were set by executives and posted in stores, eliminating bargaining and haggling at the counter. Shoppers no longer had to guess what they would have to spend to get dinner on the table or engage in a potentially embarrassing negotiation with a clerk in front of the neighbors. Fixed prices were part of a series of changes that shifted clerks' authority to shoppers. We can trace the customer service that we know today to the first chains that made shopping easier and less stressful.

In the South, Black customers derived profound benefits from chains. In fixed-price shops, they paid the same prices as white shoppers. Corporate stores also treated them more fairly. It had once been customary in mom and pops, one writer explained, for Black shoppers to wait "until all white people were served before advancing to the clerk. . . . The chains came along with a standard service for all customers and changed this condition overnight." Chain stores did not eliminate discrimination. But centralization ended some long-standing racist customs.

Chains were far from universally embraced. The stores were run by bankers and executives who might never set foot in them. Lining up at the mom-and-pop counter was a chore, and the clerk might be a patronizing jerk. But at least local stores served the neighborhood, not faraway investors. Mom and pops even allowed shoppers to run up a tab, getting a carton of eggs or a pint of milk and settling the bill later. After chains ended credit sales, customers began to see corporate stores as a threat to their communities.

Angry shoppers and small business owners launched an anti–chain store movement. By 1930, there were 260 anti–chain groups in thirty-five states. The fury crossed racial lines. Black entrepreneurs founded the Colored Merchants Association in part to defend independent grocers. Politicians and the media reflected the public mood. Senator

Huey Long declared that he would "rather have thieves and gangsters than chain stores in Louisiana," while in 1928, a *New York Times* headline read HUGE CORPORATIONS . . . ARE DISPLACING THE NEIGHBORHOOD STORE. State legislatures responded to the outrage by levying steep taxes on chains.

But corporate stores offered real improvements. Chains beat back the opposition by lowering prices, a benefit that few shoppers could resist. Even as customers embraced chains over time, they knew that the perks were coming at the cost of a loss of community.

The contradictions of community are still visible in the supermarket. At TGS, before Thanksgiving, management announced a program to collect money for the food bank. Cashiers were instructed to ask every shopper, "Would you like to help a local family in need celebrate the holiday by rounding up your purchase today?" Customers who gave to the Gobble Gobble fundraiser were invited to write their name on a piece of orange paper shaped like a pumpkin and tape it to the window. Passersby could see the pumpkins accumulate. One colleague remarked that she was collecting money for families "in need" while being a member of such a family herself. "I don't mind collecting the money," she said. "At the same time, it's depressing."

Some cashiers were more skeptical. "TGS doesn't care about hungry people. The store gets a tax break for donating to charity," Scarlet told me. Charity drives are common at the supermarket. Most shoppers have had the experience of being asked to round up their purchase for a cause. But the donations are not tax-deductible for stores since they are contributed by customers. One study on retailer promotional tactics explained that supermarkets "glean benefits associated with being viewed as socially responsible." Scarlet's critique was partly right. While TGS did not get a tax benefit from donations, the charity drive was a public relations campaign. It communicated to customers that the store cared about the community, without having to compromise profitability or commit to properly supporting their employees in need.

One evening, at Bonnie's checkstand, a shopper produced a SNAP card to pay for a roasted chicken. Funds from the program only covered food that had to be prepared for consumption. In place since the 1960s, the SNAP rule against cooked food is rooted in the idea that poor people are irresponsible and more likely to eat "bad" foods. Some customers were unaware of the prohibition or confused about which products it applied to. When Bonnie explained to the shopper that the chicken was off-limits, the woman asked for an exception. "I just got off work and have hungry kids at home," she said. "Can't you help me out?"

From a neighboring checkstand where I was bagging, I overheard the shopper's request. It was not the first time a SNAP customer had asked for an exception to buy prepared food. But cashiers had always said no. That night, Bonnie hesitated. She seemed to be puzzling over the situation. I waited to see what my colleague would do.

The shopper was lucky to have selected Bonnie's line. The longtime cashier with salt-and-pepper hair was one of the most community-minded employees at TGS. George had nicknamed her "Radio" because of the constant chatter at her checkstand. Bonnie asked about shoppers' jobs, kids, and hobbies and complimented them on their purchases. "You look like someone who knows how to spot a good deal!" Once, she told me that she was depressed about pandemic face masks—but not about having to wear one herself. "I'm tired of not seeing faces," she said. "It's hard to get to know customers when you can't see faces." Another day, when a guard caught a homeless man stealing a soda, Bonnie was angry with herself for not seeing him first. "I would have paid for it," she said.

The night the SNAP customer tried to buy a roasted chicken, my colleague waved me over. "I'm going to show you how to charge SNAP for hot food," she told me. Instead of scanning the product, Bonnie entered its price and pressed the MISC key. The checkstand registered the chicken as a miscellaneous item and the purchase went through. "I never thought of doing that," I said after the happy shopper left with her dinner. Bonnie admitted that it was not the first time she had violated the policy. "The no-cooked-food rule is pretty stupid," she said.

The incident happened on one of my first nights as a supervisor. My training had mostly consisted of trial and error. Occasionally, I followed a more experienced supervisor around to "watch and learn," as Paula had instructed. I had assumed that knowing how to operate the registers and using the override would be the most important skills. But supervising was like conducting a symphony. I had to assure that employees played their roles correctly and in the right order while balancing the needs of workers and customers. I had to decide whether to send a cashier on a break or make her wait if the lines were long, or whether to ask an employee with a bad back to sweep the floors. I worried constantly about making the right calls—would employees think that I was prioritizing shoppers' needs over theirs? In that context, Bonnie's confession was a relief. If she trusted me enough to demonstrate how to sell a forbidden chicken, maybe I was better at the job than I thought.

But Bonnie's decision put me in a difficult position. She had violated the law and put SNAP shoppers and herself in danger. Everything from the dollar amount recipients received to which products were eligible was determined by policymakers and elected officials. A manager had warned me that the state agency that administered SNAP sent secret shoppers into stores to monitor compliance with regulations. If Bonnie's transaction was discovered, TGS could lose its license to sell to those customers, and the cashier could lose her job.

That night, I thanked my colleague for showing me the trick and left it at that. I admired Bonnie's commitment to using her position behind a checkstand—as well as her technical skill—to serve all members of the TGS community. But the incident stayed with me as a sign of how ethically challenging the job might become.

During my first days at the store, I assumed that employees created community by force of will. By simply choosing to treat shoppers well, my colleagues and I could maintain TGS as a place where all were welcomed and cared for. Over time, I realized that I was wrong—employees were often constrained by rules and obligations that they didn't like but couldn't change and that determined their behavior.

One day, George saw a woman stealing chicken noodle soup from the buffet. She sipped on the cup while pushing a cart around the store pretending to shop. "This happens all the time," the guard told me. "People think we don't know what they're doing." He stopped the thief after she put the empty cup on a shelf, abandoned her cart, and headed for the exit. "I told her I would call the cops if she came back." George felt trapped between his sympathy for a hungry person and his job. "It sucks that people have to steal to eat, but we can't allow theft," he said.

One night, the radio buzzed. It was George's night off,

and a new security guard was tracking a shoplifting suspect. "Dairy case. Guy in a black coat," he said. "He went down the laundry detergent aisle, but then I lost him." The guard asked for my help. "Ann, let me know when he gets to the Front End," he said. Seconds later, a skinny guy with disheveled black hair strolled through an empty checkstand with his hands under his coat. "He's here now," I said.

The guard emerged from the front entrance to cut him off. The suspect tried to run, but my colleague grabbed him and shoved him hard against the dry ice cooler. Groceries dropped to the floor. He tried to push past the guard, yelling, "Get away from me!" My colleague wrestled the man down, smashing his face sideways against the concrete and shoving a Taser into his back until he screeched and stopped moving. The guard lifted him up, and the pair headed for the security office. A few minutes later, the police arrived and arrested the suspect.

Employees were stunned. Cashiers shook their heads and grumbled to one another as they resumed scanning. It was not unusual to see a guard chasing a suspected thief through the aisles like a scene from the TV show *Cops*. But physical altercations and Taser usage were less common. A despondent cashier gathered the groceries that had fallen out of the man's coat. The doughnut box was crushed, and the milk carton was leaking. He tossed the damaged products in the trash. By standing by while the incident unfolded, it felt as if we had all participated in the violence somehow. I felt especially implicated because I had helped the guard catch the man.

That night, and for a few nights afterward, I couldn't sleep. Every time I closed my eyes, I saw the doughnut thief sprawled on the floor with the Taser in his back. I wasn't the only employee affected. The following day, the cashier who had picked up the shoplifter's groceries told me that he was still fuming. "We tased a guy over doughnuts and milk last night," he said.

The incident shifted my view of community at TGS yet again. The store looked less like a resource and more like a perilous place. People coming into the store could put workers at risk. Workers could tell on desperate people stealing food. Worse, they also told on each another. Since I was now a full-fledged supervisor—one step below manager in the hierarchy—I was sometimes the first to hear when employees ratted one another out.

One night, George told me that Theodore, a custodian, had been caught in a mop closet watching videos. I suspected the videos were about Batman comics. The thirty-year-old was obsessed with the Dark Knight. He often passed by the Front End to share his latest theory about a storyline or character—his encyclopedic knowledge extended to the series' inception in the 1930s. "Why do people idolize Bruce Wayne, who is rich, while they despise Bane because he wants to seize the means of production?" he mused one evening to a group of cashiers, who rolled their eyes at yet another Theodore-ism. "Shouldn't it be the other way around?" he asked.

Another day, I heard a crack that sounded like someone had dropped a six-pack of soda off a forklift. A bird had flown into the window that ran along the Front End and had broken its own neck. After Theodore cleaned up the mess, he came back inside and said to me, "Do you know what kind of bird it was?" I knew what was coming. "It was a *robin*." He paused before delivering the punch line. "I hope Batman is okay!"

Now, Theodore was in trouble for watching videos. George told me that he planned to turn a tool used to catch shoplifters against our colleague. By reviewing surveillance footage from outside the closet door, the guard would determine how long the behavior had been going on. "We'll prove that he hasn't been doing his job," George said. A few days later, the guard reported his findings. Video evidence confirmed that Theodore had been spending up to an hour every night in the mop closet. Paula wrote him up (putting a reprimand in his employee file) for "stealing time" and threatened him with a suspension. Theodore promised to stop watching videos at work. After that, he still talked about Batman, but much less often than before.

Employees of all kinds were at one another's throats. Cashiers battled for the title of who suffered the most. When Gordon heard that Irene had been banished to the lobby after a customer complaint, he joked, "Irene can't stand up anymore. We're going to have to take her out back and shoot her." One bagger took a few months off work to recover from a serious illness. While he was gone, Cindy took over his spot at his favorite checkstand. On the day he returned to the job, he shoved her out of his way, nearly knocking her down. "I'm back," he declared. Another time, Darth fell down the stairs and landed on his knees. A nineteen-year-old cashier said, "Geezer, can't stay on your feet?" When Stewart (who was about the same age as Darth) heard about the accident, he said to me, "Was Darth crying like a little baby again?"

Gordon and Darth were sworn enemies, determined to best each other in the war over who was worse off—or the one most likely to tough it out. A couple of years earlier, Gordon had had back surgery—he blamed his bad back on years of working behind a checkstand. But surgery didn't help. After a few hours of cashiering, he would start wincing in pain and sometimes asked to go home early. Darth lashed out. "If Gordon is going to cashier, then he needs to stay for an entire shift!" he told me. Darth could have been talking about himself, since he regularly turned off his light to ease the pain in his arm. When Gordon heard what Darth had said, he mocked his colleague's injury. "Darth's arm will never be the same, and he's taking it out on me," he sneered.

TGS employees were not crueler or more callous than anyone else. They were trying to get by in a system that rewarded (or sanctioned) people as individuals and where there were few avenues for joining forces with others for their mutual benefit. In a zero-sum game, it took less time and was less risky to try to get by alone than to build alliances.

The battles were another sign of the barriers to organizing a union. Before starting the conversation, my colleagues and I would first have to overcome the tensions that were pulling us apart and pushing us toward individual solutions. Given the emotions built up over years of economic struggle and long-simmering resentments between workers, that task seemed even more daunting than holding a union meeting. Each worker's combination of life challenges made the foundation for organizing seem a long way off, with no clear path to get there.

A few months later, George told me that a manager had spotted an employee doing his personal shopping before clocking out after a shift. "I'm going to review the video to confirm it," the guard said. I defended the employee. "If he was shopping on the clock, then it was probably an honest mistake," I argued. It could happen to anyone. I had once made it out the door and halfway down the street before I remembered to run back inside and clock out. George said that it didn't matter whether the employee had made an honest mistake or not. I tried another tactic. "Do you really think we ought to be tattling on one another, especially when we don't have all the facts?"

He shrugged. "I'm just doing what the bosses told me to do."

Before working at the store, I might have assumed that workers' shared experience of insecurity would bring them together to fight against our bosses. But at TGS, employees' individual suffering was a source of stability for the system that abused and humiliated them, one reason the company had no interest in improving our conditions. The only way to keep our jobs was to do what the bosses told us to do. We turned on one another instead.

In the late winter of 2021, a letter went out to all employees that I hoped would improve morale. Sent by the CEO, it announced that TGS was raising wages for many workers. From then on, no one over the age of eighteen would earn less than fourteen dollars per hour. "Other cost of living adjustments are also being considered," it read. I was elated by the news. I assumed that higher pay was a good thing that would help struggling employees make ends meet. But despite being on the job three months, I was still thinking like a shopper.

To Nelly, the letter was rude and disrespectful. The fifty-five-year-old cashier was flat broke after two decades in the grocery industry. She once told me that she and her husband had hoped to celebrate their twentieth wedding anniversary by driving to a neighboring state to buy lottery tickets. "We couldn't afford the gas, so we spent the time working in our garden instead," she said. Nelly saw pay raises for new hires as a sign that her experience wasn't valued. "I'll make $0.40 more after the adjustment, bringing me to $15.40 an hour," she told me. "Someone just starting out will make only $1.40 less than I do." She had recently asked for a bigger raise but was told she had "topped out" at her rate of pay. Raising the wage floor but not the ceiling might as well have been a slap in the face. "They're just pissing off the veterans," she told me.

I had seen a photo of sixty-year-old Travis, the way he looked before I met him. He had thick white hair and a slightly rounded belly that made him look like Santa Claus. But by the time we started working together, he looked more like a weary elf. He had only recently returned to the store after recovering from a stroke. His hair was noticeably thinner, just like his frame.

Travis told me that new hires were going to earn almost as much as he did after a decade at the store. "They are boosting pay for newbies and screw the rest of us," he complained.

Cindy overheard our conversation as she walked by and stopped to commiserate. Her wage had been stuck at fourteen dollars for years. She saw no upside to the raises. "They're going to hire an eighteen-year-old to do my job at the same rate," she said.

My colleagues' views were understandable given the challenges of growing old in capitalism. Teresa Ghilarducci has sounded the alarm about the economic emergency that many of us face. In *Work, Retire, Repeat*, the labor economist described a "tale of two retirements." While the affluent are living longer, healthier lives, and retiring with a nest egg and their dignity, low-income workers are facing destitution. Since almost half of families have no retirement savings, millions must work until they die. Many would-be retirees are punching clocks in warehouses or toiling as home health aides. The number of older people still on the job spiked after 2008, when many baby boomers lost their homes during the Great Recession.

Ghilarducci's solution is a "Gray New Deal" that would expand social security and offer all workers access to a publicly funded pension. In the meantime, supermarkets are benefiting from retirees' financial desperation. For years, companies have recruited older people under the assumption that their life experience makes them good candidates for customer service roles.

Occasionally, the plight of elderly retail workers breaks into popular culture. In 2022, a Walmart contractor posted a video online from a store break room where an employee looked exhausted and miserable. The video went viral and helped to raise $170,000 for the woman. Another video featuring a homeless Kroger cashier hunched over her checkstand raised tens of thousands of dollars. The outpouring of support was a sign that shoppers are rightly horrified at the idea of people staffing supermarkets into old age.

I was coming around to the view that boosting the wage floor divided new hires from veterans, making unionizing even more complicated. But another theory circulating at TGS was more difficult to swallow. Some colleagues saw pay increases at our workplace as a sign that wages might be going up everywhere. They feared that prices would rise as a result. "Everything is going to cost more," Lucia told me. She was especially worried that the government might step in and raise the minimum wage to fifteen dollars per hour. "Can you imagine if that happened?" she said. "We would pay higher prices for groceries and everything else." My colleague told me that, if she had to choose between a pay raise or lower prices, she preferred lower prices.

George walked by and nodded. "Higher pay sounds nice, but it comes out of our ass eventually," he warned.

Research shows that most working people prefer *pre-distributive* policies, such as wage increases, to *redistributive* policies, like tax breaks that spread wealth around after it is accumulated. The choice is part of the belief that work is a foundation for self-respect and self-reliance, one reason people across the political spectrum favor a federal jobs guarantee. Lucia's and George's preference for lower prices over higher wages may have been a reflection of their place near the bottom of the labor market. Having lost hope that their conditions could ever improve, their primary concern was protecting themselves from the worst effects of a situation that seemed unchangeable.

My colleagues' comments sounded familiar. I had once encountered another version of the theory that putting money in workers' pockets would hurt them in the end. In 2015, when the Debt Collective, the organization that I co-founded, began demanding student debt cancellation, critics lashed out that inflation would follow. But a major study that examined the question found that inflationary effects would be "insignificant." Instead, research showed that erasing student loans could actually stimulate economic activity by giving families more money to spend.

At TGS, I did not tell my colleagues that I suspected their theories about slightly higher wages causing price spikes would turn out to be similarly dubious. My view was partly a result of social class and education. I had had the opportunity to study and reflect on issues in ways that most colleagues had not. I wouldn't have blamed them for assuming that my background was actually disqualifying. They might believe that I had not worked a retail job long enough to be a trustworthy source of information. Another reason was that we were in the middle of a phenomenon that I didn't yet know enough about. Too busy working to do research, I was reluctant to share my suspicions.

Later reports confirmed that corporate greed was the real reason for rising prices during the pandemic. The economist Isabella Weber called it "seller's inflation." "Large corporations . . . have used supply problems as an opportunity to increase prices and scoop windfall profits," she wrote in 2021. The Federal Reserve Bank of Kansas City confirmed that analysis, attributing 50 percent of the increases to profiteering. Prices spiked largely because corporations took advantage of the crisis to reap a windfall.

But my colleagues were also correct. Their concern about a higher cost of living was reasonable and understandable. They knew from experience that, whatever happened, they would get the sharp end of the stick. Pay raises for new hires were a clear example. A higher wage floor that appeared positive actually cemented employees' insecurity.

The TGS community was a mirage. Staffers were barely getting by. In a fog of fatigue and pain, they were trying to survive an economy where even a bigger paycheck might be a trap.

Although I was still one of the "newbies" Travis was complaining about, I wasn't sure I would be getting a raise. I had not claimed to have relevant technical experience when I had applied for the job. I was better at reading and writing than at operating machines. Now, it sometimes felt like I would never learn to master the checkstand like the veterans who punched the keys and swiped the override without looking.

Every shift was a jumble of coding mistakes, error messages, and keys pressed in the wrong order. One shopper waited fifteen minutes while I flipped through an employee manual to find out how to perform a particularly complicated transaction. "Last time this happened, a cashier called a supervisor who knew what to do," the customer said. *Calling a supervisor who knew what to do! Wouldn't that be nice?* Except I was the supervisor. When I called for help, managers arrived shaking their heads, stunned at my incompetence. Once, I forgot to put money in the registers at closing time. The morning cashier arrived to find that she could not process cash transactions. "Sorry, I can only take cards, because there is no cash in my till." Two nights later, I forgot to return some ice cream that a customer had decided not to buy to the freezer. The morning crew had to clean a gooey substance from the counter.

Though they hadn't seen me in action much, top bosses clearly doubted from the beginning that I could keep workers in line. I was being hazed. One day, a voice on the radio said, "Ann, do you copy? There is a bagger who is looking at her phone!"

I approached the employee who was still texting. "You can't use your phone at work," I said and pointed to the radio. "The boss is watching." Two hours later, during a rush, I was at the express lane when I got another call: "You have people in the lobby standing around talking." I headed outside. "I'm on it," I said.

Another day, the CEO came to TGS to inspect renovations taking place upstairs. The i-grocery department had become much busier since the pandemic. Construction workers were building walls to block off a portion of the café, creating a new workspace. A man in his sixties dressed in khakis and a flannel shirt, the head of the company could have passed for a customer. Except his smiling face was on the "managers' wall," photos of the bosses that we passed every day on our way to the time clock. If that wasn't enough to identify him, he wore a name tag that said "CEO."

That day, Paula and I had gone upstairs to meet new hires attending an orientation session. The radio buzzed. A manager wanted to know why there was no supervisor on the Front End. "The CEO wants to know where you are."

I grumbled to Paula, "She's trying to impress him."

Paula shrugged. "She's supposed to impress him."

We rushed downstairs. "The CEO saw two cashiers on their phones and two baggers hiding, refusing to work," the manager said. (She kept calling him *the CEO* like it was his name.) The phone usage might have been true. But there was nowhere to hide on the Front End. She was making up reasons to harangue me. I tried to explain that Paula and I had been upstairs for a legitimate purpose. But she didn't let me finish. "The Front End can't be left unsupervised."

I was convinced that my poor performance would mean no pay raise. But almost four months after I had started the job and soon after the CEO's letter announcing wage increases, Paula called me into the office to inform me that my wage was rising from $15.80 to $16.50. Since pay hikes had been widely discussed on the Front End, I knew that my raise was more significant than what some colleagues had received.

The boost was coming with pressure to improve my performance. Managers had filed an assessment. My highest scores were for my communications skills and reliability. But I received negative marks for technical errors, for occasional insubordination, and for not asking for help when lines got long at the checkstands. "You must call for assistance with long lines," Paula said. "We can't have frustrated customers."

It was true that I resisted calling coworkers from other

departments to help on the Front End. They were busy stocking shelves, making deliveries, or grinding meat for burgers. I wanted my colleagues to think that I was competent. Pulling them away from their jobs would have the opposite effect. But I told Paula that I would change my ways. The Front End was a black hole that sucked energy and time from other parts of the store.

Darth had become one of my closest colleagues. It had taken months to get there. At first, he had been standoffish, bordering on hostile. Once, a bakery worker came through his line to buy some flour. Darth pointed to me and said, "Here's our new Front End supervisor who doesn't have any experience in the industry." The employee laughed like I wasn't there, and Darth grinned like the Cheshire cat. I wanted to crawl under the counter and hide.

I told Kirsten about the incident. A purple-haired college student who had worked as a TGS cashier for three years, she always seemed to know what was going on behind the scenes. She told me that before I was hired, Darth had been hoping to be promoted to supervisor. "He felt snubbed when you got the job," she said. I wished that I could resign the position and demand that it be given to him instead, if only to protect myself from further humiliation. Since I knew that wouldn't work, I tried to smooth things over. One day, I let it slip that I hadn't asked to be a supervisor. "The job probably should have gone to someone else," I said. Later, after Darth confessed his repetitive stress injury, our relationship shifted. He started sharing information about which managers were okay and which ones to avoid, and spent time showing me how to run the register and correct my mistakes.

When I got the raise, I decided to return the favor by telling Darth that I was now making about a dollar more per hour than he was. I expected him to say that our wage discrepancy wasn't fair, that it was another sign of the store punishing veterans in favor of new blood. I was prepared to apologize. "I didn't expect to get a raise."

But he wasn't offended. "You're a supervisor, and I'm not," he said. "It's your responsibility to make sure that everyone gets their break on time."

His comment reminded me of another way that I was fumbling. All employees got a fifteen-minute break after two hours of work and a thirty-minute lunch in the middle of an eight-hour shift. The break cycle was supposed to flow easily, with one worker leaving for a break just as another returned. But it almost never worked out that way.

One of my first nights as a supervisor was typical. I had carefully sketched out a plan. My first move would come at 4:00 p.m., when I would close number five and transfer the cashier to the upstairs registers to relieve a colleague for a break. I didn't even get that far. At 3:30 p.m., the i-grocery manager arrived. "Do you have anyone I can use?" she said. "Orders are flooding in, and we're short-staffed." I let the manager take Christopher, who had been cashiering at number seven.

As he passed by on his way to the elevator, he said, "You're supposed to get other departments to send workers to us, not the other way around." He was saying that I should be treating the Front End like a battle position to be defended.

Since one cashier had called out sick that day, I now had two fewer cashiers than I needed. But I could still make it work. One employee's break was scheduled for 6:00 p.m. I roped off her lane at 5:50. If she came back a few minutes after 6:00, then I could give two employees their breaks before 6:30, when it was time for another cashier to take her lunch. Aurelie arrived for her shift. "Can you go and cover a break for the cashier upstairs?" I asked.

The cycle repeated two hours later when Aurelie and Zoe were both scheduled for breaks. Zoe was new to TGS and to cashiering. The nineteen-year-old had told me that her last job had been as a children's nanny. "I'm not cut out for singing nursery rhymes all day long," she said. Though I had not worked with her much, other supervisors told me that Zoe didn't seem cut out for grocery work, either. She was frequently late and regularly called out sick.

I worked in Aurelie's checkstand while she was gone, planning to relieve Zoe fifteen minutes later. But when I turned around, Zoe was gone. She had closed her register, leaving me the only cashier on the Front End. Within minutes, there were three carts in my line. "Can't you open another register?" a customer asked. I got on the radio. "Can someone help on the Front End?" No one arrived. So much for Paula's assurances that if I called, help would come. The black hole of the Front End only sucked energy and time if energy and time were available.

I scanned at breakneck speed. "Thanks for shopping at TGS. Sorry for the wait!" I didn't know who was more frustrated—the shoppers or me. When Zoe returned, I went straight to her checkstand. "You can't walk away like that," I said. "You left me alone up here." I had never raised my voice on the Front End before. She tried to say something about needing to use the bathroom, but I cut her off. "You have to wait until I tell you it's okay to go. I am in charge of breaks!" It sounded ridiculous. *I am arguing about pee breaks in a supermarket.*

It looked like I would be the most hated supervisor on the Front End in no time. But Paula soon took the title. Word must have gotten around about my spat with Zoe. Two days after that fiasco, Paula announced that extra breaks were prohibited. "Use the bathroom on your regularly scheduled break," she wrote in a mass text. A few days after that, Zoe went to the restroom. Paula told her, "You have just taken your break. You won't be getting another one." The cashier fumed. "I came to TGS to get away from small children, not to be treated like one," she said. Some came up with contingency plans. "I got Paula's message," Lucia said. "I'm going to wear an adult diaper, so I don't have an accident." The next day, when Travis's break was late, some urine leaked. He changed into a pair of pants that he had stored in his locker for emergencies.

Stewart informed me that he was tracking one employee's lunches. By accessing the online system, my fellow supervisor could see when the twenty-one-year-old had clocked in and out and when she had returned to her checkstand. "She is stealing time," he said. That day, during her lunch, the employee had been away from the Front End for a total of forty-six minutes, ten of which had been spent on the clock. "That's ten minutes she stole from TGS," Stewart said. Since I was coming on shift and he was leaving, he wanted me to keep an eye on her. "Write down her clock-in and -out times so we have a record. I'm going to report her to management," he said. My colleague hoped to make an example out of the time thief. I was relieved when she returned from her next break on time so I didn't have to report her.

Employee surveillance is common in retail. From scanners and surveillance cameras to timekeeping systems, multiple technologies track store workers' movements from the moment they enter their workplace. The tracking is a legacy of the industrial era, when factory employers broke work into discrete tasks so that individual workers' productivity could be measured and assessed. Surveillance exacerbates an already unequal power dynamic because employees may feel that they must accept Big Brother's gaze if they want to keep their jobs.

At TGS, I told myself that I was being pulled into Stewart's surveillance scheme against my will. *My colleague has got me all wrong. I'm on the side of the workers against management.* But the truth was that I wasn't so sure. I felt defeated when it came to breaks. When I first started supervising, I had not minded if someone extended a fifteen-minute break to twenty. What did I care about a few minutes? Our jobs were hard. People wanted to rest. I tried not to worry about what I considered minor infractions. But I was starting to see that small rebellions created turmoil.

Once, a cashier called from the upper level to ask when Arman would arrive to relieve her for a break. I responded that he had just come back from his lunch and would be right there. At twenty years old, Arman already seemed like a TGS veteran. He had come to the US from Syria a few years earlier and was taking college classes toward a degree in international relations. He said that he wanted to work with refugees, helping them settle in the US. "America is a wonderful country," he told me. "I love it here."

Arman asked if he could go to the candy aisle first to pick up some sweets. "The sugar helps to keep me awake."

I told him to relieve his colleague as soon as he found the candy. A few minutes later, the cashier called again. "Where's Arman? I need to use the bathroom!"

I found him in the aisle studying the hard candies like a deep-sea diver examining exotic fish.

"I can't seem to find the Jolly Ranchers," he said.

"They're right in front of your face," I said. "Now go upstairs and get to work!" Who hasn't lost track of time in the candy aisle? But Arman had not lost track of time. He had missed a few minutes of work at a colleague's expense.

At first, I assumed that employees didn't understand how extended breaks and stalling tactics affected others. I explained to cashiers and baggers that they should respect the clock on behalf of those whose breaks would be late if they didn't return on time. *We're all in the same boat.* The strategy hadn't worked. I wasn't telling anyone anything they didn't already know. No one extended a break to do harm or to make life difficult for anyone else. It was because they had to take care of their bodily functions. Or their break had been cut short in the past, so they were rebalancing the ledger and reclaiming something that they felt had been stolen from them. But rebalancing the ledger looked to others like a new round of shots fired in a competition that someone had to lose. Supervisors like me had two choices: We could do nothing, or we could harangue and denounce in an attempt to stop the cycle. Either way, it was probably pointless.

The supermarket pitted colleagues against one another while they battled for sympathy, higher pay, and the right to take a break. I wished I could go back to the days when I was just a cashier, when the store was a mystery that I might never solve. Even better, I wished I could go back to being a shopper, when the store was a haven and a community resource.

A few months into the job, my hip joints had been worn down to nubs. It felt like there was no cartilage left, just bone scratching against bone. From bagging groceries, my shoulders throbbed even when I wasn't at work. I had developed plantar fasciitis in my right foot from standing, walking, and lifting. Every step felt like being stabbed in the heel. I took solace in the idea that I was gaining experience and skills. With Darth's patient assistance, I was slowly mastering the registers. Maybe the job would start to get easier.

That was when the top bosses announced that TGS was replacing some checkstands with self-checkout machines. All the registers on the upper level were being replaced along with about a quarter of those on the Front End. The news sent shock waves through the store.

CHAPTER 3

Convenience

As a shopper, I had plenty of experience with self-checkout. I preferred the machines over the checkstand. Like many people, I picked up groceries a couple of times a week that I carried home by hand. The supermarket was a pit stop on the way somewhere else, and self-checkout felt like the straightest line between entering, buying, and exiting. Scanning my own groceries put me in charge of the time I spent in a store and got me to my destination sooner.

Self-checkout can seem like one of a series of conveniences that shoppers have come to expect. In the supermarket entryway, we grab a cart or a basket and head into a brightly lit space with tall ceilings and wide aisles. Most stores have a standard layout: The produce section is near the front, the freezer case on one side, and the dairy cooler on the back wall. Items are displayed with price tags underneath. The food aisles give way to cleaning supplies that flow into paper goods that flow into toiletries and medicines.

Thanks to barcodes and digital scanners, the cashier might have your grocery order totaled before you get out your wallet. If you have a twelve-pack of soda at the bottom of your cart, the employee may tell you not to pick it up—

you might hurt your back. Instead, a cashier comes around the checkstand with a hand scanner. You can tap your card or phone to pay. A worker might even offer to push your cart to the car. The supermarket is a marvel of streamlined efficiency.

We can trace the promise of convenience at the grocery store to Piggly Wiggly, the first store where customers walked the aisles and selected groceries from the shelves. The "self-service" shop opened in Memphis in 1916. Its owner, Clarence Saunders, was the son of a former plantation owner who had fought in the Civil War on the side of Confederate general Thomas "Stonewall" Jackson. After his father lost his wealth during Reconstruction, the younger Saunders was forced to strike out on his own. By age nineteen, he was working in the grocery business.

At first, the grocer was honest about the goal of self-service—he spelled it out in his original patent application. Self-service, it read, would "dispense with the employment of many clerks who are usually engaged to wait upon the customers." Advertisements for Piggly Wiggly made it clear that, by eliminating the clerk behind the counter, Saunders was transferring some of the work to shoppers. Something new was being born, one ad read, "not with a silver spoon in his mouth, but with a work shirt on his back." Another ad was even more direct: "Every customer will be her own clerk." The message was clear: In the self-service shop, customers worked for the store to reduce the owner's labor costs.

But Saunders had made a grave error. Shoppers weren't keen on doing the work themselves for his benefit. Barely a week after opening day, a woman came into Piggly Wiggly for butter. When a clerk informed her that she could find the product on aisle four, she turned and left. We can only imagine the shopper's shock. *Is this some kind of sick joke? Isn't shopping hard and thankless enough?* She went down the street to another store where a clerk handed her the butter. It was often irritating and even humiliating to negotiate with clerks. But counter service was still service. Piggly Wiggly felt like an insult.

Saunders needed a new sales pitch. He began promoting self-service as a time-saver. A new ad bragged that, at Piggly Wiggly, shoppers left the store an average of "every forty-eight seconds." Self-service was for busy housewives on the go. The store's ideal customer, another ad explained, was a woman "in a hurry" who "runs into Piggly Wiggly and helps herself. She pays the cashier and away she goes!" This campaign worked. Shoppers warmed to the idea of serving themselves as long as it was faster. Before long, Saunders opened two more Piggly Wiggly outlets. Since then, the promise of convenience has been central to the supermarket.

Self-checkout is a direct descendent of self-service because, to scan and bag our own groceries, we first have to select what we want from the shelves. What could be faster? If you leave your car double-parked while you run into a store for milk, or if you are simply someone who values your time, self-checkout seems built for you.

That's why, when I first started shopping at TGS, I was surprised that it only had traditional checkstands. The lack of self-checkout seemed old-fashioned, like the store was stubbornly refusing to offer a modern convenience. During the pandemic, it also felt dangerous. Wouldn't self-checkout allow shoppers to leave the store more quickly, limiting the spread of the virus? But with no other option, I had lined up at the checkstand like everyone else.

As an employee, I saw that my perspective was common. Some shoppers asked why TGS did not offer the time-saving option. Management had told us how to answer the question. "TGS wants every customer to receive the attentive service that only a human can give!" This seemed like a plausible explanation. There *was* something nice about human contact at the supermarket, especially when people were isolated at home.

Almost five months into my time at the store, the top bosses' language evolved—along with the self-checkout announcement. They now claimed that the machines made shopping faster and more convenient. To prepare workers for the change, they distributed a pamphlet with images of the machines and descriptions of their capabilities. It was like an advertisement for an exciting new tourist destination. Except the destination was our workplace, and the tourists were coming for our jobs.

On the day of the machines' installation, I arrived to find men in back braces and sensible shoes using jackhammers to punch holes into the floor. Colleagues and I watched as the crew ripped checkstands out of the floor and carted them away like old appliances. I did not expect to feel emotional or nostalgic about inanimate objects. But when I saw the holes in the concrete where twisted black wires stuck out, attached to nothing, it felt like something was being lost.

An executive from the corporate office was on the Front End to supervise the installation. Dressed in a pantsuit and wearing Converse sneakers, she looked like a prosecutor who had changed shoes after court. She explained that one cashier would be responsible for monitoring up to six machines. The corners of her mouth turned up slightly, as if she knew the news would be controversial and wanted to preempt any complaints.

Cashiers grumbled to each other about the extra work. Gordon was the only one brave enough to say what we were all thinking. "I don't like these machines," he said to the executive. "They take people's jobs away." Like an offensive line backing up Gordon, our fearless quarterback, the rest of us inched closer to hear her reply.

The executive's smile disappeared. She scrunched up her nose like she had encountered a foul smell. "Not true! I've managed stores with self-checkout. And I never had a problem staffing the Front End," she argued.

The comment was illogical. Gordon was not saying that machines would make staffing more difficult. He was saying that the new machines would require fewer people to operate them, which meant that we had to compete with them for our jobs. I followed Gordon back to his checkstand. "She just lied to our faces," he grumbled. "Do I have the word *stupid* written on my forehead?"

The self-checkout machines certainly looked impressive. Sleeker and slimmer than others I had seen, they looked like a technology you might see on a spaceship. They were silver and black with a touch screen and a white light on the top that flashed if a shopper needed assistance. Equipped with a motion detector, they greeted people in a soft feminine voice, "Welcome, valued customer." Next to the scanner was a low table that functioned as a scale as well as a theft-prevention device. If a shopper put an item on the scale without scanning it, the machine would pause the transaction and say, "Scan items one at a time before placing them in the bagging area." At the conclusion of a transaction, shoppers heard, "Thanks for shopping at TGS!" Buying groceries at the store would now be as fast and efficient as anywhere else. No human interaction required.

Like the executive who had pooh-poohed Gordon's concern about our jobs, bosses claimed that hours would not be cut and that the machines would make our jobs easier, too. But I was suspicious. Even before the machines were installed, colleagues complained to one another that TGS was abandoning the human-centered service they took pride in providing. Others groaned that employees would have to develop technical expertise. "We are going to have to learn a new skill without a pay raise," one colleague said. A staffer who had worked in another store with self-checkout told us that the machines were no faster than the regular checkstands.

I wondered what Stewart would say. My fellow supervisor's bald spot seemed to get a little bigger after each shift, like a crop circle that mysteriously spread overnight. An amateur chef, he claimed that cooking with butter was the reason he had never been sick a day in his life. Coworkers teased him about his potbelly. Once, during a downpour, Gordon said, "If the floodwaters come, we can all hang on to Stewart's belly." Stewart had laughed along with the rest of us. He once told me that, after forty years in the grocery industry, he had "no more fucks to give." Once, he admitted that, on late shifts, he sometimes locked the doors a few minutes before 10:00 p.m. so that he could get home early.

One day, when the two of us were restocking gum, candy bars, and beef jerky on the endcaps in front of the checkstands, I asked Stewart if he thought the machines were being brought in to replace humans. He saw the situation from another angle. The top bosses were panicked about a decrease in job applicants. "No one wants to work in a supermarket during a pandemic. They're going to have to raise wages," he explained. "Self-checkout limits the damage, because machines don't need to be paid."

Kirsten was working a nearby checkstand and overheard

our conversation. She was another kind of rebel. Once, when top bosses were meeting in the conference room, she said to me, "They're probably scheming about how *not* to give us a pay raise." Kirsten had her own theory about why the store was introducing self-checkout. "Employers have been trying to figure out how to keep labor costs down since the beginning of time," she argued. "They'll try anything to get us to work harder for the same pay."

She was right. We can trace this cost-cutting strategy to at least 1913, when automaker Henry Ford introduced the first automated assembly line. The invention tripled the number of cars Ford's employees produced. But the pace of work was so brutal that they quit in droves, forcing Ford to raise wages. TGS bosses were doing something similar by putting one worker in charge of multiple self-checkout machines. They were betting that we wouldn't quit. And if we did, they might try to replace us altogether.

It wouldn't be the first time the supermarket had introduced a new technology to lower costs. Self-service had reduced the number of workers required to run a store. But open aisles had created a new problem. Customers now had to carry their groceries through stores by hand. An Oklahoma grocer named Sylvan Goldman noticed that customers stopped shopping once they had filled up their handbaskets. The hand-carry system limited profits and virtually prevented impulse purchases—shoppers rarely bought more than they had come in for. In the 1930s, Goldman designed and patented a wheeled contraption that looked like two folding chairs with a basket on top. He invited shoppers to use these "folding basket carriages" in his store.

Customers resisted the wheeled baskets at first. Mothers thought they looked like baby carriages, and they were tired of pushing babies around. Undeterred, Goldman hired models to walk through his store pushing the carts and offering them to shoppers. He instructed the models to use peer pressure. "I told this young lady . . . to say, 'Look, everybody's using them—why not you?'" he said. The ruse worked. Once they heard the positive reviews, customers eagerly traded handbaskets for what they called "shopping carts."

The carts helped to turn the grocery store into an inside-out version of Ford's assembly line. Instead of parts moving down a belt where workers assembled them into cars, customers moved through the aisles selecting groceries and bringing them to checkstands. But while Ford's method added to workers' labor, in the grocery store, it was customers who took on the burden of moving and carrying. Along with self-service, carts helped to reduce grocers' overall costs.

Kirsten was right that self-checkout was part of a line of innovations intended to benefit employers. But Stewart's theory that TGS was attempting to replace humans in the short term also sounded plausible. It was undeniable that TGS was in the midst of a staffing crisis. Every day, on my walk to the store, a ball of anxiety formed in my stomach. The closer I got to the Front End, it rose into my throat and lodged there like food that wouldn't go down. I knew that I would not have enough cashiers and baggers to adequately staff checkstands and collect carts. I visualized long lines and frustrated customers. Colleagues saw that I was struggling. One evening, on my way into the store, I passed another supervisor who told me that the Front End had been understaffed all day. "It's going to be you on a sinking ship tonight," he warned.

High turnover was one cause of the labor shortage. New hires sometimes worked a few weeks and then quit, sometimes without notice. (TGS was not alone. The retail "quit rate" is 70 percent higher than in other industries, with workers citing poor treatment and overwork among the reasons for quitting.) I often walked by the conference room and saw a half dozen recruits watching a PowerPoint about everything from state liquor laws to the company's sexual harassment policy. I knew that many of those people wouldn't be around long. The staffing churn contributed to the sinking-ship feeling because it was nearly impossible to fill holes in the schedule at the last minute. Paula regularly sent out mass texts with a list of available shifts: "THE FRONT END COULD USE SOME HELP THIS WEEK."

Moreover, staffers who did stick around were not always reliable. Callouts were common. Virtually every day, someone—sometimes several people—called to say they would not be in that day for one reason or another: a car that broke down, a family emergency, a student who needed to study for an exam. Most often, employees said they were sick with COVID.

It was the weakest excuse. While virtually all employees were struggling with various physical ailments and illnesses, managers did not accept the virus as a reason for missing work. Even among employees, the general consensus was that no one had ever caught COVID and never would. Every sick callout was a ruse to get the day off. The perception was not pandemic denialism but a response to exhaustion and overwork. Absenteeism was so common that Paula threatened to write up workers who did not supply proof of illness, such as a doctor's note. It was mostly an empty threat. With the store understaffed, employees knew they could get away with occasional callouts without consequences.

On one typical shift, I arrived through the back door just before 7:00 a.m. and found that no one was stationed at the upstairs registers. I clocked in, grabbed my apron and a radio from the office, and ran downstairs to the Front End. "Who is supposed to be upstairs?" The cashier pointed to the podium. There was a note from one of the guys who stocked shelves overnight. At 4:00 a.m., he had received a callout from a sick employee. "Please go upstairs," I said to the cashier. "That area is unattended." Normally on opening shifts, I went to the bankers' office to get bags of cash and coins for the checkstands. But the callout meant that I couldn't leave the Front End. I made a radio call. "Dana, can you bring the money down here this morning? We've had a callout." I would be the only cashier on shift for at least an hour.

Between checking out customers, I perused the day's schedule on my phone. The anxiety in my throat split into tiny balls that rolled into my fingers and toes. There was no cashier coming in at 9:00 a.m. On good days, the arrival of the 9:00 a.m. cashier allowed me to give breaks. But Paula had not scheduled anyone. It wasn't like her to screw up like that. I would have to spend the morning behind a checkstand, and the other cashier and two baggers would have to wait until 11:00 a.m. to take their breaks. That was the most optimistic scenario. It was Monday, the busiest day of the workweek. The callout would create a domino effect. Everyone's break would be delayed by at least thirty minutes.

By the time Nelly arrived at 11:00 a.m., I had been cashiering for four hours straight while answering the phone and directing baggers to collect carts, in my role as supervisor. I kept scanning while other workers took their delayed breaks one at a time. When another cashier arrived at 1:00 p.m., Nelly took her first fifteen-minute break. By the time Stewart appeared at 2:00 p.m., I was so happy to see him that I almost cried. "Can you take over?" I asked. "I haven't had anything to eat today." I made a beeline for the restroom and then to the break room to inhale a sandwich, hopefully before I passed out.

After several more shifts marred by scheduling mistakes, I was convinced that something was going on with Paula. Was she stressed about self-checkout like everyone else? I stopped in her office one day and found her in front of the computer chewing on a fingernail. “Everything okay?” She told me that the store had seen a drop in profits, and she had been instructed to cut two hundred hours per week from the schedule to make up for the losses. I was stunned.

“I’ve already noticed fewer people on shift,” I said. “It’s bad.”

She nodded. “We’ll have to weather it. Maybe self-checkout will help.” Paula hoped the machines might offer a solution to staffing cuts ordered from the top.

Unfortunately, the *self* in self-checkout was a joke. It was more accurate to say that an employee operated the machines with some assistance from customers. Shoppers made errors, which prompted the light to flash. The most common included inadvertently bagging products without scanning them, putting more than one item on the scanner, or putting a personal item such as a wallet onto the scale. The extra weight confused the machine and halted the transaction.

Other times, a product could not be scanned because the UPC had fallen off or was damaged and the price had to be entered manually. A cashier had to move between machines completing transactions. As some colleagues had predicted, self-checkout was more work.

At the regular checkstand, age verification was swift. Most shoppers handed a cashier their driver’s license along with their beer. But at self-checkout, when a shopper scanned a six-pack of Mike’s Hard Lemonade, the light went off and a voice said, “Help is required for this item.” If the cashier was assisting someone else, the customer waited. If a shopper had not seen the message on the screen that said, "ID check needed," she might have to fish her ID out of her wallet when the cashier arrived.

While products sometimes scanned at the wrong price at the regular checkstand because of coding errors in the database, cashiers usually corrected the most egregious ones on the spot. It was obvious that a single can of Red Bull did not cost $10.99. But the machines did not know what anything was supposed to cost. Customers sometimes scanned, tapped their credit card or phone, and left before realizing they had been overcharged. It got so bad that if a shopper came back to the store for a refund due to a pricing error, I suspected they had gone through self-checkout.

Sometimes, after a shopper completed a transaction and left, a message on the screen read, "Remove all items from the bagging area." The machine was saying that products were still on the scale. The solution to what employees called "ghost groceries" was using a digital card to access the settings and then clicking on a link that said "Zero out the bagging area." Since the operation might have to be performed after each subsequent transaction, a cashier had to babysit the machine.

Some cashiers tried performing a "force quit" (pressing a green button on the back of the device for a few seconds). Sometimes it worked: The machine went dark, and the home screen reappeared. But the reboots could also make things worse. If the machine had glitched in the middle of a purchase, the unresolved transaction might reappear on the screen. These blockages were like a virus. A frozen machine could not accept new pricing data uploaded into the system overnight. If there was a sale on laundry detergent on a Thursday, a self-checkout station that had glitched on the previous Wednesday might still charge the old price.

Studies have confirmed what I saw on the job: Customers lack the skills to operate self-checkout without error. They don't always know which payment methods are acceptable, which produce codes to use, or how to fix common glitches. An automated voice telling a shopper what to do or a message on the screen is no substitute for a skilled worker. While self-checkout may occasionally speed up the process, there is no evidence that the machines are faster overall.

I had hoped that self-checkout might at least be easier on workers' bodies. After all, there was no scanning required. But the machines added risks and possibilities for embarrassment. Nelly had worked in another store with the machines. She warned us that bathroom breaks were about to get even more stressful. "You will have to tell everyone in the store that you have to pee," she said. It was only a minor exaggeration. If a self-checkout cashier upstairs wanted a bathroom break, she had to make a radio call. "Can someone come up? I have to go!" Downstairs, employees also had to get someone to cover their stations to use the restroom.

Once, Charles asked me to watch the machines while he went to the bathroom. When he returned less than a minute later, I said, "That was fast."

"I've been wearing a diaper since Paula said no more bathroom breaks," he said. "I prefer not to have to pee in my pants. But sometimes it's unavoidable."

Self-checkout did not eliminate pain and discomfort. When Paula first told me that self-checkout was coming, she said, "I don't know what cashiers with bad backs and sore feet are going to do." Regular cashiers stood on padded carpets that helped to protect feet and ankles. But a self-checkout cashier walked back and forth on concrete. One staffer told me she didn't know how much longer she could tolerate it. "The floor murders my feet," she said.

I asked another colleague with a bad back how she managed the demands of moving between the machines. "I wish I could take off all my skin and put it on a bionic body. I wish I could replace myself with a new machine," she said. Muscles and bones could not compete with steel and glass. In an endurance contest, the machines would win every time.

A few weeks after they were installed, a machine was glitching again. It wouldn't print a receipt. I had a clear view of the four machines to my left and could see more customers coming from the main concourse below. A shopper in a shirt and tie was standing with his grocery bag waiting for a receipt that didn't come. The "Welcome to TGS! Touch the Screen or Scan Your First Item" home screen had reappeared. As far as the machine was concerned, the transaction was over. The screen might as well have read, "Why are you still standing here, buddy? Move along!"

I waited, hoping the shopper would decide he didn't need a receipt after all and leave. No such luck. He turned to me and said, "I need a receipt." I scanned my card to access the settings and clicked on the "Reprint Receipt" button. I was the embodiment of the axiom that doing the same thing over and over and expecting a different result is the definition of insanity. The machine had glitched in exactly the same way earlier that day, and "Reprint Receipt" had not worked. Instead, I had warned customers not to expect a receipt. "We're saving trees!" Most didn't want one anyway. After a while, the receipts had started printing again. I thought I was out of the woods.

"I'm sorry," I said. "I'll have to reboot. Can you wait five minutes?"

The shopper went berserk. He gestured around to no

one in particular and called out, "Can someone come and help this idiot?" Customers waiting in line at the gelato bar turned to look. The employee working the espresso machine looked at me as if to say, "I can't believe he just said that." The man gave up and stomped off without a receipt.

At the regular checkstand, replacing the roll of paper for receipts took a few seconds. But sometimes the self-checkout sensor malfunctioned, indicating that the paper was out, even when it wasn't. A cashier could try restarting the machine and waiting for it to come back on line. The wait could feel like an eternity—and that was the best-case scenario. A reboot did not always fix the sensor. Once, a customer scolded a twenty-year-old cashier. "You should warn people not to use broken machines," he said. The cashier was worried it wouldn't be the last time the machine would break down. "People are going to blame me," she said. I shut down the offending machine to protect her from impatient shoppers, risking longer lines at the other stations.

Whether by cash, debit, credit, EBT, app, or even by personal check, the payment process at a regular checkstand usually took a few seconds. At self-checkout, options were limited, which befuddled customers and led to delays. Incomplete or unrecognizable payment methods confused the machine. If a shopper's credit card was declined, a self-checkout cashier canceled the payment and tried again. If that didn't work, she restarted the machine and rescanned the groceries. But if a shopper inserted a debit or a gift card with a balance too low to cover the total, the machine sometimes froze. A shopper would have to wait for the employee to perform a repair. I often leveled with customers. "Take your basket to a checkstand. It'll be faster."

The machines did not take SNAP or checks. And despite

large signs that screamed "NO CASH," some customers scanned their groceries and then looked for a slot to insert bills. In that case, an employee had to print a receipt with a transaction number and walk the shopper to a checkstand to complete the purchase.

The machines did, however, have a slot for paper coupons. Customers sometimes shoved cash into the slot and waited for the machine to register that they had paid. Cashiers did not have a key to open the drawer and rescue the money. They had to call a supervisor to fish it out. At the end of the day, an employee collected the coupons in the drawer and printed a report that she submitted as part of her "till count," just like a regular cashier. There was so much hardware and paperwork involved that I started to think of the machines as conventional registers in disguise. The same gears were churning underneath—old wine in new bottles.

One night, two machines froze within minutes of each other. After several failed force-quit attempts, I shut them down and sent a warning email to Paula, copying a manager. "The pricing data is not going to upload tonight," I wrote. The next day, I received a curt reply from the manager who informed me that I should have performed a "terminal transfer" to fix the problem. A *terminal transfer*? What the hell was that? I asked around the Front End, but no one else had been taught this mysterious fix, either. It occurred to me that the store didn't want to train us to perform repairs, because self-checkout was about saving on labor.

Paula responded to the email in her typical obsequious style. "Yes, a Front End supervisor should be a problem-solver!" *A problem-solver?* She was throwing me under the bus. Would it have killed her to say what was true, that I had not been trained to do a terminal transfer? Instead of the machines making my job easier, I was being patronized and disrespected.

The day that a shopper called me an "idiot" because a machine wouldn't print his receipt, I called the tech support hotline and explained the problem. "Don't tell me to reboot, because I already tried that," I said. The person on the phone was not familiar with the error. He instructed me to take a video of the malfunction and email it to him. I waited until a customer walked away, commandeered the machine, and used my phone to film the receipt tape dispenser not working. I felt ridiculous. *I'm recording a video of nothing happening.*

A few days later, employees sent by the corporate office showed up to repair the machine and to fix other lingering issues. Wearing tool belts and carrying screwdrivers and wrenches, the men opened panels and performed diagnostics like they were working on an oil rig.

Self-checkout required another piece of hardware. Employees needed a digital card to fix customers' errors. It was impossible to work the machines without it. One day, at 6:50 a.m., I was pleasantly surprised to find that the self-checkout cashier was already at her station. *This shift is starting off well.* My assessment was premature. Only recently hired, the cashier had not yet been given the card. Paula was not scheduled until later that morning, and I did not have a key to the bank where the cards were stored. I made a radio call. "We need to get into the bank fast," I said. When a manager opened the door, the card was not there.

The store was now open, and customers were in the aisles. I couldn't think of a solution, especially since I had not yet taken a drink from the thermos of coffee I had brought from home. I could not give the new cashier my digital card because I needed it to supervise the Front End. The manager had been in the store all night. If I didn't know, I could have guessed from his bloodshot eyes and hyperactive manner. Hopped up on energy drinks, he was more alert. "You'll have to move the cashier at number three upstairs and monitor the machines downstairs yourself until Paula gets here," he said. This was awful news. I had spent the prior week apologizing to customers, fighting with glitchy machines, and calling tech support. I wanted a break from self-checkout.

The first customer tried to shove cash into the coupon slot. "These are card only," I said. "If you want to pay in cash, you have to go through a register."

He frowned and said, "You know, a lot of people don't have bank accounts. You're saying that only rich people can use the self-checkout machines."

I saw his point but was too tired to care. "That's right," I said. "Only rich people can use these machines."

Later that day, when I opened my store email, I saw that a manager had sent a note the previous evening to inform me that she had left the missing digital card in Paula's office. I saw the message too late, because I had been too busy rushing around trying to find the card. Even on a day when the store was adequately staffed, the machines could create chaos.

At closing, cashiers shut down the regular registers on their own. But a supervisor had to turn off multiple self-checkout stations one at a time. Sometimes, I tried to save minutes by closing some while leaving others open. The shutdowns were a gamble. If there was a rush of late-night business, the shuttered machines became a liability. Customers had to line up at those that were still open and might still be waiting after the doors were locked.

One afternoon, I arrived to replace Stewart, who had opened the Front End that day. The first words out of his mouth were, "I'm sorry." I almost burst into tears even before he told me what he was sorry about. Two employees had called out sick. One call was from a recently hired cashier who was rumored to have fallen asleep during the orientation PowerPoint. "Not a good sign," Stewart said.

"Maybe he really is sick," I said. But my words sounded hollow even to myself. I was starting to agree with my coworkers that no one ever got sick, and every callout was suspicious. After another employee called out, I was down to two cashiers for the night shift.

Before self-checkout, I might have been able to get through the crisis by performing the usual juggling act: filling in for workers when they took their breaks and hoping customers didn't complain about the lines. I could also pull a rabbit out of a hat by calling a manager of the stocking crew who knew his way around a checkstand, thanks to a prior role on the Front End. My colleague wouldn't like being pulled away from his job unloading trucks and ordering inventory, but I knew he wouldn't say no. He probably knew, like all the managers did, that I had been told to call for help. Self-checkout was still a glaring hole in my plan. Since the machines needed a constant babysitter, I still wouldn't have enough people.

I called a top boss. "Can I come and talk to you?" In her office, I explained the situation. "I may have to shut down self-checkout while cashiers—" She didn't let me finish the sentence.

"No, you can't do that," she said. "I'll get you some help from i-grocery." She dialed the department manager and instructed her to send a member of her crew to cover cashiers' breaks. I was relieved, even as I recognized that the i-grocery manager was now the one scrambling. Self-checkout moved people around to plug leaks caused by self-checkout.

Eventually, I got used to some technical glitches and learned how to fix others. But the social impact of the machines never got easier. Once, a customer tried to pay with a Visa gift card. The message on the screen read, "Insufficient funds." When I explained the situation, the customer said, "You stole my money!" I assured him that I had nothing to do with how much money was available on the card. He raised his arm as if he might hit me. I felt no fear, only a numbing fatigue. *I'm about to be punched by a customer who is mad at the machine.* "You stole my money!" George heard the commotion, rushed over, and escorted the guy out the door.

Once the shopper was gone, I took a closer look at the error record. The customer had only been a few cents short. If I had deleted one item from the order, he could have purchased the rest of his groceries and left without incident. But the man was so unhinged by the time I arrived that the possibility did not occur to me. When I told George that I was kicking myself for not looking more closely at the transaction, he said, "That guy was a scumbag." He was telling me to let it go. Self-checkout gave shoppers and workers more reasons to despise one another. There was nothing we could do about it.

One of the biggest issues caused by the machines had to do with shoplifting. Before self-checkout, since all shoppers had to go through a checkstand to exit the store, thieves had limited options. They could pay for some items while hiding others under a coat. More brazen methods were easier for security guards to spot. Once, a customer wearing a backpack brought groceries to the checkstand and opened his wallet. "I thought I had enough cash, but I don't," he said to the cashier. "Can you hold these groceries for me while I go to the ATM?" The cashier let the customer walk away. Security guards stopped him at the door and pulled off his backpack. It was full of stolen goods.

The self-checkout machines were like a big, flashing sign that said, "SHOPLIFTERS WELCOME." One method was scanning a less expensive product in place of a pricier one. A cashier once reported seeing a customer scan a container of yogurt in place of a rib eye steak. Other thieves entered the wrong produce code. A shopper buying mushrooms might enter the code for potatoes, ensuring herself a discount. More daring thieves put a phony credit card in the machine and walked away. If they were stopped, they could say they had forgotten their card in the machine. When the card didn't work, they would produce another one to pay for the order.

Some shoplifters stole without touching a machine. They put groceries into a bag brought from home and walked out the door. When the self-checkout area was crowded, a customer who looked confident and unhurried might not be stopped. Employees were supposed to call security the moment we saw suspicious behavior. But stopping every thief was impossible.

Before I worked at TGS, I had not seen shoplifting as a moral failing. I figured that anyone who stole from a grocery store was probably just hungry. On one hand, I was right. In my experience, the most common type of theft at TGS was a person putting food directly into their mouth. But once, a self-checkout shopper scanned and bagged seventy dollars' worth of groceries and ran for the door when I turned my back. Before he bolted, I had noticed his expensive-looking watch. While I might have been sympathetic to shoppers who appeared down on their luck, it was humiliating to be taken advantage of by a cheat who could probably have afforded to pay. As angry as I was, I feared that, if I reported the theft, I might be accused of not being vigilant enough at self-checkout. I used the override to delete the order. Both of us got away scot-free. Supervising had its advantages.

After a few shifts, I understood why retailers are giving up on cashierless systems. A 2022 study showed that theft is rampant at self-checkout, with companies attributing as much as 23 percent of losses to the technology. Stores, including Target, Walmart, and Dollar General, have all cited theft as a reason they are limiting or replacing cashierless checkout.

Companies may also be responding to the threat of government regulation. In 2025, Long Beach, California, became the first city in the country to mandate that stores adequately staff self-checkout. The law prohibited a single employee from monitoring more than three machines. The United Food and Commercial Workers International Union (UFCW) endorsed the law, noting that companies use self-checkout to try to cut labor while putting workers in the position of stopping thieves. It may not be the last time that cities impose some sanity on retailers.

One day, Nelly told me, "Someone stole from me today." She had observed a new technique at self-checkout. A customer had filled a large container of soup at the buffet and then only charged himself for a small one. I suggested that it could have been an honest mistake. Nelly didn't agree. "He knew what he was doing." My colleague had a real disdain for shoplifters. "My lot fees go up every year," she said, referring to the cost of renting the land that her trailer home sat on. "But I don't steal!" To stymie soup thieves at self-checkout, Nelly wanted barcodes printed on the bottom of the containers. "Will you pass the idea to management?" she asked. It was a smart idea, but I had never seen the store act on any suggestions from employees. I told her that I didn't think managers would want to spend more money on a system that already looked like a bust.

Days later, Nelly told me about another incident. At the salad bar, a woman had filled a container with salad along with two cups of dressing on the side. She did not put the cups on the scale. "You have to pay for those," Nelly said.

The shopper argued, saying, "But this is just salad dressing."

Nelly stood her ground. "Salad dressing is not free."

The woman refused to pay.

"So, we had to shrink it," Nelly said, using the industry term for throwing food in the trash. "But at least she'll know that she can't get away with it next time."

Given my own experience with shoplifters at self-checkout, I didn't blame my colleague for throwing food away instead of letting a thief win. No one wanted to feel duped.

It felt like we already had been duped by the whole system. At the checkstand, chatting with customers was one of the pleasures of the job. Many cashiers had "regulars," shoppers they knew by name and enjoyed serving. But at self-checkout, there were no regulars. Conversations were rarely friendly banter or catching up with the neighbors. By the time I got to a machine with a flashing light, a shopper might be ready to berate me. Most shoppers took delays in stride and laughed when I joked that "this machine has been grumpy today!" But the few that did not could ruin a shift.

A self-checkout shift was wildly unpredictable, and yet the outcome was certain. I knew that the light was going to go off. I just didn't know when, what the problem would be, or what I would have to do to fix it. I blamed customers who made mistakes. This was irrational. There was no reason that a shopper should know how to use the machines, even though they were also working on behalf of the store.

Self-checkout only works if customers do. The machine wants to know how many mangoes you are buying. If you are purchasing loose mushrooms, you must select shiitake, oyster, brown, porcini, and so on. Is that cucumber regular or organic? American or English? (If you don't know the answer, you have to ask the human cashier.) Would you like a printed receipt, or would you prefer it by email? Please enter your email address. Other instructions, from "Scan your items one at a time" to "Don't forget to scan your rewards card," treat you like an employee.

Knowing the skilled labor required to operate a self-checkout station, I still watched with a combination of contempt and amusement as TGS customers fought with uncooperative machines. Sometimes, I waited a few seconds before stepping in to help. I turned self-checkout into a game for which only I knew the rules. *Will this shopper be able to fix this issue himself? Or is he just the usual idiot?*

Shoppers often seemed as frustrated as I was. It is not hard to sense when a store employee is less than enthusiastic about helping you or when a technology doesn't live up to the hype. There are signs that customers everywhere are reaching the limits of what they are willing to put up with. In 2020, Amazon introduced a cashierless supermarket in Seattle. Shoppers used their phones to enter the store, which tracked their purchases using sensors and scanners. After they were done shopping, they exited without passing through a checkstand. The "just walk out" technology was eventually installed in about twenty Amazon stores nationwide.

By 2024, the company announced that the experiment

was over. Amazon was removing the technology and closing physical stores. It turned out that shoppers were creeped out by the sensors and cameras that followed their every move. They also rejected the labor required to make "just walk out" work. Customers drew the line at weighing their own produce and performing other tasks once done by employees. They recognized that a "cashierless grocery store" didn't mean there were no employees—it meant that *they* were the employees.

It was a twist that Clarence Saunders might have warned about. In the 1940s, the grocer had a new idea for boosting profits. He worked with engineers to design an automated store. The Memphis outlet stocked products vending machine–style behind glass, which customers selected by inserting a key into the display. A clerk then inserted a second key into a master slot that sent the selected products down a chute and onto a conveyor belt to the checkstand. Saunders hired only two employees to stock displays and accept payment. He called his new shop Keedoozle. Others dubbed it the "robot grocery store."

The mechanics were endlessly glitchy. Odd-size products fell and broke, which required stopping the conveyer belt to clean up the mess. Regular breakdowns required assistance from electricians, increasing the grocer's labor costs. A phenomenon that today's grocery workers know well, customers often changed their minds. They sent items down the chute that they decided not to buy at the counter, forcing a worker to restock them.

Like Amazon's "just walk out" stores decades later, Keedoozle was a flop. The store drained Saunders's bank account, he declared bankruptcy, and the government seized his assets for unpaid taxes. The entrepreneur's walkable aisles and open shelves had changed the industry forever. Now he was humiliated and broke. Saunders blamed shoppers, suggesting they were too stupid to recognize his genius. Keedoozle "was too much for the average mind to comprehend," he said. But customers wanted real convenience, not a cheap substitute.

It may turn out that today's promised "revolution" in the supermarket was more like a detour into a social nightmare that we are just waking up from. As my sixth month at TGS began, I didn't like the person I was becoming. And I was not alone. During one of my shifts at self-checkout, Christopher passed through to empty the trash. He told me that he preferred the machines over the checkstands. I had never heard anyone say that. I told him that I thought I was losing my mind. A few shifts earlier, while monitoring the machines on the upper level, I had caught myself feeling sorry for a shopping cart abandoned in the produce section. "The poor thing was just sitting there, alone and rejected next to the cucumbers," I explained.

Christopher said that he was not bored or deluded during a self-checkout shift. He made the situation work to his benefit. "Working the machines allows me the opportunity to be condescending to customers who don't know what they're doing," he said. I didn't know whether to laugh or cry.

Instead, I built an emotional wall. My choice was not an improvement, but it felt more wholesome than being openly condescending. The next time a shopper with a wad of bills said, "It doesn't take cash?" I pointed to the sign that was staring her in the face. "That's why it says 'NO CASH' right there at the top," I said.

So far, self-checkout has not replaced workers. Even as the machines have become ubiquitous, employment figures for the retail industry as a whole have remained stable over time. Innovations from self-service to shopping carts effectively reduced costs, but companies may have reached the end of the road. The implications go beyond the supermarket. The lesson of the "cashierless" grocery store is that human intelligence cannot be easily replaced. And even in cases where automation is a time-saver, such "convenience" may come with a social cost that isn't worth paying.

So why do supermarkets keep trying to automate labor given all the drawbacks? As Kirsten had warned, automation is an excuse. Just because machines can't always replace people doesn't mean companies won't keep trying. The staffing crisis at TGS was not only an outcome of the pandemic, or an anomaly in the industry. Retail workers everywhere are being similarly squeezed. One 2024 study reported that more than half of employees said that their stores were understaffed. And the problem was especially serious in stores with self-checkout. The UFCW has correctly argued that automation at the supermarket is not just an employment issue. It's bad for everyone.

TGS employees were not Luddites afraid of innovation. Our anxiety was as old as the first automobile assembly line that sped up work and provoked mass resignations. My colleagues and I feared that our already difficult jobs could turn into something worse. We wanted to participate in the community life of the supermarket. But the machines severed a social connection between us and our customers and created an environment where we judged and mistreated one another.

It's hard to give up the promise of convenience. Even after I left TGS, I continued to use self-checkout machines. The technology still *seemed* faster, even though I knew the truth. Few of us would want to give up the option to scan, swipe a card, and be on our way. It's only when we zoom out to take in the full picture that our dilemma comes into focus.

Our desire to save time is understandable. On average, customers today spend more hours buying food than on housework, cooking, cleaning, or answering email. But most of the time we spend shopping happens *before* checkout. We have to walk or bike to a store or find parking, browse the aisles, make selections, make a payment, and push a cart to the car or carry bags home. Making the process more convenient would require shortening all those steps or assuring that everyone has the time to complete them without feeling rushed or impatient. A person waiting in line at the checkstand or using a self-checkout machine is already at the end of the process. The minutes saved at that stage don't add up to a real benefit. If buying groceries feels like an imposition, it is because free time is a luxury that most of us don't have.

In the meantime, retailers are enticing shoppers to participate in the latest round of the convenience game. Companies are experimenting with programs that promise to save time—for a price. Since 2020, Walmart has offered same-day grocery delivery to customers who pay a monthly fee. Amazon (which purchased Whole Foods in 2017) entered the market in 2025, announcing a same-day grocery delivery service for paying members of its Prime program. It's hard to predict how long those gimmicks will last before they, too, end up in the trash can of "convenience" history. From the failure of Clarence Saunders's robot grocery store to the disappointment of self-checkout, the promises of automation are more fantasy than reality.

At TGS, many shopper complaints were related to a lack of time. One morning, I arrived on the Front End just as another supervisor was hanging up the phone. The caller was a customer who had asked to speak to a manager. "The customer comes in the early morning for coffee," my colleague said. "He griped that there is just one barista." The customer was right. Lines could be painfully long during the morning rush. "The customer requested at least two baristas at all times," my colleague said.

I laughed. "You should have told him to apply. We're hiring!"

My coworker shook his head. "Supermarket employees don't grow on trees, buddy!"

Later, I regretted laughing. My colleagues and I had a lot in common with the customer. We were also suffering from understaffing. "Convenience" at the supermarket wasn't working out for anyone.

At TGS, workers blamed Paula for the staffing troubles. "She's not a good Front End manager," Gordon told me one day. "She doesn't know how to put cashiers behind checkstands at the right times."

I defended my boss. "Paula has a hard job," I said. "She is doing what she's been asked to do."

Gordon was unmoved. "She signed up for it, didn't she?"

The comment would have once seemed callous. We both knew that Paula had been fired from her previous job after marking down the price of some hamburger meat and buying it for her food-insecure family. But now I sympathized with Gordon's view. The bosses had told Paula to cut staffing hours, and she had followed through without complaint. She wasn't defending us from the higher-ups or from the machines that were making our jobs harder. It didn't help that her crackdown on bathroom breaks had increased tensions without solving absenteeism.

My shifting sympathies about everything from callouts to scheduling to breaks were a sign that I was integrated into the TGS culture. I saw that the lines of acrimony were linear and went only in one direction. If your job sucked, you blamed your colleagues or the person directly above you in the hierarchy, someone with whom you toiled day in and day out, not those you rarely saw who set the policy. I would have once seen such a view as irrational. *The top bosses and executives are to blame! Workers have to unite to demand fair treatment!* But months into the job, I understood why colleagues blamed one another.

The sociologist Michael Burawoy made a similar discovery while working as a machine operator in a manufacturing plant in the 1970s. He wanted to know why assembly line workers often risked "life and limb" to advance their employer's interests. Why did they acquiesce to a system that exploited them? He determined that workers' dedication was linked to a culture of individualism in the factory. Since they were paid as individuals, and their work was evaluated or rewarded based on individual performance, they learned to "face one another in conflict and competition" instead of as part of a group with shared concerns. We often think of the retail industry, where workers serve customers, as separate from the industrial factory, where employees make things. But employees may be toiling at different versions of the same assembly line—and shoppers are working, too.

Paula wasn't around long enough to win her colleagues' respect. A few weeks after the self-checkout machines were installed, she put in a transfer request to a new store. She was laser focused on saving money. "The store is closer to my house," she told me. "I'll save a hundred dollars a month on gas!" Another reason for the transfer was that she had had a falling-out with a banker. "Dana is pissed because someone has been sending the loan till to the office too early," Paula told me.

The *loan till* was a locked drawer full of cash that supervisors used to refill the checkstands when they ran low. Every night, the till had to be sent to the bankers' office to be counted and logged. But if you sent it too early, cashiers might run out of money. Once, a supervisor had knocked on Dana's door. "Can I get the loan till back? We're out of twenties." Dana had slammed the door in his face. "I'll never make that mistake again," he told me.

I defended myself to Paula. "I've never sent the till too early—not once," I said.

"Well, *someone* has made a habit of it, and I'm getting the blame," she said.

I suspected Stewart. The "no more fucks to give" veteran was frustrated about the time it took to shut down the self-checkout machines. He was sending the loan till early to save time. I thought about telling Paula that he was the culprit. But her transfer request had already been approved, so what did it matter? She was leaving, but I still had to work with Stewart. The Front End was entering a new era. It felt like I was starting over.

A forty-five-year-old cashier named Whitney applied for the job to replace Paula. She told me that she was trying to dig out from under $30,000 in credit card debt and was desperate for a promotion. "The pandemic has been rough because they closed the plasma clinic," she said. Before COVID, Whitney had donated plasma twice a week, earning about $400 extra per month to help pay bills. Now she was struggling to get by.

I told her that I hoped she would get the job. "My fingers are crossed for you." I knew that she had been hired when I arrived at work one day and saw her photograph had been added to the managers' wall. Whitney's bio said that she was a NASCAR fanatic and that she and her granddaughter were learning to play the guitar.

Whitney had been on the job for about a week when I was bagging at Lucia's checkstand. "I saw you called out sick a couple of times last week," I said. It was an innocent question. I wanted to know if Lucia had caught the virus. She admitted that she hadn't really been sick. Her dog, Sparky, had died, and she couldn't bring herself to come to work. "I *hated* that dog. He chewed up everything and got hair everywhere. But now I miss him so much that I can't stop crying."

I was about to ask Lucia to show me a photo of the dearly departed when George arrived with news. "I just saw Whitney fall and break her arm." It was raining, and the new Front End manager had slipped in the lobby. George was shaken by what he had witnessed. "It's bad," he said. "The bone was all twisted up under the skin." One of the bankers drove Whitney to the emergency room.

Later that night, the phone rang on the Front End. Whitney's voice was shaky. She was calling from the hospital. "I'm in so much pain," she said, "and I can't work now." I had already suspected that her arm was broken by how shaken George had been. But her last phrase sent the anxiety ball thumping in my chest. "You're going to have to take charge for a while." Whitney told me to get a pen so I could make a to-do list. By the time we hung up, I was in shock. Was she saying that I was now responsible for the Front End? She did not mention a pay raise to go along with the extra work. How was I going to get out of this?

CHAPTER 4

Abundance

At 5:00 p.m. on the day before the Super Bowl, a security guard called from the parking lot. "Every spot is full. And more cars are lined up outside waiting for people to leave," he said. "I've never seen it like this before." I was not yet acting manager, but as a supervisor, managing crowds was still my responsibility. A bagger approached with another chilling update: "I went to collect carts, but there aren't any to collect." It wasn't unusual for carts to disappear from the lobby. But from the parking lot?

On the Front End, carts were lined up two deep at checkstands—common during the afternoon rush. The store had scheduled extra cashiers for the day—almost every lane was staffed. But a manager was pacing and looking down the aisles. What could he see that I couldn't? As a supervisor, I usually did not work as a cashier. I kept lines moving by assisting others. But no carts in the parking lot could only mean one thing: As many as three hundred of them were in the aisles. I got behind a register and started scanning.

Minutes later, customers with carts surged toward the checkstands from all directions. The line snaked down the aisles almost to the dairy case. Shoppers couldn't find the end of the lines. Some abandoned their groceries and walked away, while others crowded around the Front End waiting for a path to clear.

"This is an SOS call," I said into the radio. "I repeat. This is an SOS call from the Front End." Christopher was cashiering at number five. "We're going to DEFCON one!" he declared. Managers started yelling on the radio, talking over one another. "Everyone to the front for instructions!" An SOS call instantly catapulted the Front End supervisor to the top of the store hierarchy. I was about to be in charge of TGS on Super Bowl weekend, an event that retailers everywhere treat like an unofficial holiday because sales of snacks are through the roof.

Earlier that afternoon, I had arrived for my shift to find the store transformed into a football party resource center. The stocking crew had loaded shelves with extra cases of soda and beer. Managers had set up displays of chips and salsa, while deli employees had been on the job since dawn making pounds of TGS's seven-layer chip dip and slathering it into containers. In the bakery, sheet cakes with green-and-white frosting looked like gridirons. In produce, colleagues were using chocolate icing to make strawberries look like tiny footballs. Freshly ground hamburger patties were dotted with blue cheese or cloves of roasted garlic or flecked with truffles and mushrooms. Fatty hunks of bratwurst were lined up next to jars of mustard. Trays of chicken wings bathed in neon-orange sauce and accompanied by ranch dressing adorned a table along with plates of shrimp and vats of creamy crab dip. I wondered if TGS was overdoing it. Would all the party food sell?

By the time I made the SOS call three hours later, I knew the answer. Before I pulled the trigger that day, I had only seen it done one other time. It had happened the day before Thanksgiving, a shift that rivaled the Super Bowl for the busiest of the year. Paula had arrived on the Front End to find carts three deep at the checkstands. She grabbed the radio out of my hand and made the call. Within seconds, employees from every department arrived for marching orders. Those with cashiering experience got behind registers, while others bagged or collected carts.

When I made the call on that Saturday in February, I took a page from Paula's playbook and gave orders like an army general. "You're cashiering at number three! You can bag at number seven!" Other colleagues helped customers to their cars or headed to the parking lot on the hunt for carts.

It felt like TGS was being looted. Except shoppers paid for the loot. When I locked the door at closing time, every party food display and shelf had been ransacked, picked clean. One of the last transactions of the night had been a customer buying a plate of cocktail shrimp. He had accidentally spilled it on the checkstand. Shrimp rolled down the counter, and the pink sauce had spilled into the crevice between the belt and the counter.

The next person in line saw an opportunity. "That's the last cocktail shrimp," he said to the customer who had spilled it. "If you don't want it now, I'll take it off your hands." I informed both shoppers that we would not be selling food that had fallen onto the counter. "It's not safe. We're in a pandemic," I said. The customers appeared to be evaluating whether getting the last plate of shrimp for their Super Bowl party was worth the risk of catching COVID. I used a rag to wipe the shrimp into the trash, ending the discussion.

The supermarket offers virtually everything you want to eat in varieties you didn't know existed. Typical stores today sell tens of thousands of items. There may be more than a dozen types of pasta on a shelf stocked with as many sauces. Breakfast cereals lining multiple shelves feature every conceivable combination of flake, fruit, and grain. Dairy products of every variety clamor for your attention. Eggs are white, brown, organic, pasture-raised, or cage-free. Yogurt is Greek, nonfat, low-fat, sugar-free, and even dairy-free. The beverage aisles overflow with domestic varieties and international brands. You can buy produce, fish, and fresh-baked bread in one store. The abundance can make the supermarket seem like capitalism's greatest achievement.

None of it would be possible without the workers who drive trucks, stock shelves, cook the food once it arrives in stores, and sell it at checkstands. The process begins on the farms and ranches and in the factories where workers keep supply lines moving. The food industry employs more people than any other. Disproportionately women, people of color, and immigrants, frontline food staffers earn low wages and, like their peers in the supermarket, have high rates of food insecurity. They are also at risk of injury from repetitive labor and heavy machinery. Wandering the aisles of the grocery store, we see products that tempt and delight. We are also seeing the handiwork of an industry that has the second-highest rate of employee amputations.

Consider the shrimp that two TGS customers coveted on Super Bowl weekend. It might have come from Thailand, a major producer of the global supply. Slave labor is involved in up to 60 percent of Thai shrimp production. One writer reported on unpaid shrimp workers imprisoned on boats where they were beaten and threatened with death if they stepped out of line. The men slept together in a crawl space and worked twenty-hour shifts.

Much of the food for sale at the supermarket ends up in

the trash. In the US, up to 40 percent of food produced for consumption goes uneaten, while hundreds of millions around the world go hungry. The waste is also linked to environmental damage. The largest contributor to landfills, food accounts for up to 10 percent of greenhouse gas emissions.

Losses occur all along the supply chain, from farms, where food is mishandled, to transportation and storage, where it may come into contact with rodents or insects. But according to one USDA study, 31 percent of waste—or 133 billion pounds—occurs after food has already reached stores. One reason is that retailers cull damaged goods for shoppers who prefer undented boxes and unblemished fruits and vegetables.

Stores also over-order to create the appearance of abundance. At TGS, deli employees roasted chickens in industrial-size ovens and displayed them in a heated case. A worker once told me that, since the display had to be kept full even when business was slow, the store might throw as many as a dozen unpurchased chickens in the trash at the end of the day. Such waste won't change as long as employers don't have to pay living wages. Cheap food industry labor, from farmhands to cashiers, allows stores to over-order and toss out what shoppers don't buy.

On the day before the Valentine's holiday, TGS managers set up a table on the Front End where shoppers could choose from a half dozen varieties of fresh flowers as well as cellophane balloons. By midday, customers were lined up at the table, and red and pink balloons that had gotten away floated above the Front End like shimmering clouds. The flowers sold out by midafternoon, prompting a manager to suggest fresh fruit as an alternative.

The flower industry has a significant carbon footprint. Most flowers are grown in the global south and then shipped. The lead-up to Valentine's Day is what the writer Margaret

Renkl called an "environmental crime." Refrigerated planes and trucks crisscross the globe to bring the flowers to stores in the US and Europe. A bouquet of roses grown in Latin America and sold in the north does more damage to the planet than an eight-ounce steak. These days, some stores advertise pledges to sustainability. But selling fresh flowers is a sign that those promises are more marketing than genuine commitment.

As an employee, I saw the positive side of abundance. The store fed the neighborhood seven days a week. At lunchtime, people lined up at the deli for macaroni and cheese, fried chicken, or lasagna with garlic bread. They ordered hot dogs, corn dogs, or slices of pizza. Or they selected from a cooler stocked with ham, turkey, chicken salad, salami, and cheese sandwiches.

Others opted for the salad bar where four kinds of greens and two dozen toppings were available. Dispensers of ranch, Thousand Island, and vinaigrette the size and shape of bowling pins assured a constant supply of dressing. At the "wok bar," shoppers chose between kung pao chicken, sweet-and-sour pork, fried rice, or hot-and-sour tofu. Upstairs, a gelato shop offered a dozen varieties while, a few steps away, shoppers lined up at the grill to order chicken sandwiches and hamburgers served on ciabatta buns with house-made mayo.

At the height of summer, temperatures soared into the triple digits and stayed there for days. The city declared a heat advisory followed by a drought warning. Public buildings and some homeowners stopped watering lawns. Fourth of July celebrations were canceled because of the fire risk. At the checkstand, shoppers said, "Thanks for the air-conditioning!"

Customers stampeded into the beverage aisles. They filled carts with cases of bottled water, soda, juices, and energy drinks. It was not uncommon for cashiers to scan hundreds of dollars in beverages in a single order. One customer spent more than $500 on Topo Chico mineral water, an amount so high that I had to authorize the purchase by scanning the override. "Do you think I'm overdoing it?" he asked. "On the contrary, you win a gold medal in the drought preparation Olympics," I assured him. Sleep apnea sufferers purchased jugs of distilled water for home humidifiers and CPAP machines. Workers from a nearby construction site left the store carrying cases of bottled water or Gatorade over their shoulders.

Like hospitals, schools, and sewage systems, the supermarket was essential infrastructure. It allowed people to survive, thrive, and live with dignity—at least those who could afford their grocery bill. But everywhere they turned, shoppers acquired products linked to low wages, injury, environmental destruction, and even slavery.

The manager's suggestion that Valentine's shoppers consider fresh fruit in place of flowers was not an improvement for the climate. The produce department marked the holiday by selling strawberries in heart-shaped boxes. I assumed the fruit wouldn't sell. How good could berries taste in the middle of winter? But all weekend long, strawberries the size of golf balls passed through checkstands along with pink boxes filled with whipped cream.

Like flowers, fruit is a major contributor to carbon emissions. Fruits and vegetables have a greater environmental impact than other foods because they have to be kept cold over long distances. The idea that we can limit the ravages of climate change through vegetarianism alone is misleading. The key is eating food that is in season and produced or grown close to home. Of course, many shoppers do not have that option.

Today, about fifty million shoppers live in "food deserts," an urban neighborhood with no grocery store within one mile, or a rural area where people have to travel at least ten miles to shop. In New York City, three million people live in food deserts. One in four Atlanta residents does not have access to a store that sells fresh produce. Rural communities are particularly burdened. About half of North Dakota residents live in a food desert. Across the country, more than two million people are in the double predicament of having no store and no car. These shoppers must get a ride to a store and buy enough food to last until the next trip, an impossibility for the cash-strapped. For millions, the supermarket's bounty is a cruel taunt.

Most food deserts are located in low-income neighborhoods, and Black customers are twice as likely as whites to live in one. What the food justice activist Karen Washington calls "food apartheid" is part of a legacy of racial inequality going back to the era when a grocery clerk might overcharge a Black customer or sell her rotten meat. Now, discrimination looks like Black shoppers in food deserts paying higher prices for basic goods.

Like price gouging and food waste, food apartheid is not a natural occurrence but an outcome of public policy. Until the 1980s, independent grocers flourished across the country. Antitrust laws like the 1936 Robinson–Patman Act protected small entrepreneurs by banning large retailers from cutting prices to undersell competitors. The regulations assured that people everywhere had access to a store even when corporations did not invest in their communities. President Reagan stopped enforcing antitrust laws, arguing that they held back corporate expansion. Since the 1980s, regulators have largely followed that line. There were signs of a change during the Biden administration, when Lina Khan, the chair of the Federal Trade Commission, sued two companies for violating the Robinson–Patman Act. But the Trump administration dismissed the higher-profile case against PepsiCo, suggesting a return to a laxer enforcement of the law. That means that, when a Kroger or a Trader Joe's comes to a neighborhood, small businesses scattered around the area are often forced to close, leaving shoppers without a store.

For TGS employees, "abundance" required materials and labor. One morning, I arrived at work to find Stewart in a state of despair. "We're screwed," he said. The cubbies underneath the checkstands were nearly bare. "We are out of paper bags." My colleague had already been to the back room where the bags were stored on a shelf reachable by climbing on top of boxes of dented cans and other damaged merchandise. It was empty.

I took the elevator upstairs to another storage area where bags could sometimes be found. Nothing. *Am I asleep and having a nightmare?* Trying to run a supermarket without shopping bags was like trying to operate an airport without runways. The normal disruptions from staffing shortages to glitchy self-checkout machines were minor mishaps by comparison. "We *are* screwed," I said to Stewart when I returned to the Front End.

TGS did not use plastic bags. The top bosses explained that the store was committed to sustainability, and paper was better for the environment. It's true that paper is biodegradable while plastic bags end up in landfills. But paper is not always an improvement. According to one study from the UK, since it requires trees and water to produce them, paper bags must be used at least three times to become truly sustainable. At TGS, whether offering only paper was better for the climate depended on what happened to the bags after they left the store.

While Stewart called the warehouse to try to find out why the bags hadn't been delivered, I checked the day's schedule. A note read, "Gordon called out because his back is acting up again." A missing cashier was not uncommon. But there was another problem. Scarlet was scheduled to work number three. But she had stopped showing up for her shifts the week before. The no-shows should have led to her replacement on the schedule. But after Whitney fell and broke her arm, administrative tasks were falling through the cracks. The manager who had written the schedule didn't work on the Front End and probably didn't know that Scarlet had stopped showing up. I was going to have to run my department with two fewer cashiers and, apparently, without shopping bags.

When I first started the job at TGS, my attempts at bagging had been disastrous. Groceries rolled toward me and piled up faster than I could bag them. The packaging and the size, weight, and shape of goods were paralyzingly diverse. An order of laundry detergent, milk, toothpaste, cereal, apples, and frozen corn felt like a calculus exam that I was doomed to fail. If I put the milk next to the detergent next to the corn with the apples on top, I knew it was all wrong but didn't know how to fix it. My filled bags bulged and tilted. Some were too heavy, while others had only two or three items.

I hoped that customers didn't notice that I was botching the job. Once, I was so frazzled by a large produce order that I bagged the fruit while moving the vegetables to a neighboring checkstand to clear space. I forgot the vegetables. The customer was a chef. He didn't notice the error until he got to his restaurant and realized that he couldn't prepare some of the dishes on the menu. He had to come back to TGS in search of the vegetables that he had paid for. At the time, I wondered how I could supervise the Front End if I was stumped by bagging.

Managers sent me to baggers' reeducation camp. Alone in the conference room, I watched a thirty-minute training video on proper technique. The video instructed me to put "hard stuff on the bottom and lighter items on top," as if theory was the same as practice. A can of soup counted as a "hard" item, sure, but what about plastic containers of mayonnaise and olive oil? Frozen chicken tenders? A bag of confectioner's sugar?

Experienced colleagues came to my rescue. One bagger demonstrated how to "build walls," placing canned goods or cereal boxes on the inside edges. The walls created a space in the middle to tuck medium-hard objects like pasta, carrots, or bags of rice. Eggs, bread, and potato chips went on top. Another coworker told me that bagging was not about individual items at all. "Focus on the big picture," he said. He advised me to assess the number of products in an order and talk to the customer. If the shopper was going home in a car, a bagger had to pack more groceries in fewer bags that would fit more easily in trunks or in back seats. If the person was on foot, it was essential to create a consistency of weight. Placing salsa and cat food in one bag and doughnuts and pita bread in another made carrying difficult.

It was critical to package cold products together and to keep them separate from cooked food. "The frozen hashbrowns go on top of the frozen shrimp next to the ice cream and underneath the frozen waffles," a bagger explained. Bagging was serious business. Making a poor decision could mean sending a shopper home with lukewarm milk or a half-melted carton of Rocky Road. Thanks to my colleagues, in time, I developed a method that was adaptable.

We owe the invention of the paper shopping bag to a machinist named Margaret E. Knight. Born in Maine in 1838, Knight did not follow the typical path of women of her era. She worked in a cotton mill where a colleague's accident prompted her to invent a safety mechanism to prevent workplace injuries. By the 1860s, Knight was employed in a factory in Massachusetts, where her creativity came in handy again. She designed the machine that mechanized the production of the flat-bottom bags that are ubiquitous in stores today.

A few years later, a Scottish immigrant named Robert Gair was manufacturing paper bags in New York. One day, a malfunctioning machine sliced horizontal lines through a stack of bags. Gair realized that the cutting created cartons that squared off at the bottom. He went on to automate the production of easily foldable boxes. Food manufacturers seized on the invention of cardboard. They no longer had to ship products in bulk or in burlap sacks. Individual packages of cereal, crackers, and more flew off factory assembly lines and onto store shelves. The modern supermarket wouldn't exist without bags, and bags helped to pave the way for the prepackaged food products that now line the shelves of the supermarket.

At TGS, I separated the two sides of a bag and reached to the bottom to create volume so that it could stand up on its own. Next, I detached the paper handles to make them vertical. The motion had to be quick but gentle, since pulling too hard risked tearing the handles and rendering the bag virtually useless. If the customer was buying several heavy items, I opened a second bag and slipped it inside the first.

Double bagging assured that handles didn't rip off when the bag was full. After filling the bags, I lifted them into the shopper's cart, placing the remaining ones on the bottom shelf. The opening-detaching-filling-lifting-kneeling motions were repeated dozens of times during a shift.

Like cashiering, bagging requires standing for long periods, awkward postures, and repetitive hand and arm motions. If you want to know what bagging is like, try setting an assortment of items of different sizes and weights on a table about a foot in front of you and then pick them up and put them back down again repeatedly for hours. You will quickly see why, in one study, more than three-quarters of baggers reported a work-related injury. Almost no part of the body is spared. Employees reported pain in the feet, upper back, shoulders, lower leg, lower back, neck, and upper arm. The most experienced baggers are prone to wrist injuries since they repeat movements at a higher velocity.

At TGS, fast-moving fingers sometimes slid across a bag's razor-sharp edges. The cuts burned when I applied soap or hand sanitizer. If I was working multiple shifts in a row, they wouldn't heal. Once, two cuts on my right hand merged and became a larger wound. I spent several shifts trying to keep a bandage on the bleeding finger. Another time, when the first aid kit was short on bandages, I worked with a towel from the produce department taped around my finger.

Some baggers wore latex gloves. At first, I assumed that they were trying to limit the spread of the virus. But COVID had nothing to do with it. They wore gloves to protect against cuts. (It didn't always work, and the gloves made bagging more difficult.) I had also assumed that the first aid kit mounted on a wall was for stockers using box cutters or meat department employees working with knives and saws.

But baggers used the antiseptic, bandages, and finger dressings more than anyone. Once I watched a custodian dump a checkstand trash can into a larger bin. The can contained balled up receipts, scraps of food, and bloody Band-Aids.

It may seem like baggers benefit from invisibility. They don't interact with customers the way cashiers do. But baggers are among the most surveilled employees in a supermarket. Some TGS shoppers watched the process as if they expected the bagger to put the Budweiser on top of the Cheetos. Their fears were sometimes justified. Once, a man got to his car before realizing that his apple pie had been crushed under a pineapple. He came back inside understandably grumpy, asking for a new pie.

Shoppers' anxiety about how their groceries are bagged can lead to false accusations. One customer accused an employee of tearing open a package of pancake mix while putting it into a bag. I defended my colleague. "It was probably damaged before you put it in your cart," I said. Most rips and tears happened before a product got to the Front End, a casualty of the blades that stockers used to open boxes. But baggers got the blame anyway.

One day, a man came through my line with a cart. Hesitant to touch the PIN pad, he grunted and sighed his way through the payment process while Cindy bagged. "I can do it myself!" the shopper said. My hard-of-hearing colleague kept working. The customer took a step toward the cart, making sure not to get too close. "Get away!" He took over the job and then doused his hands with sanitizer. "My God," he said. "We're in a pandemic, and that woman is lingering over my food!" The shopper had clearly never given much thought to how supermarkets work or how items get to the shelves. Groceries passed through several hands before customers selected them. Since the man didn't see or interact with the people who unloaded trucks or stocked shelves, he lashed out at the bagger, the last employee who touched his groceries.

One afternoon, I arrived at work to find Gordon in a panic. A manager had moved a bagger from his lane to self-checkout. "Everyone needs to train on self-checkout," the manager had said. Gordon pleaded with me to send the employee back. "There is no reason to train a bagger on the machines," he groaned. "I need help!" For Gordon, every shift was a battle with his aching back that he started to lose as the day wore on. A bagger was pain management. If he didn't have to bag his customers' groceries, the cashier could usually make it to the end of a shift. Without help, his chances were slim to none. "This just isn't right," Gordon said. He took the manager's decision personally. "Does TGS want me to do my job or not?"

I opposed training the bagger on self-checkout, because they typically earned a lower wage than cashiers. One former bagger had already complained to me that she had been promoted to cashier without a pay raise. But I was hesitant to reverse a manager's decision. "Let me think about it," I said. Gordon shot back. "You want to *think about it*?" He said that I was confused about how things had changed. "After Whitney's accident, everything went to hell around here," he complained. "*You* are the Front End boss now and should act like it."

It wasn't true. The top bosses had not informed me that I was in charge. While I had taken on some of Whitney's tasks, such as sending weekly reports to the corporate office, most of her duties had been transferred to a manager. The most likely explanation was that the top bosses were trying to avoid raising my wage. But Gordon wasn't talking about what was technically true. He was saying that the Front End needed leadership from someone on the ground. The bosses didn't want to pay to promote me, but workers still needed me to step up.

I sent the next cashier on shift to self-checkout and moved the bagger back to Gordon's checkstand. But the damage had already been done. When Stewart showed up to replace me for the night shift, Gordon asked to leave early. "I need to sit down!" To which Stewart replied, "People in hell want ice water!" The cashier took the joke as a yes and turned off his light. A shortage of baggers created a domino effect that would have consequences for the next hour. Until Gordon's replacement arrived, the Front End would be short one cashier.

On the day when TGS ran out of shopping bags, the crisis was mercifully short-lived. At 8:00 a.m., a truck delivered them. *Hallelujah!* A manager explained that the warehouse was having COVID-related supply chain issues made worse by the popularity of grocery delivery during the pandemic. In addition to stores offering their own services, delivery companies saw their profits explode. One start-up, Instacart, saw its sales jump 500 percent, leading to a flood of venture capital funding. (By 2022, the boom had faded, and Instacart's valuation crashed.) While I worked at TGS, the popularity of home delivery meant that i-grocery fought regularly with the Front End over bags, with each department jealously guarding its supply.

When the bags arrived on the day of the near disaster, I planned to send a young employee to collect and restock them. The phone rang. The employee said that he would be thirty minutes late. I didn't ask why. It didn't matter. Cashiers couldn't wait for bags.

I went to the stockroom and grabbed a wheeled pallet mover that I pushed into the elevator. On the upper level, reams of bags about the size and weight of a bale of hay were stacked on a wooden plank and covered in plastic. I tore off the plastic and situated the pallet mover next to the plank. Since I was not strong enough to lift the bundles, I knocked one off the pile and adjusted it to lie flat. Then I knocked over a second bundle. Eventually, I managed to get six reams onto the pallet mover, which I guided back into the elevator.

Back on the Front End, I pushed the reams off the pile one by one and tore off the cardboard packaging so that the bags fell open like a stretched-out accordion. I knelt and restocked the bags under each of the nine registers and put the remainders in slots next to the self-checkout machines. Finally, I tossed the packaging into the baler, a growling machine with a mouthful of teeth that shredded cardboard, or employees' fingers if they got too close.

I turned my attention back to the problem of the missing cashiers. After months of moving workers around to cover the gaps, I was out of ideas. I made a radio call. "Is there anyone in the store who can run a register?" A former Front End employee who was now a supervisor in the deli arrived to help. A shift that might have been a world-historic disaster became a day like any other. TGS could feel like a machine that let nothing stand in its way.

Other parts of the job were looking up. The store's top boss began copying me on emails to managers, a sign that, in my seventh month, I had risen in status. (I suspected it was partly because I had learned how to fix the self-checkout machines.) I had even developed a rapport (if you want to call it that) with Dana, the surly banker who had once slammed a door in a cashier's face. I made pleasing her a priority. No matter what else was happening on the Front End, I sent the loan till to her office at the same time. I could tell she appreciated the consistency, because when we crossed paths, she pretended not to see me. I had been too stressed out to notice crossing the threshold from neophyte cashier to competent supervisor. But being ignored by Dana was a sign of respect. It meant that another achievement had been unlocked.

I was earning points from colleagues across the store. On one opening shift, I discovered that no cashier was on the schedule until 10:00 a.m.—three hours later. *Are managers trying to make me go insane?* In between serving shoppers, I made a radio call. "I'm the only cashier this morning. Can anyone lend a hand?" A stocker named Kevin appeared. I was surprised to see him. The sixty-two-year-old had shoulder-length red hair with streaks of gray. After decades in the industry, Kevin walked with a slightly hunched back and complained about foot pain. A few weeks earlier, he had told me that he needed a less strenuous job. "My body doesn't work anymore," he said. The day of the missing cashier, Kevin started bagging.

Minutes later, a deli worker with cashiering experience logged in to number three. He nodded at me as if to say, *I've got you covered.* For the next two hours, my colleagues neglected their own jobs to help me keep the checkout lines moving. I was so humbled and grateful that I felt like I might never leave TGS. My supermarket was a beautiful place.

Later, after the staffing crisis had ended, Kevin passed through the Front End during his break. I apologized if I had seemed panicked at the start of the day. "You handled it well," he said. "Getting through something like that means that you're on our team now." Stockers like Kevin were well above me in the TGS hierarchy. Even the top bosses sometimes deferred to them. It was a thrill to know that Kevin had noticed and appreciated my progress.

My new status came with a downside. One day, two new cashiers were working registers for the first time. The women looked nervous as they rang up customers. I reminded them to press CLEAR twice after making a mistake and to make use of the "miscellaneous items" cheat sheet that was taped to the top of the register. I tried to be relaxed and encouraging. "It seems challenging now, but you'll be experts in no time!"

But it was excruciating to watch them work. I constantly stepped in to help with basic functions, which led to slow checkouts and long lines. Had I needed this much help when I was new to cashiering? I doubted it, even though I couldn't remember those days anymore. One cashier was so nervous that, anytime she had to give change, her hands shook as she counted the bills. Once, she almost gave a customer a twenty-dollar bill instead of five dollars. "Make sure you take the time to get it right." I didn't raise my voice. But I was on edge and short-tempered. *I don't have time for this.* The supermarket was turning me into a judgy, ill-tempered person.

Another day, a longtime cashier called me over to help with a bottle return. When I was new to the job, I had once bungled the transaction so badly that it had taken fifteen minutes to sort it out. Now that I was more skilled, there was no reason to get annoyed at others. But my blood pressure spiked when I saw that the cashier had mistyped the code, creating a string of problems for me to fix. Instead of showing him how to do the transaction correctly, I completed it myself. After all, I had to pay attention to the big picture. How long are the lines? Who was due for a break? Was it time to send the loan till to the bank? It wasn't my fault if a cashier didn't know what he was doing.

Colleagues became a target of my disdain. One day, I arrived to find George and the manager of the frozen department giggling. "What's so funny this early in the morning?" I asked. The manager told me that an employee from i-grocery had called out sick. When he reported the call to the manager, she burst into tears. "It's so hard to run i-grocery short-staffed," she said. The image of the manager crying over a callout was hysterical. My coworkers and I howled with laughter. "There's no crying at TGS!" the frozen manager said.

Months earlier, I might have felt guilty or even admonished my colleagues for mocking our coworker. I knew as well as anyone that callouts could turn a shift into a nightmare. The manager's response was understandable. There was also the issue of gender. I had joined two men in mocking a woman in an industry where women are overrepresented in the lowest-paid roles and earn less than men even when they do the same jobs. The i-grocery manager was working in an environment that was already hostile to her interests. I should have defended her.

But I did not feel guilty for laughing. Staffing shortages were common. It was silly to shed tears over them, just as it was important not to show weakness. Word got around about the manager's breakdown. Hours later, Darth approached me and said, "If I start crying, will you send me home early?" We belly laughed until tears streamed down our cheeks.

Pain explained some of the workers' attitude, including my own. My arms and shoulders ached twenty-four hours a day, and my plantar fasciitis was getting worse. It felt like a nail was pushing into my heel with every step. There was never enough downtime between shifts for the injury to heal. I bought a new pair of sneakers that promised extra heel support. And once my health insurance kicked in, I saw a doctor. She examined my heel and asked about my symptoms. "You really need to stay off the foot for a while, if you can," she said.

I thanked her for the advice but felt like cackling. The only reason I had insurance was because of a job that caused the pain that sent me to the doctor in search of relief for my pain. I was starting to doubt that it was worth it. I had entered a territory that many colleagues knew well. Pain could not be prevented, only endured. I was also experiencing a fundamental dilemma of wage laborers everywhere. Earning a living caused harm that imperiled my ability to earn a living.

One night, when business was slow, I told Aurelie that TGS had gotten into my body and head in ways that I had not expected. "Someone should make a TV show about supermarket employees," I said. "I haven't seen many series that accurately portray retail work." I was thinking about comedies like *Superstore*, about employees in a big-box store, and *Ten Items or Less*, about a failed businessman who returns home to run a local supermarket. These shows featured a sanitized version of the job where injuries were rare to nonexistent and conflicts were usually resolved by the end of the episode. I was offended by those portrayals of the industry. It wasn't right to set a lighthearted comedy in a supermarket.

Aurelie told me that she had grown up poor. She and her sister used to fantasize about getting locked in a store overnight. "We spent hours describing to each other the different foods we would taste up and down every aisle," she said. I said the game sounded fun, but a little sad. "It's different now," she said. "I feel overwhelmed by it all." The supermarket had once symbolized unattainable plenty. Now Aurelie was drowning in other people's groceries.

The writer Edouard Louis told a similar story about the supermarket as a source of pleasure and fantasy. In his autobiographical novel, *Change*, he described growing up in poverty and finding happiness at the supermarket. Unable to afford anything but a can of soda, the young Edouard enjoyed being surrounded "by an infinite accumulation of goods" that he could never afford. "Wealthier people went to the theater or the opera," he wrote, while poor shoppers "dreamed of the supermarket."

From checkstand number five, a cashier overheard my conversation with Aurelie. He recounted a recurring dream where he got trapped in an underground tunnel that connected TGS with his bedroom. "Once I get into the tunnel, it's an endless loop," he said. "All I can do is go back and forth between my bedroom and the checkstand. I have no other life except work and sleep." He paused. "Actually, I'm so tired after work that the dream *is* my life."

I hoped the bleak vibe on the Front End was temporary, and things would get better for all of us when the real supervisor came back to work. I had heard from a top boss that Whitney's return was on the horizon, an event that would allow me to resume my role as her assistant. The change would not cure foot pain or paper cuts or miraculously improve my attitude. But it might tip the scale so that the positive parts of the job outweighed the bad.

Around that time, I ran into Whitney shopping at the store (her employee discount was still valid) with her arm in a sling. She was making slow progress and hoped physical therapy would help her regain mobility in her hand. "I have a metal plate in my wrist," she said. "I can't play my guitar anymore, which means that, for now, those lessons with my granddaughter are over." So was the hope that I would soon be able to slip back into the crowd.

CHAPTER 5

Autonomy

It was a Thursday in June, just after the evening rush, when I knew that I was about to get chewed out. I didn't know which one of the bosses would be the one to do it. But I knew it would happen like I knew that shopping carts in the aisles ended up in the parking lot or that paper bags sliced fingers. Minutes earlier, the "sweep buzzer" had gone off on the Front End. The hourly reminder that it was time to assign someone to sweep the floor, the alarm provoked sighs and grumbles. Baggers wandered off or made themselves small, while cashiers took extra time with their customers. *I'm definitely too busy to sweep*. Felix had startled me by volunteering. "I'm happy to do it," the twenty-one-year-old said. I had never heard anyone say they were happy to sweep. I should have known that something was about to go wrong.

During my first days on the job, I had learned how to grip the industrial broom in one hand while carrying the "sweep buzzer" in the other. The device listed thirty locations that were marked with a numbered tag. A sweeper tapped the buzzer along the walls and shelves to log the sweep into the system—a process that took between thirty to forty-five minutes depending on a worker's fitness level and stamina. After completing the sweep, an employee shook out the broom in a corner next to a supply closet out of shoppers' view. (Sweeping was mostly moving dirt from one area to another.) Since the buzzer went off every hour, someone was almost always sweeping or trying to avoid sweeping.

When I was still thinking like a shopper, I assumed that the purpose of sweeping was clean floors. But after a few trips through the aisles with the broom, I saw that the job was also a form of hazing. It took a few days to feel the physical effects of scanning and bagging. But a sweeper quickly regretted every life decision that had led them to the job. The simultaneous reaching and stretching motions were instantly agonizing. A sweeper returned to the Front End already feeling the initial effects of the backache that he would wake up with the next day.

Once, Paula sent a new hire to sweep. When the buzzer sounded again a few minutes after she had finished, Paula sent her again. "You'll learn where the tags are after a few more tries," she said. The look on the worker's face suggested that she saw no difference between sweeping and medieval torture. The next day, she called to say she had an "emergency" and would not be in for her shift. "The emergency is that she doesn't want to do sweeps," Darth said.

For me, sweeping prompted childhood memories. When I was born, my dad was employed in a supermarket, mopping floors on the overnight shift. Later, he told me stories about coming home at dawn exhausted and determined to get an education. Thanks to the Servicemen's Readjustment Act of 1944, otherwise known as the "GI Bill," my dad earned a college diploma and left his mop bucket behind for a job in a school library. But his stories came back to me at

TGS. Even after two decades of white-collar jobs, cleaning the floors of a supermarket felt like a familial destiny. It didn't help that sweeps could not be faked. Due to the tagging system, it was impossible to say you had swept if you had not done it.

But on that late spring day, it looked like Felix had cracked the code. Two minutes after he set off, I caught a glimpse of him in the housewares aisle. *How did he get there so fast?* Something else wasn't right. *Where is the broom?* Felix didn't have anything in his hand except the sweep buzzer. I watched in disbelief as he tapped the device before turning the corner to the pet food aisle. My colleague was logging a sweep into the system without sweeping. It all made sense now. Felix had volunteered to do the job because he had no intention of actually doing it. The most brazen act of insubordination I had ever witnessed at TGS was happening before 6:00 p.m.—when managers would still be in the store.

The voice on the radio belonged to the bakery manager. "Front End. Do you copy?" The manager always referred to her subordinates by their department name. It was her way of anonymizing and dehumanizing people. In return, we called her "Bakery Bitch" behind her back. "Your sweeper is tapping but *not* sweeping!" she said. I played dumb. "I didn't see him doing that," I said. "I'll talk to Felix." When I said those words, I believed them. I couldn't allow an employee to fake working on my watch. *Does he think I won't notice what he's doing?* I planned to tell the cashier that his impertinence was blowing back on me and send him back into the aisles with the broom. But by the time he returned to the Front End, I had changed my mind.

Felix was an unlikely candidate to break the rules. A competent and reliable employee, he had never caused trouble. One day, I asked him about his college studies. A musical theater major, he dreamed of a career on a Broadway stage. If that didn't work out, Felix said that he counted on his degree to provide a path to a good life. "Education is how I don't end up in a job like this when I'm older," he told me.

The comment stung. My colleague was admitting that he saw "older" supermarket employees as role models in reverse. He was working hard to avoid a life that we had apparently stumbled into. I didn't tell him that grocery work was a socially necessary and even a noble occupation or that our working conditions and low wages were the real problems. There was never time for nuanced conversations at TGS.

On the day that Felix faked the sweep, I thought back on that conversation. It occurred to me that his academic background might explain the ruse. Used to singing and dancing in front of an audience, he treated sweeping like a role open to interpretation. He was saying, "I can choose how I perform this part of the play." I decided to let him get away with it. I did not reprimand him even though I had told the Bakery Bitch that I would. For one thing, ignoring the manager felt good. Front End workers had to have one another's backs. For another, Felix's "sweep" was a form of resistance to the store's control over our time.

The control began with scheduling. Managers published the schedule about two weeks in advance. It was a rough draft. When I arrived for a supervisor shift, the first thing I did was compare the online schedule with the printed version posted on the Front End. There were often discrepancies that reflected last-minute changes, callouts, or resignations.

The comparison wasn't always clarifying. While the online version was more reliable, it sometimes contained errors. The schedule that listed a cashier who had already left the job was most likely wrong, while the version that listed someone else in the spot was probably correct. I treated the schedule as a list of likely possibilities instead of accurate information.

Employees worked days, nights, or a combination depending on factors from their availability to managers' preferences. The worst-case scenario was what staffers called a "clopen," a closing shift followed by an opening shift. The dreaded schedule meant closing the store at 10:00 p.m. (late-night shoppers could keep workers on the clock even later), and then rolling out of bed the next morning to make a 7:00 a.m. arrival time to open the store back up.

A worker who needed a specific day off had to ask at least two weeks in advance and wait for approval. It didn't always come. Once, I wanted to take my mother to lunch for her birthday. Since the day fell on a holiday weekend, my request was denied. Once, an employee bagged groceries while wiping away tears. "I wanted to go to the cemetery to see my mom today. It's the anniversary of her passing," he told me. "I asked for the day off but didn't get it."

In cases of emergency, employees were responsible for covering their own shifts. One morning, on my day off, I woke up to a series of panicked texts from Darth, who was at work. In the middle of moving apartments, he had been sleeping at his new place while moving belongings from his old one whenever he could get help from a friend with a truck. The previous night, burglars had broken in and stolen some property at his old place, including a gaming console and a monitor. Darth pleaded with me to come in and cover for him. "I want to file a police report and move the rest of my stuff so there's nothing left to steal," he said. I texted back, "You sure you want to do this? You're going to lose the hours." Darth replied that he would figure out how to survive on less money that week.

The retail industry views workers as widgets that have no lives beyond the store. By plugging them into the schedule according to a store's immediate needs and giving them virtually no authority over when they work, companies only pay workers when they are absolutely necessary. But such "just in time" scheduling means that many employees do not know their schedules more than a week in advance and sometimes less. Some retail workers are required to stay "on call," ready to clock in on short notice but with no guarantee of hours. A person may even be assigned a "split shift": working during a busy period, clocking out during a slowdown, and then returning later when business picks up again.

Workers have had to come up with creative ways to survive. In many stores, next to the time clock, employees post notes asking for additional shifts from colleagues looking to give them away. Others use social media to navigate scheduling uncertainty. Grocery workers have set up Facebook pages to find extra hours or to get shifts covered. The unpredictability and horse trading means that retail employees essentially have two jobs: one serving shoppers and one navigating the uncertainty about when, or if, they will be assigned to serve shoppers. Unfortunately, only one of those jobs is paid.

Being a widget creates burdens beyond low pay. Unpredictability at work means falling in and out of eligibility for public benefits. And workers subject to an employer's short-term demands are more likely to rely on payday loans or other high-interest financial products to make ends meet. The writer Adelle Waldman saw the harms while working in a big-box store to research a novel. Retail workers, she wrote, are "trapped in jobs that don't pay enough to live on and aren't predictable enough to plan a life around." When a parent's work schedule is erratic, children suffer. Unpredictability at home has been linked to higher rates of childhood depression, sleep disorders, and obesity.

When I first started at TGS, Lucia was in a long-running fight with Paula over her schedule. The cashier had requested Sundays off because she did not have a car and city buses were limited that day. But Paula often scheduled her anyway. "I worked Sunday last week!" Lucia said one day. "It's not fair that I have to do it two weeks in a row."

Paula shot back, "I don't have anyone else available."

Lucia offered an olive branch. "I'll work if I can punch out by 7:00 p.m.," she said, "so I can get the last bus."

Paula wouldn't budge. "If you leave early, I will cut your hours next week."

Lucia was trapped. She would have to spend most of Sunday's wage on a taxi. The shift would pay in sore feet and an aching back instead of in dollars.

One night, I introduced myself to a new bagger. About twenty-five years old with blond hair, she wore long, fake eyelashes and light purple eye shadow. It looked like her eyes were framed by the wings of an exotic butterfly. "Let me know if you have any questions," I said.

Butterfly Wings took me up on the offer. "When I was hired, I said that I was only available on Tuesday and Thursday," she said. "But I'm scheduled on Wednesday next week."

Scheduling complaints were common, but this was a case of a mistaken identity. "I don't make the schedule," I said. "You need to speak to a manager."

The employee kept talking while groceries rolled off the belt and piled up on the counter. "TGS has a bad rating online for this type of treatment," she said. "Employees say that you don't honor schedule requests."

Who was this "you" she was talking about? I could have

explained that she had not been singled out. I could have said, "We're all in the same boat when it comes to scheduling." Months earlier, I might have even offered to talk to the boss on her behalf. But late in my seventh month, I had lost my patience. The bagger wasn't listening. "Again," I said, "you will have to talk to a manager." The employee took off her apron and tossed it on the checkstand.

"I quit," she said, with dramatic effect, and fluttered out the door.

The cashier was despondent. "My bagger left me?" But before I could even respond, she started bagging the groceries herself.

The incident reminded me of a phenomenon the media referred to as the "Great Resignation." While I was working at TGS, employees of all kinds began walking off the job in record numbers. About forty-seven million people quit in 2021 alone. Some commentators hailed the trend as a positive sign of growing worker power. But at the supermarket, high turnover and walkouts didn't feel empowering. They shifted burdens onto others and added to the unpredictability.

At TGS, scheduling signaled to workers that their needs, their personal lives, didn't count. The job always came first.

One day, I overheard Nelly and another colleague commiserating about how they never got anything done on workdays. "While I'm at the store, I start making plans about how I'm going to work in my garden later," Nelly said. "But by the time I get out of my car at home, I'm so sore and exhausted that all I can do is rest." The other cashier said that a shift made her feel "out of it" but unable to sleep. "A lot of times," she said, "I'm a zombie until bedtime. An eight-hour shift lasts sixteen hours." Once, the cashier admitted, she fell asleep after work and woke up covered in urine.

Some may wonder why retail employees don't just go out and find better jobs. But bad jobs are like quicksand. If you can't be sure of your schedule, it's difficult to sign up for college classes, enroll in job training, or to know when you might be available to interview. Just getting through the day may already feel impossible. In one study, more than half of retail employees reported sleep problems and unhappiness. In *Nickel and Dimed*, Barbara Ehrenreich wrote about working a series of low-wage jobs. She had expected the financial strain but was surprised by the existential toll. "What you don't necessarily realize when you start selling your time by the hour," she wrote, "is that what you're actually selling is your life."

I had a more predictable schedule than most colleagues. Since managers knew they needed at least one supervisor on every shift, they couldn't "just in time" our schedules. My shifts fluctuated between days and nights, but I usually knew what I was in for a couple of weeks in advance. But selling my life by the hour still messed with my head. Once, on my eighth shift in a row, I looked at my phone and saw that it was 7:00 p.m. I panicked. Hadn't it been 7:00 p.m. the last time I looked? *The clock has stopped*. I was losing my sense of time, stuck in a real-life version of my colleague's dream about being trapped in a tunnel that connected the checkstand to his bedroom.

That wasn't a rational thought, but it was like a hand that gripped my throat and wouldn't let go. Even after the shift ended, I was haunted by the possibility that I might not make it out the next time. It occurred to me that the anxiety was an outcome of routine. Outside the store, novel or unexpected occurrences marked the passage of time. But the Front End was a repetitive motion machine. Cashiering was the same thing all over again, shift after shift.

As the months went by, my moods were getting harder to control. My white-collar jobs had offered an autonomy that was impossible at the supermarket. I could usually arrange to see a doctor, do laundry, or do my grocery shopping during the day. At TGS, I was either on or off the clock, but either way, my time didn't feel like my own. I wondered if my mental struggles were a product of my former occupational privilege. I considered that I was overreacting to a situation that millions of service employees took in stride.

Except that my colleagues were also obsessed with the clock. Being paid by the hour infected our language. When offered a chance to go home early, a cashier might decline by saying, "I need the hours." She really meant, "I prefer to eat three meals a day instead of one," or "Rent is due in a week, and I'm short." The cliché *time is money* was no longer just something people said. It was my lived reality.

One night, I asked a colleague if she could stay a couple of hours late to cover for a callout. She agreed, saying that she needed the money immediately. "My car is out of gas." In *Maid*, Stephanie Land described a similar double bind. The single mother needed gas to make it to the housecleaning jobs that didn't pay her enough to afford gas. TGS workers made such calculations every day. From food to transportation to leisure activities, everything was debited in hours. "Thirty more minutes on the clock, and I can order a pizza for dinner," someone might say. Or "Two more shifts and I'll have enough money for new shoes."

A lack of autonomy over our time produced contradictions that might seem odd to those who have never worked retail but were logical at TGS. Workers might need all the hours they could get, but no one wanted to stay on the clock past closing. The extra minutes at that hour were not worth it when we were tired and just wanted to go home. Closing time was always a dash to the exit.

George was at perpetual war with late-night shoppers. Each night, an hour before closing, he started nervously pacing in front of the checkstands. Thirty minutes later, he made an announcement on the public address system. "This store is closing in thirty minutes," he said. "Please bring your purchases to the checkstand." Another announcement came fifteen minutes later, followed by the last at 9:55. "TGS will be closing in *exactly* five minutes." Between announcements, he walked the aisles urging shoppers toward the Front End. "Time to go." George may not have had a voice in his wage or working conditions, but he could assert authority over late-night shoppers. Most customers did not argue with the security guard with the linebacker physique and an expression that said he would not take no for an answer.

One night, a customer did not follow instructions right away. "I just have to pick up a couple more things," he explained. I overheard George invent a lie on the spot. "The registers are on a timer," he told the shopper. "They shut down at 10:05. Get to the checkstand now, or you'll go home empty-handed." The look on the shopper's face suggested that he didn't believe the guard's story, but he headed for the Front End anyway. Best not to take any chances.

Some might assume that George was being unreasonable, that people who come into a store before closing should be able to finish their shopping. It wasn't that simple. My colleague believed, as we all did, that late-night shoppers were being cruel, forcing us to work past all reasonable expectation. The security guards even held a running contest over who could get out of the store the quickest. The night he lied to the customer, George clocked out at 10:08 p.m. It was the fastest exit ever, a record that likely still stands today.

Closing time was the culmination of a battle with the clock that had been unfolding all day. One evening, Arman was gleeful. "Time is passing fast tonight!" he said. An hour later, his perception had shifted. "It's slowing down now." A few minutes after that, he announced that the clock had "completely stopped."

I responded with my own version of the psychosis. "Arman, the minute you say that time is going fast, it starts to go slow. If you want the shift to pass quickly, then don't talk about it!"

He considered my theory. "You think so?" he said.

"It's important not to mention the clock," I said. "Then everyone becomes aware of what time it is."

He promised to tone down his running commentary. It was perfectly logical to both of us that time sped up or slowed down as a consequence of how we talked about it.

Arman couldn't kick his addiction. A few nights later, while I was bagging at Bonnie's lane, he whispered to us, "I don't want to mention it, but I think the clock is moving really fast tonight!"

I glared at him. "Saying you don't want to mention something is the same as mentioning it," I said. "I thought we discussed this!"

Bonnie was not amused. "Everyone knows that talking about the clock slows down the clock," she said. "The first rule of TGS is: *Do not talk about the clock.*"

A chastened Arman slunk away from her checkstand. Everyone revered and respected Bonnie for her kindness and skill. If she said that a rule should be followed, that was the end of the discussion.

Time distortions are not unique to the supermarket.

Most of us have experienced the clock slowing when we are doing something tedious, and picking up the pace when we are having fun. Scientists call the sensation "perceptual illusions." At TGS, the illusions were a source of deep anxiety because we knew which one we were likely to get.

Another day, Nelly was monitoring self-checkout. She glanced at the clock on the wall and grimaced. "Are you sure that clock is working?" she said. "I swear I had twenty minutes left on my shift twenty minutes ago." We laughed. But it wasn't funny. Nelly knew, just as I did, that the clock had not stopped. But rational thinking might not protect us from getting trapped in a time loop where we were forced to watch customers scan and bag their groceries for an eternity.

Cindy's version of the time panic involved earnestly begging for help. In a typical incident, I arrived for the evening shift to find her staring at the clock. I knew what was coming. "Thank God you're here," she said. "The hands on the clock aren't moving. Can you fix them?" I chuckled like I usually did even though, with eight hours to go until my own shift ended, I found her desperation unsettling. When a manager walked by, Cindy continued to plead her case. "Can you bring a ladder so we can climb up and move the hands of the clock? They're stuck."

Sometimes I broke my own rule and gave into the urge to talk about the clock. One evening, when Bonnie was not on shift, I called out, "One more hour before we shut the doors!" Including others in my anxiety lessened my sense of isolation. But my comment sent Willow into a tailspin. "It's going to take ages." She closed her eyes and bowed her head like she was saying a prayer for mercy. Others groaned, saying that the slow night was about to get slower.

It had only taken a handful of shifts to learn that a "slow night" was as bad as a hectic one—it might even be worse. With less to do, we focused on the fact that we had less to do and that our time was controlled by the store. Boredom might seem like an unpleasant but benign emotion, nothing to get worked up about. But neuroscientists associate it with a quickening heart rate and emotional distress—a fight-or-flight reaction to a hazardous situation. Human beings crave novelty and intellectual challenge. We are averse to experiences that deprive us of stimulation. At TGS, a slow clock could ruin our evening and, in the long term, our lives.

The time clock was another inhumane feature of grocery work. A device the size of a cigar box, it was posted on the wall near the public restroom and across from a photograph of the cashier of the month. Staffers punched in and punched out by placing a finger on the scanner. The biometric system linked our bodies to the store's timekeeping mechanism.

Fingerprint scanning permitted our employer to track our movements with precision. The top bosses and some managers and supervisors could log in to the system to learn what time an employee arrived, took a break, and went home. The system blocked most attempts to manipulate it. There was no way to clock in on behalf of a colleague, a technique that retail workers call "buddy punching." During my first week on the job, I arrived at the time clock to find a line that wasn't moving. I asked the person in front of me what was happening. "Why isn't anyone punching in?" She told me that people scheduled at 2:00 p.m. couldn't punch in because it was only 1:53 p.m. If workers punched in early, the store's labor costs would soar.

Once, Felix showed up for a cashier shift and reported that he had not been able to punch in. "That's because you're late," I said. He had misread his scheduled start time as 5:00 p.m. instead of 4:00 p.m. It was an honest mistake. But the clock barred anyone who arrived more than fifteen minutes late from punching in. To ensure that he got paid for the shift, Felix would have to see a manager and explain himself.

Another day, a cashier arrived on time but was still blocked from punching in. A manager had accidentally scheduled him for 4:30 a.m. instead of 4:30 p.m. There was no way to immediately fix the problem. But if the employee went home, the Front End would be dangerously short-staffed. I promised that I would make sure the error was corrected. "Please don't go. I'll text the manager right now," I said. The cashier confirmed that I had sent the message before heading to his checkstand. I didn't blame him for being cautious. Punching in set the shift clock ticking, turning a person into an employee. Off the clock, standing on the Front End in a uniform felt ridiculous. It was like showing up for a costume party that wasn't one and that you hadn't been invited to anyway.

Timekeeping mechanisms like fingerprint scanners are part of a multibillion-dollar workforce management industry that surveils employees of all kinds. Companies like Kronos and Cornerstone on Demand have developed scanners and trackers that monitor everything from retail workers' punches to how often nurses wash their hands, to how long call center staffers are on the phone. Some forms of surveillance are directly tied to work requirements and pay scales. Journalist Esther Kaplan reported on a rash of back and shoulder surgeries at UPS after the company installed tracking devices in vehicles and increased quotas. Amazon has even patented augmented reality eyeglasses that could be used to track warehouse workers' exact location, assuring they are never free from Big Brother's gaze.

The fingerprint-scanning technology used in many retail stores was first introduced by Identimation (now called G4S), a security firm with ties to the private prison industry. In 2016, G4S protected the Dakota Access Pipeline against protesters at Standing Rock in North Dakota. And since 2003, it has provided security for Immigration and Customs Enforcement (ICE). The links between policing and workplace timekeeping are a sign that employers view workers not as people but as a problem to be managed and controlled.

Employees have found creative ways around surveillance, often through old-fashioned sabotage and subterfuge. In her 2022 book, *Data Driven*, Karen Levy reported on long-haul truck drivers who smashed the in-truck surveillance systems that monitored their movements. Other drivers disrupted GPS tracking devices on their trucks by covering the transmitter with tinfoil. In one study, retail employees foiled biometric time clocks by telling a manager the fingerprint scanner was down and manually entering their time.

During my first weeks at TGS, I had arrived in my work shirt, punched in, and headed directly to my checkstand. But such efficiency was a rookie mistake. The veterans knew better. They punched in and then went to the locker room to change. At the end of a shift, they ran the play in reverse, changing back into civilian clothing *before* punching out.

Lunch breaks were another opportunity to beat the clock. A few staffers bought food before punching out. The tactic was more dangerous because it was easy for managers to spot. There was a direct line of sight between the deli and the Front End, making it nearly impossible for workers to linger at the counter without being seen. Paula once sent out a mass text: YOU WILL PUNCH OUT BEFORE PICKING UP LUNCH.

The fingerprint scanner broke down one day. "We're

going analog," a manager said as he tacked a notepad onto the bulletin board and instructed us to write down our punches. Workers took advantage. An employee who got to the store late noted an on-time arrival, while someone who left early assured that he got paid for a full shift. These adjustments did not feel dishonest. They were tactical countermeasures in low-paid jobs that stayed with us at all times in the form of sore feet, aching backs, and the general indignities of service work.

Punching in early was impossible, but punching out late was permitted. Some colleagues took advantage via a trick that they called "padding a paycheck." Darth was the resident expert. Instead of punching out at the end of a shift, he lingered on the Front End restocking bags or offering to push shoppers' carts to the car. "I can get an extra ten dollars a week by slow walking to the time clock," he told me. Since padding a paycheck raised labor costs for the store, the tactics were discouraged. Darth had to be careful to clock out a few minutes late, but not late enough that it looked like a deliberate act.

One day, I saw what looked like a book tucked under a cashier's hand scanner. A book? On the Front End? I was sure that I was hallucinating. Texting was forbidden but tolerated, but reading material was prohibited. "No customer wants to feel like they have to interrupt a reading cashier to be served," a manager had told me.

The second time I passed by the register, I saw that the book was real: *Brief Interviews with Hideous Men*. The contraband was just out of sight of customers but close enough that the cashier could read a few lines between transactions. Like when Felix had faked the sweep, my first response was exasperation. *If she gets caught, it will be on me.* I opened my mouth to say, "I am impressed with the effort, but I can't let you do it." But my will flagged. The cashier was claiming some autonomy over her time. I was envious. Luckily, she wasn't caught that day.

Another time, a manager covering a cashier's break noticed some paper sticking out from underneath the keyboard. She called me over. "Can you believe this?" she said. "It looks like he is writing a play!" The employee had scrawled some notes and lines of dialogue on a piece of receipt tape. "He can't be doing that," she said. "I should throw this in the trash."

I argued for saving the writing. "Don't throw it out," I said. "I'll talk to the cashier. It won't happen again."

When the employee returned from break, I said, "You can't leave this on the checkstand. Are you crazy? A manager almost tossed it out." He said that he was writing a script for a faux documentary in which a camera crew followed supermarket workers around a store. "Like the *Real Housewives* series," he explained. "*The Real Cashiers of TGS*." I wasn't sure the pitch was right. "That sounds like an art film," I said. "Lots of repetition." He shoved the paper in his pocket.

Workers took back time in small, unofficial ways because most didn't have paid time off. During the pandemic, retail employees were briefly heralded as heroes, a long-overdue acknowledgment of their importance to society. But they have never been valued enough for paid vacations. European workers of all kinds are provided up to thirty days per year along with paid holidays. But in the US, about one in four of us can never take a paid leave from our jobs. Our "no-vacation nation" is especially harmful for those on the economy's bottom rungs. The lower a worker's wage, the less likely they are to get paid time off.

At TGS, part-time workers did not qualify for paid time off. And full-timers had to work a year to begin earning points toward "vacation days." Colleagues reported to me that a year of full-time work earned about ten paid days off. Cindy never took a real vacation. She used her paid time off whenever her ankles swelled up, a symptom of her kidney disease. Once, she called the store to say that she would not be in that day because she could not walk. But one missed day put her next rent payment at risk. "Mark it down as a vacation day," she told me, "or I'll end up on the street."

Those who did take vacations seemed like members of an alien species. Once, I overheard a conversation between George and a bakery employee, who had just returned from a week off. "You went on *vacation*?" the guard asked. "I've never been able to figure out how that works. Don't you have to make more money than you spend?"

The bakery employee replied, "You have to have a little bit saved up."

George was stumped. "How does anyone save money?" he asked. "I work full-time and have never had a vacation in my life."

The conversation stayed with me because George seemed suspicious of the story. How had a coworker been able to afford time off while he could not? "You have to have a little bit saved up" seemed to the guard like an accusation. The bakery employee might be saying that George wasn't good at managing a budget or maybe he was a profligate spender who just needed some willpower. In the absence of paid time for everyone, personal discipline was the only explanation for why one colleague could afford a vacation while another could not.

Instead of paid time off, TGS bosses offered employee-appreciation programs. The most common were games and contests. One day, I arrived at work to find a stack of "self-love bingo" cards next to the time clock. The squares included activities like "Taking a shower," "Getting eight hours of sleep," "Meditating," and "Taming negative thoughts." Managers encouraged us to cross off the squares as we accomplished these "acts of self-love." Once a worker reached bingo, their name was entered into a raffle for a ten-dollar deli gift card.

A couple of times a year, TGS celebrated Employee Appreciation Week. A manager set up a table on the Front End with a sign: "TGS Appreciates You!" She distributed mini Snickers bars and Doritos while the Tina Turner song "The Best" blasted out of her cell phone. Employees were invited to fill out a raffle ticket. Winners got a box of TGS's homemade pasta or five dollars off any deli item. The next day, a "mindfulness expert" led employees on a meditation exercise to "soothe nerves and calm minds." Since the sessions were only available during breaks, most workers skipped them. They preferred to spend the time eating or sipping on a coffee while looking out the window—the most common forms of "meditation" at TGS.

During another Employee Appreciation Week, someone from the Humane Society brought two "therapy dogs" that workers could pet on their breaks. A top boss explained that interacting with animals produced endorphins and made people happy. The next day, a manager invited workers to "de-stress" by making paper airplanes and sailing them off the mezzanine onto the sales floor. The planes landed in the aisles and sometimes in carts.

Individual rewards were especially prestigious. The store hired customers to evaluate workers' politeness and helpfulness. They stopped employees in the aisles to ask questions and assessed cashiers' customer service. One day, Aurelie received word that one secret shopper had passed through her checkstand. For her "professional" and "friendly" performance, she was awarded a ten-dollar gift card. Nelly won the title of "cashier of the month." The reward included her photo on the wall next to a "With Gratitude" card signed by the top bosses.

Such games and rewards in the workplace may seem positive. What's not to like about being appreciated? Bosses are showing that they care about their employees! But most workers don't win awards. They toil away in obscurity. In low-wage industries, the programs are a form of emotional abuse. At TGS, being appreciated felt like another job that we weren't being paid for—the job of acting like we were happy and carefree no matter how we really felt. In fact, getting us to suppress our real emotional states felt like the main purpose of the initiatives.

Take self-love bingo. Being urged to "get eight hours of sleep" and "tame negative thoughts" was an underhanded way of telling us to show up to work well rested and with a positive attitude, even if we were assigned a clopen or had to come in on a day we had requested off. Other activities encouraged a certain outlook. My colleagues and I were being ordered to enjoy ourselves, but only while participating in boss-sanctioned "fun" activities on our breaks. Some games were ridiculous. How much stress was relieved by throwing a paper airplane? Instead of real attention to our problems, we were being treated like children.

Some critics have noted that employee appreciation can even be harmful. Workers can develop an "infantilized dependency" on praise and rewards. But those who don't win or who aren't recognized may see themselves as failures, deepening the mental health struggles that are common among low-wage workers. One critic noted that the pursuit of external validation may leave workers unable to separate "their own desires and ambitions" from those of their employers. It's not hard to imagine that such employees may be less likely to ask for a pay raise or to complain about poor working conditions.

At TGS, no one participated in the games and contests with complete credulity. It was no secret why Nelly was named cashier of the month. "The store is rewarding the Front End because our jobs are the worst," she told me. "And me in particular because I am not getting paid what I deserve." She knew, like we all did, that her photo on the wall was supposed to serve as a substitute for the bigger raise that she did not receive when the store increased wages for new hires.

Public displays of bosses' gratitude confirmed my sense that trying to unionize was ill advised, possibly even dangerous. It was clear that workers would never be rewarded for making collective demands to improve their conditions. The more time I spent at the store, the more I saw games and contests as a veiled threat. A company that invested in therapy dogs and meditation sessions instead of pay raises would also take the next step and bust a union or punish employees for organizing. The real lesson of being appreciated was that we were on our own.

George may not have been able to afford a vacation, but he was a master of a tactic known as "my Friday." He often worked twelve shifts in a row, a punishing schedule that allowed him up to five days off without reducing his take-home pay. During the last shift before a "vacation," he announced to coworkers, "Today is my Friday." (It didn't matter if it was Friday according to the calendar.) He bought frozen hamburgers and liters of Dr. Pepper. "I have to feed myself until Monday," he said. (The day of George's return might be a Wednesday or a Saturday, but it was always "Monday" to him.) On one of his "Friday" shifts, I asked George what he was going to do with his time away from the store. He told me that he planned to stay off his feet and watch his favorite movie, *Face/Off*.

Other employees adapted the "my Friday" strategy, working multiple shifts in a row to finance time off. One colleague liked to take his dog, Rufus, on camping trips. "We sleep in my truck, so I don't have to pay for a hotel room," he said. Once, after he returned from four days off, he showed me photos of Rufus in a stark desert landscape a hundred miles from the nearest town. "It was like we were on another planet where TGS didn't exist," he said.

Once, I worked seven shifts to get three days off. I called it a "long weekend." Another time, I worked ten shifts straight to get four days away from the job. But I was so spent by the time "my Friday" came around that I came to doubt that it was worth it. What good were days off if I spent them in bed? The cycle of work and recovery was another maddening routine. Aurelie told me that she had come to a similar conclusion. "Four is the magic number for me," she said. "Once I've worked four shifts, my legs have had enough. I can't sleep because they ache so much." I gave up "my Fridays" and went back to working five shifts followed by a two-day "weekend" that might fall in the middle of the week.

Some colleagues claimed that taking a late lunch shortened a shift. During my first days as a supervisor, the tactic appeared to contradict the principle that breaks were sacrosanct. "I'm scheduled for lunch at 6:00 p.m.," Lucia said one day. "But I want to wait until at least 6:30 to take it." Another worker flat-out refused an on-time lunch. "Time for your break," I said.

"I'll go when I'm ready," she said.

I was so shocked that I stammered, "Sure, go whenever you want."

Eventually, I came to understand the logic of the late lunch even if I didn't believe it could work. A break normally cut a shift in half: four hours of work, lunch, and then four hours until freedom. But a break five hours into a shift meant that there were only three hours between lunch and freedom, while a break five and a half hours in was even better. Since top bosses didn't care when workers took their breaks, the strategy was a low-risk way to beat the clock.

Once, I forgot to close Bonnie's checkstand for lunch. She waited two hours to remind me—and was ecstatic. "Only two hours to go when I get back!" she said. Since my colleague had not actually reduced her hours, I told myself that the tactic was silly—an eight-hour shift was eight hours long no matter what.

Except when it wasn't. One day, the self-checkout cashier asked to use the restroom. I watched the machines while he was gone, planning to take my break as soon as he returned. Twenty minutes later, the lunch rush started. But he still wasn't back. "He must have fallen in," Gordon said. Every self-checkout machine was in use, and lines were forming at the registers.

Two cashiers were due for breaks. I was going to have to close off those lanes and move shoppers. But how could I do that while still monitoring the machines? For the next thirty minutes, I sprinted back and forth between self-checkout and the registers helping to complete transactions, sending employees on breaks, and apologizing to customers for the inconvenience. I was sure self-checkout shoppers were taking advantage by entering the wrong produce codes or walking away without paying. When the cashier finally returned to his post, he apologized. "Sorry. It was an emergency." *A fifty-minute bathroom emergency?* I didn't ask, because I didn't want to know.

That day, I worked well past the point when my stomach started growling and I felt lightheaded. But the experience was not entirely negative. Maybe it wasn't negative at all. I had to admit that part of me *liked* it. My colleagues were right. A late lunch was oddly satisfying. The anticipation of relief mitigated the agony that preceded it. As I got hungrier and more fatigued, a feeling of calm washed over me. *It will be over soon.* The repetitive nature of cashiering may also have had something to do with it. Neuroscientists have asserted a strong link between repetition and time perception. Events that are predictable seem to last longer than those that are rare or strange. A late lunch was a novel occurrence that sped up the clock.

Another tactic was urging everyone around me to move faster. Once, a cashier called me to his checkstand. He had charged a shopper for poblano instead of serrano peppers. I elbowed my way behind the register to enter the correct code. I should have taken the time to show the cashier how to fix his mistake. I might have once drawn the customer into the conversation as a friendly gesture. "What do you make with these spicy peppers?" But my battle with the clock made me desperate for speed. The sight of the customer standing there, waiting to pay and be on her way, made me uncomfortable. I blamed the employee. *A cashier should know the difference between a poblano and a serrano pepper. They don't even look alike!*

My impatience was not on the customer's behalf. I was

practicing a variation of my colleagues' belief that time could be manipulated to our benefit. Getting to the end of a shift more quickly was a matter of eliminating frictions at the checkstand. A cashier who made a mistake was not a person who needed mentoring but an obstacle to *getting the hell out of here.*

Some tasks slowed down the clock no matter how fast I did them. It was a supervisor's responsibility to order gum, candy, and beef jerky for the shelves along the checkstands. But focusing on the minutiae of which items and brands were low turned a shift into a slow crawl. Just *thinking* about doing it felt like capitulation to the enemy clock.

I remembered a work-avoidance strategy from Mark Twain's *Tom Sawyer*. In the novel, Tom gets out of painting his Aunt Polly's fence by convincing another kid that the work is a barrel of fun and not to be missed. His performance is so convincing that the kid offers Tom an apple for the privilege of doing the job. Twain called such trickery "the slaughter of innocents."

One day, when a nineteen-year-old stocker passed by the Front End pushing a pallet mover, I saw an opportunity. "What are you up to?" It was a dumb question.

"I'm about to throw this product," he said, using the grocery industry term for stocking shelves. "What about you?"

I told him that the checkstands were running low on beef jerky and gum. "I wish I could do the order," I said. "I love ordering. But we're short a cashier today." I paused, wondering if I had overplayed my hand. I half expected him to say, "Nice try, Larson. But I've read *Tom Sawyer*, too. Do the order yourself!"

Instead, he fell into my trap. "I'll take care of it," he said. I was overjoyed.

A week later, I punched out for my lunch. The radio

buzzed. "I'm sorry to bother you," Gordon said, "but I really need your help with a transaction." Even though I was off the clock, I put my apron back on and headed to the Front End. My colleague was trying to do a return but kept pushing the wrong buttons. I fixed the problem, but there now were too many shoppers in his line. I got behind another register and started scanning. For the next thirty minutes, I worked through my lunch break. It felt like the clock was punishing me for slaughtering an innocent the week before.

Shoppers who came into TGS within fifteen minutes of closing became objects of my contempt, much like they were for George. *What are those people doing here? Don't they realize that I want to go home?* One night, two minutes before closing, I performed my usual check for late-night shoppers. The aisles were empty.

"We should get out on time," I said to Aurelie.

"Thank God," she said.

My elation transformed instantly into dread when a customer who had been blocked by a pillar turned in to an aisle. I was devastated when I saw that her cart was full. "Don't count your till yet," I said to Aurelie. "There's a giant order coming." The shopper was casually reviewing some protein bars, oblivious to the torture she was inflicting on us.

My colleague sighed. "We're *never* getting out of here."

The shopper rolled her cart into the checkstand ten minutes after closing. Given the situation, I was impressed with Aurelie's customer service. She went through the motions of asking the customer if she had found everything she was looking for and reminded her to scan her frequent shopper's card. Once bagged, the woman's groceries didn't fit into a single cart.

"I'm getting a second cart," I said.

The shopper and I headed to the elevator with the carts. When we reached the lobby outside the parking garage, the door was locked. George had not realized that there was still a customer in the store. Or maybe he had locked her inside as a warning not to ever do this again. "Can you come and unlock the door?" I said into the radio. "We can't get out with these carts."

While we waited for the guard to arrive, the cashier working self-checkout called. "When are you coming up?" He couldn't punch out until I shut down the machines and printed the reports.

"I'm sorry to keep all of you," the shopper said and thanked me for staying late. She had done nothing wrong. But I still blamed her for my frustration. *She should have known better.*

The incident put shoppers in my line of sight. I convinced myself that I could speed up the clock by micromanaging their decisions. A surprisingly large number of customers didn't verify that they were in the shortest line. Or maybe they lacked my ability to scan carts and baskets and instantly know which lines were likely to move the fastest. I tried to stamp out the exasperating behavior by directing carts like a traffic cop. "Go down to number three," I might say. "The person in front of you has just a few items. It'll be faster." I stopped people who were buying only a handful of products from making the preposterous decision of getting in a regular line. "Go on down to the express lane! *It'll be faster!*"

Micromanaging didn't work. No combination of speed at checkout, "paint the fence" tricks, or late lunches alleviated the sense that I was rowing against the current. Like a casino gambler addicted to the game, I might win back time one day but lose it all the next. *Should I admit defeat and quit?* I had considered leaving the job before. The store had ended its mask mandate, a sign that the pandemic was waning. I could afford to take some time to look for a new job (though I would have to give up my health insurance to do it).

While I considered my future, tensions spiked on the Front End. Managers accused us of neglecting sweeps. It was true. I had started ignoring the sweep buzzer. When it went off, I pretended not to hear it. I told myself that I didn't have a choice. If I didn't have enough employees to keep checkstands staffed and carts in the lobby, who was supposed to sweep?

One solution came straight out of the "employee appreciation" toolbox. The top bosses called Stewart into a meeting to propose an idea. They suggested a contest to reward the employee who did the most sweeps with a free sandwich. When Stewart told me about the proposal the next day, I lost it. "That's the dumbest idea I've ever heard in my life," I said. "Everyone here is old or injured or in pain. That's why the physical labor doesn't get done." I felt silly for saying it out loud. Naming a root cause of our problems was a waste of time. We both knew what we had to do.

"I'll make a spreadsheet so we can record the names of sweepers for the contest," Stewart said. His bald spot looked a little bigger than it had the day before.

I did not quit, because suddenly, the news was not all bad. Cindy called to report that she had recovered from her stroke and was returning to TGS. She was anxious to get back to her customers and was out of paid time off. "I don't have enough vacation days saved up to cover all the days that I've missed anyway," she told me. Cindy's return would be something of a restoration. The Front End would feel more like the place where I had first been hired. I was nostalgic for those days.

Whitney also called to say that she was finally returning.

"I still don't have full motion in my hand," she said. "But my insurance won't pay for more physical therapy, so I'm coming back to the store. If I have to, I'll work with one hand." I was sorry that the real Front End boss was returning before she was ready. But this was good news for me. Keeping the gears churning would be her job, not mine.

The reprieve never arrived. A top boss called me into his office. I thought he was going to reprimand me for ignoring the sweep buzzer, or maybe he had heard that I had let an employee fake a sweep or that cashiers were reading books and writing scripts on the job. Instead, he said, "Whitney will need to ease back into things, so you'll take over training cashiers." He had signed me up to attend an event at the corporate office, where I would learn the training system. The new role would blow up my plan to just be a regular supervisor again. But it would also grant me a new status at the store. I knew how I wanted to use it. I thanked the boss. "When do I start?"

CHAPTER 6

Choice

On one of my first night shifts at TGS, two shoppers rolled into a checkstand near closing time. George cursed when he saw them. I thought it was because their cart was full. This was going to take a while. But that was not the only reason for his reaction. Like other longtime employees, he had developed the ability to tell the difference between shopping carts that had been filled intentionally and those whose contents had been tossed in at random. The random carts spelled trouble almost every time.

That night, the shoppers' cart was a strange mix. The bottom was lined with two dozen cans of beans. Next, the customers had tossed in a pair or reading glasses, some vitamins, stuffed animals, a puzzle, candy bars, lunch meats, chilled soups, and containers of lemon custard. There were two dog collars and two kinds of shampoo. On top of the pile was cooked food from the deli: a salmon dinner, fettucine alfredo, lasagna, and roast beef sandwiches. With more experience, I would have recognized the problem, just as George had. *Who buys so much prepared food late at night? Who buys multiple dog collars and more than one kind of shampoo?*

As soon as the cashier started scanning, one of the shoppers put up a hand. "We aren't buying all of this stuff," he announced. The couple began to reconsider everything in their cart. They handed some of the items back to the cashier. "We don't need this salmon dinner," the woman said. "And we don't want all these containers of lemon custard." The culling continued for the next several minutes. The cashier put the unwanted items on the counter behind him seamlessly, like he had expected this. "We don't need the glasses. I have a better pair at home," said the man. The cashier took the glasses. "And this dog collar is too expensive."

The scene played out as if someone else had put the groceries in the couple's cart when they weren't looking, and they were only now being given the opportunity to decide what they really wanted. The shoppers ended up purchasing only about half of the products they had brought to the Front End. "What the hell was that?" I asked my colleagues after the shoppers left.

"Some people are like this," George said. "They change their mind after they get to the checkstand." The cashier nodded. "I hate when it happens at closing."

I had just had my first encounter with a species of customer that I came to call "the choosers." Such shoppers first made selections from the shelves and then chose again, for real this time, at the checkstand.

"These marshmallows look delicious," a customer might say as he handed the bag to me. "But I need to limit my sugar consumption." Other choosers offered no explanation except a changed mind. "On second thought, I'll pass on the tahini sauce." A few intentionally put more products in a basket than they could afford. "Can you stop scanning at fifty dollars?" someone might say. "Fifty dollars is all I can afford." Once, a child carried a toy to the checkstand. His mother whispered to me, "We're not taking the Matchbox cars." I put them behind me. The child would be none the wiser until he got home and found the toys were not in the bag.

The psychologist Barry Schwartz has argued that, contrary to the American idea that a variety of options is a key to individual freedom, choice is not always a good thing. We may believe that selecting between different kinds of jeans (relaxed, slim fit, easy fit, boot cut, button or zipper fly, and more) makes us happier, or that choosing between electricity and phone service providers assures the best price. But the experience becomes negative when acquiring goods feels like a multiple choice quiz that takes up our time and energy. Too many options can lead to feelings of regret and inadequacy and even depression. There may be no better example of this "paradox of choice" than selecting a health care plan, a process so stressful and reviled that it has spawned an industry of providers that promise to help bewildered consumers decide.

At TGS, some choosers may have been genuinely indecisive. Others may have enjoyed making decisions so much that they wanted to do it twice. Or they were enacting a wish-fulfillment scenario. The checkstand was where they left the fantasy of what they wanted to buy and entered the reality of what they actually bought. Whatever explained their behavior, the choosers created labor for workers. Everything shoppers decided not to buy had to be reshelved. Once the pile at each checkstand got large enough, an employee moved the unwanted items to a shopping cart behind an unused register. Like the grate at the bottom of a storm drain, the "gobacks" cart collected debris dislodged from its place of origin that didn't make it out the door.

Frozen gobacks were an emergency. The moment a shopper abandoned ice cream or waffles, a call went out. "Frozen goback!" Once, when no one responded to the call, a top boss got on the radio. "Who's taking care of those waffles? I'll keep asking until someone volunteers." Another time, when no one volunteered to restock some frozen pretzels, an executive who happened to be in the store did the job herself. Frozen gobacks were an event almost on par with an SOS call.

The urgency was not only about preventing spoilage. One night, a shopper changed her mind about some Popsicles. The cashier failed to make an emergency call. Instead, she tossed the box in the gobacks cart like it was cereal or crackers. Two hours later, I noticed that the floor was wet. The melted Popsicles had oozed out of the box, covering a dozen other gobacks with a dark, sticky substance. Most of the groceries had to be thrown out, and a bagger had to wipe down the other products in the cart.

One night at closing time, a shopper at self-checkout took a long, slow look at his basket. "I'm not going to take the fried chicken," he said and left it on the machine. Arman, the cashier, ignored the chicken. George came back from locking the front door and also pretended not to see it.

"Guys," I said, "we need to restock that chicken."

The guard shook his head. "They can put it away in the morning."

I could already hear colleagues arriving in the morning and cursing me out for leaving the chicken. "It will be inedible by then," I said.

George glared at me, picked up the box, and headed for the deli. "New rule," he said as he passed. "From now on, shoppers have to buy everything they bring to the Front End. No gobacks."

Arman laughed. "Is George really going to tell people they can't change their minds?"

The idea was obviously silly. But the following night, I half expected the guard to make an announcement on the public address system warning shoppers about the new rule: "Please bring your items to the checkstand where you will be required to purchase all of them."

A few cashiers coveted the job of restocking abandoned groceries. An employee might say, "Since business is slow, I'll turn off my light and do some gobacks." At first, I didn't understand the choice. Cashiers already handled thousands of groceries each day. Restocking looked like more of the same. Or worse. Gobacks regenerated like bacterial spores. A worker could spend hours in the aisles and never get to the bottom of the cart. One day, I asked a cashier why she volunteered. "It's a change," she said. "It's a break from scanning." I should have realized that restocking was relief from repetitive motion. Pain was the answer to almost every mystery at TGS.

TGS employees' relationship with gobacks may seem extreme. After all, moving groceries from one place to another is part of a worker's job. But our experiences were far from unique. When I first started at the store, I searched online to see what other grocery employees were saying about their work. I discovered forums where employees discussed their jobs anonymously. A surprising number of conversations were about gobacks.

One employee said that abandoned products made him feel as if he was being buried alive. "Sometimes I'll come to work in the morning, and the gobacks cart will be overflowing," he wrote. "I end up having to put it ALL back. I have asked for volunteers, but nobody ever helps. I feel like I can never get on top of it." Another worker complained that shoppers were clueless about how their changed minds and whims affected him. "Today I found a number of items in the wrong locations," he wrote. "Probably because customers decided they didn't want to purchase them, so they just put them anywhere. It's like they think elves come out at night and restock everything."

A common theme was how gobacks might lead to poor customer service. Workers lamented being interrupted while restocking products that shoppers had changed their minds about. "Today, no fewer than ten shoppers asked for help while I was on the sales floor," one wrote. "I happily assisted them. But when I returned to the Front End, a manager criticized me for taking too long doing gobacks." The employee wanted to know how others managed the impossible task of helping shoppers while restocking items.

Researchers have documented the mental toll of gobacks. In the 2023 book *Worn Out*, Madison Van Oort interviewed retail workers who said they felt like they were losing their minds. One employee described wandering around a department store unable to find where an abandoned shirt belonged. After twenty minutes of frantic searching, she asked a coworker for help. He pointed to the shelf. The employee had become so frazzled and disoriented that she couldn't see what was right in front of her. Van Oort wrote that returning gobacks often means "meander[ing] in circles" in a process that makes workers "feel crazy."

After reading about other retail employees' experiences with gobacks, I asked a colleague what she thought. "Until I worked here, I could never have imagined how many products get abandoned," I explained.

My coworker refused to have the conversation. "I don't want to talk about gobacks," she said. "Too traumatizing."

Most choosers at TGS probably didn't realize how their behavior affected employees. To them, groceries existed only as an idea until they paid for them and took them home. Walking through the aisles, shoppers saw possibilities instead of things. When they changed their minds about a product, it disappeared. But to workers, groceries were always concrete objects that had to be picked up, shelved, and restocked whether customers bought them or not.

The choosers might have been surprised to learn that the supermarket offers fewer options than we think. Many popular brands and varieties are owned by the same parent companies. When we walk the aisles reviewing and selecting, we are participating in an elaborate illusion. We might linger in the pasta aisle deciding between brands and varieties. But no matter which package we bring to the checkstand, we are likely buying from one of only three producers that sells almost 80 percent of all pasta products. It's the same in the cereal aisle, where three mega-companies control two-thirds of the market. In the dairy section, where numerous varieties of yogurt beckon for our attention, just four entities produce about three-quarters of yogurt sold.

The beverage aisles are among the most misleading. However we quench our thirst, our dollars are lining the pockets of a small number of producers. Today, just two companies sell 70 percent of beer sold. Anheuser-Busch, the world's largest brewer, owns seventeen craft beer makers, including international brands. That brew from Belgium may look like a boutique brand. But it was produced by the same company that distributes Budweiser.

The soda, water, and juice selections are equally deceptive. Ninety-three percent of the soda we buy is sold by just three companies. Coca-Cola is a major player in the bottled water and juice business. It owns Dasani, Smartwater, Vitaminwater, Minute Maid, and Simply. Its top competitor, PepsiCo, owns Tropicana and Aquafina.

Think you're in new territory when you move on from the beverages to the snack food aisle? PepsiCo, which owns Frito-Lay, also has a lock on a popular treat. The company sells 88 percent of dips, including Fritos, Lay's, and Tostitos.

Our cats and dogs have as few choices as we do. Animal lovers might be surprised to learn that Mars, the candy conglomerate that makes Snickers bars, M&Ms, and more, is a leader in the pet food industry. Mars is behind brands including Whiskas, Pedigree, Sheba, and Cesar.

We can trace the concentration of the grocery industry to the 1930s, when the Great Atlantic and Pacific Tea Company, or A&P, operated sixteen thousand grocery stores in every corner of the country. The shops were part of national culture. Customers treated A&P like a member of the family, nicknaming it "grandma." When the writer John Updike needed a name for his coming-of-age story about a cashier's moral dilemma, he went with "A&P," a title that signified a common American experience.

A&P grew into the largest retailer in the world by buying out competitors. Starting in 1919, it opened a coffee-importing business, assuring that its coffee became a bestseller. It went on to take over a Wisconsin milk maker, which put the grocery giant in competition with other milk suppliers. Next, A&P bought bakeries, modernized their equipment, and created a precision bread-delivery system. Within a few years, it was offering salmon, producing peanut butter, and more. Much like shoppers today, A&P customers who thought they were choosing among different brands were actually purchasing products manufactured by A&P.

The company's aggressive methods infuriated competitors and led to a crackdown. In 1949, the Justice Department called A&P a monopoly and asked a judge to order its breakup. The government accused the company of illegally using its size and power to pressure food manufacturers to give it lower prices than other stores received. If a supplier refused its demands, A&P declined to sell its products. But losing access to the chain's shelves could put manufacturers out of business.

The case was more than a skirmish between the federal government and a grocery company. It launched a national debate about fair competition and led to laws against the bullying tactics that had made A&P so powerful. It was also a battle over what kind of society shoppers wanted to live in. Should stores that sold basic goods serve the public, or should they seek to get as large and rich as possible? It's a debate that is still playing out today.

These days, even a store's name is an illusion. As late as the 1990s, many of us could still choose between a chain or a locally owned competitor. By 2019, just four corporations took in around two-thirds of all grocery sales. When we steer a cart through the aisles at Ralphs, Dillons, Food 4 Less, Fred Meyer, Harris Teeter, King Soopers, and more, we are patronizing Kroger. Vons, Safeway, Lin's Fresh Market, and Pavilion are all owned by Albertsons. Californians who flock to Foods Co. for the organic produce, and Manhattanites who swear by the Camembert at Murray's Cheese may think they are visiting a specialty store. But they are shopping at Kroger.

The pandemic was a peek behind the curtain into how corporate concentration harms shoppers. During the crisis, customers paid about 13 percent more for groceries. We were told that high prices were related to supply chain disruptions, that manufacturers were simply passing on their increased costs. But company balance sheets told a different story. The meat producer Tyson Foods doubled its profits after it raised prices by up to 30 percent. One egg company saw its profits explode more than 700 percent as the cost of a dozen eggs more than doubled. Retailers' profits also spiked. But instead of lowering prices to help struggling shoppers, Kroger offered buybacks to shareholders, lining the pockets of wealthy investors.

The illusion of choice at the supermarket brings us back to the TGS customers who changed their minds. While it's impossible to know what motivated the choosers to abandon groceries, for shoppers everywhere, consumer choice may appeal because it's the only kind we have. We can't choose living-wage jobs or affordable health care and education—but at least there are a dozen brands of coffee to choose from at the supermarket. Fake variety on the shelves may be a substitute for real material goods that are less and less available to us all.

My colleague's "trauma" comment about gobacks made me wonder why she even worked at the supermarket. Why had other colleagues chosen the retail industry instead of another line of work? I decided to conduct an informal survey. I asked coworkers about their prior experiences and what had led them to apply for a job at TGS.

A couple of cashiers had worked at Walmart. Bonnie told me that she preferred TGS because the pay was better. Another former Walmart cashier, Aurelie, had broad experience in the retail industry. "Grocery stores are not the worst," she told me. "I always tell people, whatever you do, do *not* get a job in a department store. Your life will be hell. You'll spend your whole day picking up clothes that shoppers drop on the floor."

One twenty-two-year-old cashier had recently worked as a hotel housekeeper. She told me that she got tired of being called "maid" by hotel guests. "I would be walking down the hall," she recalled, "and someone would yell, 'Maid! Maid! I need new towels!'" Selling groceries was less humiliating than cleaning rooms. Some TGS customers were demanding, but "no one has ever called me 'cashier,' so that's a win," she said.

A stocker in his thirties told me that he had recently worked in a law firm as a paralegal. "One of my jobs was calling people to tell them that they had been denied their claim for public benefits—Medicaid, disability, stuff like that." He said the pay had been "decent," but the job was depressing. "Many times," he told me, "by the time I made the call, the person had already died from whatever it was they had been trying to get benefits for." He preferred TGS, where he felt like he was providing for people's needs instead of denying them.

A few colleagues saw the supermarket as a source of stability. One cashier in her twenties had recently worked at home for a pharmacy start-up. She liked the job—taking calls from customers who had questions or complaints. But after the company flopped and laid off its workforce, she didn't want to go through that experience again. Nelly found another kind of stability at TGS. Years earlier, she had quit a call center job after it had made her gain weight and feel sluggish. "Standing and walking all day is bad for you," she told me. "But sitting is worse."

Amazon was a funnel that sent burned-out, injured people to the supermarket. Before TGS, I had considered working in an Amazon warehouse. But once colleagues told me horror stories, I was glad I had chosen the supermarket instead. "Amazon treats you like a robot. You have to make quotas," George told me. At the warehouse where he had worked, employees were surveilled, their every action timed and cataloged. "I was required to box ninety items a minute," he recalled. "It was insane. If I didn't meet my quota, I had to work overtime. It felt like they owned me."

George hung on at Amazon for a year for the insurance. He told me that he and his wife were hoping to have a baby via in vitro fertilization, and they needed the benefits. "Amazon's health care policies are not bad compared to what you can get elsewhere," he explained. When the pandemic started, George got laid off. "I don't know if we'll be able to afford to have a baby now," he said. "But TGS is a little easier on the body."

One cashier had recently been employed as a "picker" at a company that sold clothes online. "I walked ten miles a day through a giant warehouse picking clothing off the shelves to send to customers by mail," he said. "Eventually, I just couldn't do that kind of walking anymore." Another worker overheard our conversation. "I slung a sledgehammer in an oil field for a few years," he told me. "I burned out on that by the age of thirty." One employee said that he had once been employed as a "cleaner" at an oil refinery. The job required crawling into a pipe with a broom and a rag and scrubbing the walls. "It was dirty, hard work over twelve-hour days," he said. "But the pay was good." He quit only after he got too old to sweep and crawl.

For my colleagues, occupational choice was as illusory as the "variety" on the store shelves. Employees who found cashiering less demeaning than other jobs were still working in customer service roles where poor treatment was hardly unheard of. Those who had come to TGS for stability didn't really have it. There were no protections against layoffs or having our hours cut. Cashiering might be less immediately taxing than boxing ninety items a minute at Amazon, swinging a hammer, or crawling through a pipe. But repetitive stress and other supermarket injuries would develop eventually. Workers who came to the store for a less strenuous job were buying themselves time that might run out.

Their jobs also set them up for long-term economic pain. There are many variables that determine whether a person will receive a promotion or a pay raise at work, or whether they will see their wages stagnate. An employee's education level, gender, and race are contributing factors. (For example, racial discrimination in job assignment and pay is a long-standing problem in the retail industry.) But neither workers' backgrounds nor their individual decisions completely explained their economic precarity. The main reason supermarket employees get trapped in poorly paid jobs is so simple that it can be hard to see: Employers pay as little as they can get away with. And retailers have been allowed to get away with everything.

Talking to my colleagues shed light on my own case. I was stressed out. But TGS was not, as Aurelie put it, "the worst." The store satisfied some of my immediate needs for an income and a place to contribute to my community. I had been telling myself that I was just waiting for the pandemic to end to find a new job. But I wasn't sure where to begin. An academic position would be virtually impossible to land. And part-time college teaching paid so little that it felt like a lateral move rather than an improvement. I was facing a variation of the dilemma that many coworkers knew well. Age had given us experience and skills, but our options were dwindling.

My perspective on my workplace had also evolved. At first, I had seen TGS as a place to earn a paycheck until I found my "real" job. But the Front End had taught me that cashiering *was* a real job, more important to society than many occupations that paid better and came with a higher social status. I hesitated to quit partly because I valued the skills I had developed and the knowledge that I had gained. I didn't want to give them up.

Maybe I just needed to think differently about my own choices. Inspired by coworkers who were making the best of limited options, I tried to think of ways to improve my situation by helping others. In my past life as an organizer, I had acted in solidarity with student debtors to "turn alienation into connection" and "oppression into strength," according to one definition of the term. I also recalled a lesson that the educator and organizer Mariame Kaba had learned from her father. "You have a responsibility to live in this world," he told her. "Your responsibility is not just to yourself. You are connected to everyone."

What might responsibility and solidarity look like at TGS? *Solidarity* was mostly a collective term—one reason "Solidarity forever!" is a rallying cry for unions everywhere. But I also knew that individuals could be in solidarity with a group or with another person, such as when a customer refuses to cross a picket line or when people take turns grocery shopping for an elderly neighbor. Could something like that work at TGS? I decided to try to find out. I would work on being a more sympathetic colleague and supervisor, even if that meant breaking rules and policies. I could choose not to become the person that the job was turning me into.

I started with my first cashier training a few days later. I had often walked by the conference room wondering which of the trainees would last more than a month. Now, I was leading the event for a half dozen people who were depending on me to get them ready to work on the Front End. Their crisp, unfaded uniforms made me feel wistful for my first days, when customer service was a pleasure and the supermarket community was a source of pride.

As soon as I launched the training PowerPoint, I saw the problem. The first slides about how to sell food to SNAP recipients had not been updated in years, while those about the regulation of alcohol were confusing. I skipped those slides, telling the trainees in a few sentences what they needed to know. Next, I was supposed to go through the steps for returns. It might have been because I was traumatized by returns, but the idea of teaching the skill made my skin crawl—especially because it wasn't necessary. "This is a waste of time," I said to the group. "Cashiers never perform returns. You'll have to call a supervisor." I skipped those slides, too, and moved on to a video about best practices for avoiding trips and falls and other accidents.

By midmorning, I had already completed the all-day training. I sent everyone on a break and lingered over my lunch trying to figure out what to do next. Part of me wanted to stay in the conference room and try to make the time go faster. The trainees and I could watch more videos until it was time to punch out. Instead, I decided to give my new colleagues the kind of training I wished I had had when I started the job.

On the Front End, I assigned the new cashiers to a checkstand and moved an experienced employee to the bagging station. I put a notice on the front of the register that said "Cashier in Training." At first, the trainees worked haltingly. But after a couple of hours, most looked confident enough that I removed the "Cashier in Training" signs. Instead of showing pointless videos, I was teaching practical skills. By the time I punched out that day, I was convinced that I had a model for solidarity and responsibility at TGS. I could make better choices for everyone.

A few days later, I saw another opportunity. An executive was hovering around the Front End. His name tag said that he was the company's risk avoidance officer. "Do you know what the safety theme of the month is?" he asked me. I didn't know what he was talking about. "Every month, we educate employees on a theme around safety," he said as if putting the words *safety* and *theme* in a different order in the sentence would explain everything. "This month's theme is bloodborne pathogens." I expected him to share some guidelines about how to avoid contact with blood in the store, like what to do if a worker cut themselves while sawing up a side of beef. I was about to ask the executive if he knew about baggers' paper cuts. But he had already changed the subject. "I'd like you to go around and ask everyone if they know the theme," he said. "If they know, give them a coin." He handed me a stack of dollar coins. "Later, I'll come back to see how many people knew the answer."

I headed to Darth's register to tell him what Risk Avoidance Guy had said. My colleague had never heard of the safety program, either. "You should tell everyone what the theme is while I'm on break," I said. "When I get back, I'll distribute the coins." When I returned to the Front End, I went around and asked about the safety theme. Each person said, "Bloodborne pathogens." I gave Darth a thumbs-up and went into the lobby. The cart collector had been in the parking lot when Darth was providing the information. I gave him a coin anyway.

When the executive returned, I said, "Every employee knew the answer. Can you believe it?" He was full of smiles and compliments. "You're doing better than a lot of other stores," he said. "In some of them, *no one* knew the theme of the month." I had made the executive happy and improved our store's reputation. And all it took was colluding with Darth and a harmless lie.

Another evening, a manager called me to his office, where he told me that the cart collectors were rebelling. Three of them were refusing to be trained as cashiers. They preferred to work in the parking lot instead of on the Front End. The manager was furious. "When employees don't want to cashier, it limits our scheduling options," he told me. It was true that the store desperately needed more cashiers. But why was the manager telling me about the rebellion?

"I need you to clamp down on cart collectors wearing AirPods," the manager said. The cordless headphones were prohibited on the job because they might make customers feel like they had to yell or tap a worker on the shoulder to get their attention. (Only stockers on the graveyard shift were allowed to wear headphones.) The manager planned to punish the workers with write-ups and suspensions. "Maybe they'll see that cashiering is not so bad," he said.

"Sure, I'll report AirPods when I see them," I said.

I went directly to the lobby, where a teenage employee was spraying a cart with disinfectant. I told him that I had just been called to the manager's office. "Do you know what he wanted to talk to me about?" I asked.

"I have a pretty good idea," he said. The worker was a ringleader of the rebellion. And he had taken AirPods out of his ears to talk to me.

"Look, I don't care if you listen to music at work," I said. "Let's make a deal. Cart collectors keep wearing AirPods but not in the store." I pointed to the headphones in his hand. "If you only wear those in the parking lot, then I won't get blamed for not reporting it. Understand?"

He nodded. "Only outside," he repeated.

"Tell the others the deal. It starts now," I said.

From then on, I never saw cart collectors wearing AirPods, and no manager ever mentioned the topic again. The workers continued to refuse to train as cashiers—it was the only collective rebellion I saw during my time at the store. After most members of the group quit, managers made training to cashier a requirement of the cart-collecting job.

Weeks later, another manager called on the radio. I could tell by the tone of her voice that this was not a friendly call to tell me how much she valued my contribution. "You have two employees standing at a register doing nothing but talking! Can't you find some work for them?"

Lucia and a bagger were chatting animatedly at number seven. I said, "A manager is mad that you two are not working."

Lucia threw up her hands. "What are we supposed to do? There are no customers right now."

I told my colleagues that I understood they felt demeaned. "But I'm going to have to send one of you on a job to get the boss off my back." The gobacks cart was sitting a few feet away. "Why don't you work on gobacks?"

The bagger disappeared with the cart. Later, I ran into her at the time clock. "Managers are on my case all the time," she said. "It's not fair. I wasn't doing anything wrong."

I told her not to worry about it. "We just have to look busy when the managers are around." I was announcing to my colleague that I was on her side against our common enemies.

Part of me knew that I was blaming individuals for a systemic problem and giving my coworkers the wrong impression about the source of their mistreatment. TGS was no different from other workplaces. Managers carried out orders passed down from the top bosses who did the bidding of executives who followed common practices in the retail industry. But treating those just above me in the hierarchy as a stand-in for everything that was wrong at TGS seemed logical at the time. It also felt good.

So did defying my fellow supervisors. One day, Stewart announced that he had prepared a written exam for cashiers. "I want everyone to take it," he told me. The test began with a list of produce items, including broccoli, brussels sprouts, and kiwifruit. Employees were supposed to list the correct produce code for each item. A second part asked cashiers to write down how to perform special functions, such as changing the price of a weighed item or voiding an entire transaction. Stewart had already given the exam to staffers that morning. He wanted me to ask evening workers to take the test. "We'll be able to find out which cashiers really know their jobs and which ones need to improve their skills," he said.

The test was another one of the pointless policies that I had vowed to ignore. I didn't need to give the exam to know what the result would be. Cashiers with the most experience would correctly answer the questions, while the newest would perform poorly. It made no sense to draw attention to staffers' weaknesses so we could learn what we already knew.

I suspected that Stewart was trying to curry favor with the higher-ups. Months earlier, he had surveilled the punches of a cashier who extended her breaks, intending to turn her in to management. Now, he was coming up with test questions for the same reason. While Whitney was off the job, Stewart, like me, had been given more responsibility and authority. But Whitney's return had put him back in his regular role. While I was now a cashier trainer, Stewart probably felt like he had been demoted. Giving the test and passing the results to the bosses was a way to remind them that he was manager material.

"Sure, I'll give the test," I said. After Stewart left, I waited for the crowds to thin out and then filled in the sheets myself with correct (and a few incorrect) answers. I put other employees' names at the top. Since I had to work fast, I didn't bother to change my handwriting. I figured if Stewart really wanted to know if the cashiers had filled out the forms, all he had to do was ask them. I tried to head off that possibility by telling colleagues what I had done. "If Stewart asks, you took this test and learned a lot," I said to the cashiers. I told myself that my fellow supervisor wasn't thinking clearly. It was up to me to protect others from his irrational behavior.

Unfortunately, Stewart was still on his quest to distinguish himself a few days later. He fumed that employees were using their phones at work. "They think we can't see them texting behind the register or scrolling Instagram when they're supposed to be monitoring self-checkout." My colleague was getting worked up over behavior that had always been common. Virtually everyone checked their phone on the Front End. "I'm keeping a list of people," Stewart told me. He showed me a sheet with the names of a half dozen phone violators. "You should add more names to the list tonight," he said. "Tomorrow, I'll take it to the managers." I agreed to the plan, hoping that he would forget about it. But the next day, Stewart asked for the sheet. I dug it out of the drawer where I had left it.

"You didn't add any names to the list," he complained.

"I didn't see anyone using a phone last night," I lied. "Word must have gotten around that you are keeping tabs."

Stewart was satisfied and did not mention the list again.

Timothy was never going to be cashier of the month. The nineteen-year-old had a thin frame and blond hair that looked white when it caught the afternoon light that came in through the window. Once, when the two of us were cashiering next to each other, he told me that he was taking college courses in computer science. "I like machines better than people," Timothy had said. "They don't need to be sweet-talked into getting work done."

My colleague's appreciation for the work ethic of machines was surprising given that he was a distracted employee. He often stared out the window with his back to the Front End and had to be reminded to serve shoppers. It was possible that he was just confused about how to keep himself busy when no one was telling him what to do. Timothy took instructions literally. Once, a cashier told him to "stay right there until I get back." He froze in place like a statue, not moving a muscle until she returned. He refused work that didn't appeal to him. Once, I approached with the sweep buzzer. "Please do a sweep."

Timothy shook his head. "No, I don't want to."

I was so taken aback by his defiance that I didn't make him sweep.

One day, a manager passed by the Front End. "How is Timothy doing over at self-checkout?" she asked. I reported what was true: Everyone loved our newest colleague. "He works hard and always does whatever he is asked." (I meant it literally.) But praise for Timothy wasn't what the manager wanted to hear. She told me that there had been a spike in thefts at the machines. Customers were pretending to pay and then walking out when the cashier wasn't looking. "Only specific people should be assigned to self-checkout," she said. "They need to be alert. I don't think Timothy is up to the job."

This criticism was a reminder that my colleagues and I

worked on the border between the store and the outside. Shoppers might enter the building in the front or back, but once inside, they had to pass through the heavily surveilled Front End to exit. This design originated with Clarence Saunders, the entrepreneur behind Piggly Wiggly. Shoplifting had been virtually impossible in mom-and-pop shops, where goods were kept behind the counter. But the inventor of self-service recognized that walkable aisles presented a theft risk. That's why he designed his store with separate entrances and exits and gates that shoppers had to pass through to exit.

Today, anti-theft architecture is standard in stores of all kinds. Grocery shoppers may not realize they are walking into a space that treats them like potential criminals. But employees know the reason that customers can only exit in the front. At TGS, the geography meant that my colleagues and I doubled as security guards. No manager had said, "Self-checkout cashiers must stop shoplifters." Instead, we were instructed to be "alert" and "ready to call security."

The manager's instruction about Timothy troubled me. She was putting workers in danger. A thief trying to flee might push a cashier to the ground to get to the door. Or a shoplifter might throw a punch. Since I had already seen such behavior from customers who hadn't been accused of anything, it was easy to imagine it from a person accused of stealing. I decided not just to ignore the manager but to do the opposite of what she wanted. I approached the cashier. "If you see anyone stealing, let me know. I'll call security," I said. "But you should never stop anyone yourself." Timothy agreed to steer clear of anyone who might be stealing.

Managers were determined to reduce the theft rate at self-checkout at cashiers' expense. The next day, Whitney sent a memo detailing a new policy from the top bosses. "If a customer scans items but doesn't pay, cashiers should zero out the transaction," it read. (Many thieves approached a machine and began scanning, waiting for the cashier to turn her back before running for the door.) The new policy was worrying news. "Zeroing out" told a machine that a customer had paid. But if no payment had been made, the transaction created a discrepancy between payments and receipts, or what cashiers called a "short till."

Regular cashiers were punished with a write-up or even a suspension when their tills were "short." But they accepted the consequences because the discrepancy likely meant that they had made a mistake, such as by giving a shopper too much change. But at self-checkout where a short till might be the result of a theft, the zero-out rule was unfair. The top bosses were refusing to take into consideration that self-checkout created more opportunities for shoplifting.

A few days after the policy was announced, Darth was at self-checkout. When he turned his back to help a man retrieve a card that had become stuck in the ATM, a shopper walked out without paying. "I zeroed out the order," Darth told me. "Now my till will be short." I was furious at the top bosses. But the words that came out of my mouth still surprised me. "Next time, call me over. I'll void it," I said, using the term for completely deleting an order. I had been thinking about using the override to void thefts instead of zeroing them out. But I had not wanted to implicate coworkers in my decision.

For all I knew, Darth would report what I had said to a manager, saying something like, "A supervisor is defying the zero-out policy." Though Darth and I were friendly and he had recently helped me deceive the risk avoidance officer, this was a more serious policy breach. I didn't learn what my colleague had decided until two days later, when another theft occurred. A cashier had noticed a man dawdling near the machines examining a display of cinnamon bears. When she turned her back, he sprinted out the door with a six-pack of beer. "Don't zero it out," Darth said to her. He called me over and explained what had happened. I slid my override across the scanner and erased the order like it had never happened.

Word got around. From then on, a couple of times during each shift, self-checkout cashiers asked for a void. Except they didn't explicitly ask. They said something like, "This transaction was started but, uh, not completed by a customer who has since left the store." We both knew what had happened. I voided without a word. I never asked cashiers to explain themselves or said, "Try to pay more attention next time." I did not care whether the employee saw someone stealing and was afraid to intervene, was distracted by another customer, or was looking at their phone. It was unfair to expect cashiers to stop thieves, and I could mitigate the injustice. I swiped the override like a gunslinger using a pistol, with great abandon and a sure hand. No one was going to tell me how to run *my* Front End.

One night, Willow called on the radio from the upstairs registers. "Where is that chair?" she asked. Everyone knew that chairs were forbidden. Better to have this conversation face-to-face. "I'm coming up to talk to you," I said.

Willow told me that she had recently fallen down the stairs at home and was bruised and sore, on top of the eczema scars up and down her arms. "I need to sit down tonight," she said. "You have to wait until after the last manager has left to sit down," I said. "I'll bring the chair to you then." Willow agreed to wait. But I felt angry and guilty. Why shouldn't an injured cashier be able to sit down? I went back upstairs and dragged a chair from the café to her station. "If a manager comes by, tell them I told you it was okay," I said. "They can take it up with me." From them on, I didn't offer chairs on the late shift. But if a cashier asked for one, I didn't say no.

The sweep buzzer went off one afternoon, prompting the usual sighs and grumbles. At that moment, two young employees from i-grocery passed by the Front End. "What are you two up to?" I asked. They were headed back to their department after filling an order. I handed one of them the buzzer. "You can do a sweep first." I told them to pair up. "One of you can carry the broom, and the other can tap the tags."

I was a little worried the strategy might catch up to me. I was taking labor away from another department. But acting in solidarity with my Front End colleagues was my priority. The i-grocery manager would probably just assume that her workers were slow. It was a win-win.

Another day, Stewart argued with an eighteen-year-old employee who had refused to do a cart run. "I was hired to bag," he said. "And it's hot out there."

Stewart was furious. "I do cart runs all the time," he said. "And I'm an old man!"

The bagger gave up the fight and headed to the elevator.

"Make sure he stays on it," Stewart said to me. "We all have to do things we don't want to do around here."

My colleague had a point. I often did cart runs, as did many others not as young or able-bodied as the teenager. It wasn't fair to let him off the hook.

At the same time, I resisted Stewart's method of berating workers. Since there were few ways for us to negotiate our workloads, supervisors like us had to make better choices. When the bagger came back inside with sweat pouring down his face, I pulled him and another bagger aside. "Listen," I said. "Stewart was too hard on you. But carts have to get done. There's no way around it. I'm offering to let you share the job. Have a discussion and figure it out." For the rest of the shift, the staffers took turns getting carts. The incident was a sign that standing with workers was a matter of will, plus a convincing performance of good-cop-bad-cop.

Solidarity was a superpower that I kept in my pocket and pulled out whenever I wanted. Soon after Whitney returned from her injury, I started looking for ways to use it for her benefit. The Front End manager was struggling to keep up. Possibly due to too many painkiller-induced naps or just a lack of practice, she had lost a step or two. Employees complained that they didn't always get their schedules two weeks in advance, and there were often last-minute changes.

Managers were also making impossible demands on Whitney's time. A typical incident occurred one day when she was working in her office. A voice crackled on the radio. "Where's the Front End manager? The lines are too long. Whitney, we need you up front." I looked up and saw a top boss on the mezzanine, observing us from above.

Seconds later, Whitney appeared and got behind a register. I was annoyed at the manager who didn't even know how to operate a checkstand. "There's no need for you to be down here," I said to Whitney. "I've got things under control."

She shrugged. "The boss wants me behind a checkstand, so I'm behind a checkstand." Minutes later, she changed her mind and closed off her lane. "If anyone asks where I am, tell them I'm on lunch," she said to me.

I knew that she would clock out and spend her thirty-minute break in her office completing the schedule.

It was not the first time Whitney had worked without pay. In fact, she was making a habit of it. I sometimes received texts from her when she was at home. She might remind me to place an order for shopping bags or ask if anyone had called out sick that day. For a while, I figured it wasn't my place to tell my boss how to run her life. But after I decided to be a better colleague, I tried a new approach. The next time she texted me from home, I texted back: "You aren't being paid to send these messages." She replied with a laughing/crying emoji and kept texting.

I knew what was happening—Whitney was a victim of "wage theft," when employees are required or pressured to work off the clock, or when they do not receive mandated overtime pay or tips. Some companies purposefully misclassify hourly workers as managers to avoid paying overtime. Wage theft is especially common in the retail industry where employers steal billions each year in unpaid wages. More people are victims of employer lawbreaking than of robbery or other street crimes.

Like with shopper price gouging, the solution is robust enforcement of the law. But we are moving in the opposite direction—and not just at TGS. The first Trump administration rolled back efforts to protect workers from the crime. Senators Elizabeth Warren and Sherrod Brown responded by opening an investigation into twenty-three companies they accused of wage theft. But during the second Trump term, the Department of Government Efficiency (DOGE) continued the assault, cutting funds for programs that enable the Department of Labor to enforce the law.

It's easy to despise politicians and companies that steal from low-wage workers. But wage theft also implicates those of us who do not work in supermarkets. TGS shoppers benefited from Whitney's unpaid labor. Everyone who came into the store had a better experience when she worked off the clock to ensure that employees got their schedules on time or when she worked from home. Customer service was propped up by exploitation.

The next time a manager called Whitney to the Front End to help with the lines, I saw an opportunity. This time, she didn't answer the call right away. She was probably in the bathroom, or maybe her radio was out of batteries. I picked up the call. "This is the Front End," I said. "We've got everything under control. We don't need Whitney's assistance. Thank you for your concern." I expected the boss to march downstairs to reprimand me or say, "It's not appropriate to second-guess my decisions." But he didn't come. Nothing happened. Whitney never showed up, and the Front End rolled on without her, just like I said it would.

A few days later, I arrived at work to find several colleagues in an intense discussion about events that had taken place the previous evening. They told me that a manager had caught a cashier on the upper level looking at his phone. He had screamed at the worker and then marched downstairs to confront the supervisor. The person running the Front End that night was a kind, timid man in his thirties who had only been on the job about a month. An oversharer, he had recently told me that he didn't know how long he could stay at TGS due to his irritable bowel syndrome. The lack of bathroom breaks was becoming a problem.

The previous night, the manager had lashed out at him. "You need to pay more attention to what cashiers are doing," he had said.

The supervisor defended himself. "I can't see the upstairs registers from here."

The manager wasn't listening. "The next time I see a cashier on their phone, I'm going to rip it out of their hand and smash it on the floor," he warned the supervisor.

By the time I found out what had happened, the cashier had already called out in protest of his treatment, and the supervisor was threatening to quit. "This is the kind of abuse that might push me out the door," he told me.

The thought of losing two reliable employees because of an out-of-control manager was unbearable. I told my colleagues that I would make sure this never happened again. "We're not putting up with this shit," I said.

I climbed the stairs two at a time. In the top boss's office, I reported what had occurred the night before. "This behavior from a manager is unacceptable," I protested. "Everyone knows phones aren't allowed. But if cashiers can't be treated better, we're all going to quit." I expected her to tell me that I was out of line, that I needed to remember my place, or that it was my job to smooth things over with the staff.

Instead, she listened. "I'll speak with him," she said.

The next evening, the manager who had threatened to smash a cashier's phone came to the Front End. "If you need any help tonight, don't hesitate to call," he told me. This was his way of apologizing. The boss had not just said she would reprimand him for his behavior. She had actually done it.

Something was going on. My relationship with the higher-ups was changing.

Each night at closing, I shut down the registers one at a time while leaving others open for the last shoppers. The process required some guesswork. It wasn't always clear how many open registers would be necessary. I usually erred on the safe side and kept three stations open. But one evening, I tried to save time by closing all but two checkstands. It was a mistake. A half an hour later, lines formed, and more shoppers were in the aisles. We were about to get buried.

I got behind a checkstand and waved customers over. Most paid with cards until a man with a six-pack of beer offered cash. I owed him twelve cents in change. When the register kicked open, I realized what I had done. There was no cash in the drawer. I had already dropped it in the vault. My effort to save time had come back to bite me. I gave the customer back one of his dollar bills. "You're getting a discount on the beer tonight because I messed up," I said.

There was now a ten-dollar bill in an empty till. I was going to have to admit my error to Dana. I dialed the number for the bankers' office. I was hoping she wouldn't be there so I could just leave a note. When she answered the call, I took a deep breath and explained that I had collected cash for a closed-out till. "I screwed up."

To my surprise, Dana was not angry. "It's no big deal. Just bring it up as soon as you can." I checked out a few more customers to thin out the lines and then headed upstairs. Dana reminded me of the rock star Joan Jett. She had pale skin and dyed black hair blow-dried stick-straight. That night, she was sitting at her desk in a windowless room surrounded by stacks of cash. I felt as if I had stumbled into the backroom of an illegal betting ring instead of the accounting office of a supermarket. When Dana saw me, I could have sworn she almost smiled. "Have a good night," she said as she took the cash from my outstretched hand.

The kindness emboldened me. A few days later, a supervisor lamented how long it took to process returns. "I can't believe the bankers want us to follow all of these steps," she said. I decided to try to convince Dana to simplify the process. I knocked on her office door. "We're spending a lot of time on returns," I began.

She did not let me finish my next sentence. "Look," she said. "It's clear that you are not an idiot." *Wait. Is Dana paying me a compliment?* The banker was so rarely kind or encouraging that I wondered if she was setting a trap. "I don't expect you to follow the rules to the letter every time," she continued. "Just do it if you feel like the transaction is suspicious. Use your judgment." I was speechless. In thirty seconds, the meanest boss at TGS had told me that I was *not* an idiot and that she trusted me to use my judgment. *Is this really happening?* I felt like I had just been let into a secret club of managers who were kind and respectful to one another. Or maybe they put up emotional walls between themselves and employees like I did with customers.

Another night, a boss of the nighttime stocking crew passed by the Front End on his way home. "The new guy is closing tonight," he told me. He was referring to a new assistant manager, the same man who had recently told me about his previous job at a law firm. "I can tell he's overwhelmed to be closing alone for the first time," he said. "But I'm trying not to show him that I can tell he's overwhelmed. Can I count on the Front End to be understanding as he learns the job?"

I laughed and assured him that we would be kind. "We'll take care of him."

I could hardly believe what I had just heard. The stockers normally steered clear of the Front End to avoid being asked to bag or sweep, tasks they considered beneath them. They certainly never shared any details about their department or admitted anxieties or weaknesses. But the manager had sought me out to tell me about a colleague's mental state and to ask for my help. He was teaching me what he already knew: The store didn't have to be a battleground where workers competed with each other in a war for survival. Instead, we all shared circumstances and needs. Even more shocking, the manager was admitting that the stockers needed more than muscles and gallons of energy drink to do their jobs. They needed respect and emotional support just like the rest of us did.

Everyday incidents started to feel extraordinary. A few shifts later, a bagger and I were pulling reams of paper bags off a shelf and onto a pallet mover. Several stockers came to help. Within seconds, our small group had moved the bundles. Such collaborations happened every day at TGS. It was the only way anything got done. But this one moved me. I had assumed that solidarity would have to be built from scratch. But now it occurred to me that collective identity and shared struggle were already present in the labor that kept the store running. It wasn't that solidarity didn't exist; it was that we used it to the benefit of our bosses and shoppers instead of ourselves.

A few evenings later, I was working with Aurelie, Christopher, and some others. The stubborn clock would not move. Christopher said, "We could just close the doors and go home."

Aurelie agreed. "We could walk away," she said. "No one can stop us. The store doesn't run if we don't work."

I had never heard such comments on the Front End. I was intrigued. "We could shut the doors and leave," I joined in. "If we were really organized, we could demand a lot—pay raises and more."

A bagger got excited about the possibilities. "We could

say, 'We won't work anymore unless you give us five dollars more per hour!'"

A customer rolled into Aurelie's lane, so the conversation ended. But solidarity was in the air.

I loved my job. Every other job in the world was trivial compared to working in a supermarket. I was doing work that really mattered in society, even if society didn't know it. I had found a sweet spot at TGS: I had responsibility and respect, but I could make some demands and break with protocol, at least some of the time. My aching back and sore heel were badges of honor. I was proud to be a real grocery worker. Maybe I would have to reconsider my decision not to organize a union.

The following day, on my walk to work, I received a group text from Whitney. Bonnie was dead. She had passed away in the hospital where she had gone for treatment for a heart condition. I knew about my colleague's illness. She had told me that, a few times a year, a doctor stuck a probe into her leg and pushed it through a blood vessel to her heart. She had described the procedure so casually that I had not realized the seriousness of her condition. Now, I recalled one night when Bonnie had broken her own rule not to talk about the clock. "I might drop dead before the end of this shift," she said. It turned out that she wasn't joking.

Bonnie had never given in to the worst impulses of the supermarket. Devoted to her customers, she had made everyone feel special and unique and broke dumb rules to serve shoppers long before I did. She even tried to see thieves before they got caught so she could offer to buy them food. How would the TGS community survive without her?

When I got to work that day, no one was talking about the news even though I was sure it had traveled through the whole store by then. Finally, I ran into Kirsten, who had been on the group text. "I'm shocked about the news," she told me.

"Yes, it is awful," I agreed. "And so unexpected." On the Front End, I reviewed the schedule like I always did to start my shift. Bonnie had been scheduled to work number three. But her name had been crossed off with a pen.

CHAPTER 7

Solidarity

George looked as pale as a grocery receipt when he approached the Front End a few minutes before closing. "This is going to sound crazy," he said. I expected him to say that he was thinking about locking the doors early so we could punch out and go home. Instead, he told me that he had just seen Bonnie's ghost. He had opened the door to the walk-in cooler and caught a glimpse of a woman with salt-and-pepper hair standing inside amid boxes of yogurt and cottage cheese. "It was Radio for sure," he told me, using Bonnie's nickname. "She turned to look at me and then disappeared," George said.

"Why would Bonnie come back to TGS as a ghost?" I asked. "And why would she be in the walk-in?"

The security guard said that ghosts liked cold places, and the walk-in was the coldest place in the store after the freezer.

Days later, another colleague told me about a similar experience. "Today, I turned a corner in the produce department and thought I saw Bonnie," he said. "But it turned out to be a customer who looked like her."

I assured my colleague that he was just mourning our colleague's passing. "You just have Bonnie on your mind."

He acknowledged that was the likely reason for the sighting. "But I swear she is still here," he insisted. "She is trying to send us a message."

The supermarket operated according to its own rhythms regardless of which customers came and went, which employees worked the registers, or whether workers lived or died. Even the incident that had prompted me to start taking notes about the job was an exception that proved the rule. The intrusions didn't only come from shoppers. They included gaslighting, control, and exploitation from management. But disruptions from outside were also not as rare as I had once assumed.

"Since it's after 7:00 p.m., I think I'll sit down," Lucia said one night. By that hour, managers and top bosses had gone home. Without waiting for my answer, she dragged the chair from a corner and put it behind her checkstand. "It's nice to get off my feet," she told me. Not every employee could sit every night. But over time, a system developed where cashiers took turns using the chair. Cindy was also working that shift—she was her old self again after recovering from her stroke. Between customers, the bagger flipped through a magazine called *Baby Boomer*. The actor John Wayne was on the cover.

Gordon teased her for staring at the photograph. "Someone's in love," he said.

"John Wayne reminds me of my dad," Cindy replied. "A real man's man!"

Gordon was back at work, too, after missing a few shifts to rest his back. His jokes were a sign that he had also returned to form. When a customer came into his lane, he gestured to Cindy. "Be gentle with the bagger. She's older than dirt!"

The shift passed smoothly until 9:00 p.m. when I got

behind a checkstand to help with the late-evening crowds. I had checked out several customers and was preparing to turn off my light when a woman entered my lane. Her cart was full of filled TGS bags. She had already paid for her order, so why had she come back into the store and rejoined a checkout line? "I wanted to tell you what a wonderful staff you have here at TGS," she told me. The customer had recognized me as a supervisor from my uniform. "My cashier, Aurelie, was fantastic," she said. "Such a positive attitude!" The shopper went on to praise other employees by name. "You have fantastic people here."

I thanked her for the compliment, still thinking that it was strange that she had gotten back into a checkout line to say nice things about employees. "Have a pleasant evening," I told her. But the shopper didn't leave. She glanced over her shoulder to confirm that there was no one behind her. "Since you have the time, I'll tell you a story," she said.

For the next ten minutes, the customer stayed at my checkstand recounting the story of how she had lost her "one true love" decades before, when she was fifteen years old. "We were so much in love," she said, sighing. She explained that she and her boyfriend had been forced to break up over religious differences. Their families didn't want them to be together. "Like Romeo and Juliet," she told me. The shopper went on to marry someone else, as did her former boyfriend. "We kept in touch over the years, even though we were married to other people."

She continued, "Later on, I got divorced. And my one true love began having problems in his marriage. I told him that he should try to work things out with his wife. But if he couldn't . . ." She paused to make sure I was still paying attention. My eyes had wandered over to the next checkstand. Something was happening. Willow was heading in my direction. "I told him that if he couldn't work things out, then he should come back to me," the shopper said. "We could finally be together."

Willow said that an item wasn't ringing up correctly on her register. Could I come and take a look? "I'll be right there," I told her. The cashier turned to go, but the shopper called after her. "Excuse me," she said. "You just interrupted a conversation." The woman who, minutes earlier, had cheerily complimented employees' customer service had transformed into someone else. Willow turned around. "What people with good manners do in such a situation is say 'excuse me' before they interrupt a conversation!" The cashier muttered an apology and gave me a look that said, *What is going on?* "It's okay," I said to her. "I'm right behind you." I addressed the customer. "As you can see, I have to go back to work."

I tried to step out from behind the checkstand, but she blocked my path. Her tone had gone from breezy to angry to distraught. "Did I do something wrong?" she whined. "Was there some other way that I could have handled that situation?" *Is this customer asking me how to improve her communication skills?* "People interrupt me all the time when I'm speaking, and I am so tired of it," she harrumphed. "So tired!"

I was sympathetic to her complaint about being interrupted. But the shopper was still in my way. "It's been a pleasure talking to you," I said, "but we don't have time to chat." I squeezed past her. When I looked back a few minutes later, she was gone.

I had navigated awkward encounters with customers before. But this incident jarred me more than most. I knew nothing about the woman, but she had seemed desperately lonely and had looked to me for relief.

Another night, a shopper went to the deli, selected a container of macaroni and cheese, and started eating with her hands straight out of the carton. George approached her and said something that I couldn't hear. The two of them came to the Front End. "I'm going to call an ambulance," the guard told me. That was when I saw that the customer had bruises and scratches on her face. "This shopper has been beaten," George said. "She won't tell me who did it."

The woman shrugged. "A man hit me. I didn't know where else to go." The shopper did not want an ambulance. "I can't pay for it," she said. "I'll be all right in a minute. I just need something to eat."

George turned his attention to the macaroni. "You have to pay for that."

She kept eating. The guard didn't stop her.

"Are you sure we can't call an ambulance?" I asked. "The store is closing soon. You'll have to leave."

The shopper refused the ambulance. A few minutes later, she exited into the chilly evening.

When I got to work the next day, a colleague told me that a woman had been found sitting outside the door. She had apparently been there for hours. "The stockers called an ambulance," a manager said. "It looked like she had been beaten up." I told the manager that the woman had been in the store the previous evening. "We offered to call an ambulance, but she didn't want one." The manager didn't blame us for not calling. "It's not your job," she said. But I regretted not doing what the morning crew had done. I had wanted to punch out and go home, and calling for help would have extended my shift.

I already knew by then that the store was not really a community resource, even as workers did their best to take care of customers and one another. But now I wondered what my obligations were to customers who needed more than groceries. Should I have let the shopper tell me her tragic love story, or forced the customer who came in with injuries to accept medical attention?

It's not surprising that my job posed such dilemmas. The supermarket has long functioned as a replacement for social support systems that do not exist or that have failed to protect us from everything from loneliness to economic immiseration. The first supermarket arrived during the Great Depression, when millions were out of work and desperate for affordable food. Its owner, Michael Cullen, brought food and household goods under one roof, selling as many as one thousand products at his store in Jamaica Estates, Queens. No one had ever seen anything like it.

The secret to King Kullen's success was low prices in a large space where, like at Piggly Wiggly, customers chose for themselves. Using the high-volume sales methods that he had learned as a top employee at A&P, Cullen's store sold popular brands for less. The company motto "Pile it high and sell it cheap" (along with free parking) brought in the crowds—one ad bragged that King Kullen served as many as "15,000 housewives" a day. Given the effort that companies like Kroger had put into customer service, King Kullen's success was surprising. Customers entered to find a bare-bones space with fewer employees than in other chains and without personalized service. But within a few years, Cullen owned fifteen outlets from the Bronx to Long Island, a testament to the supermarket's wild popularity.

It's easy to see why shoppers eagerly accepted the trade-off. The Great Depression had changed everything. Customers were willing to push a cart through the cavernous supermarket, doing the labor of moving products to the checkstand, if it meant saving money. Other grocers were skeptical at first. They assumed that Cullen's supermarket was a fad that would not last. But after King Kullen's smashing success, they swiftly transitioned to the one-stop-shop model. Within six years, there were 1,200 supermarkets across the country. Small-business owners admitted defeat, and mom and pops closed their doors. The supermarket had arrived.

Today, for those of us who have access to a supermarket, this is a story of progress. One-stop shopping is a time-saver, and stores are so much a part of our daily lives that it would be hard to imagine getting by without them.

But as much as we might appreciate the supermarket, and as essential as its workers are, stores are not a substitute for real social rights and protections. Michael Cullen saw people's need as a business opportunity. But low prices on groceries could not end the Great Depression. That took millions of people demanding government action. In the years after the 1929 stock market crash, unemployed workers marched and organized sit-ins. From New York to Cleveland and Philadelphia, thousands rallied at city halls and clashed with police. Shoppers raided food warehouses, looted supermarkets, and declared hunger strikes. Such protest was a critical part of the social movement that pressured President Franklin Delano Roosevelt to pass economic relief legislation.

TGS's role as a public space was an echo of the supermarket's historical legacy. These days, many of us feel overwhelmed by high prices and jobs that don't pay enough to live on. As long as that's the case, retail employees will encounter shoppers whose needs are bigger than they can meet. Shoppers who sought help at TGS did not mistake the store for a hospital, a therapist's office, or a shelter. It was more likely that they came to the supermarket because hospitals, therapists, and shelters are often inaccessible. Open most hours of the day and full of food and welcoming smiles, TGS was available to people who had few other options.

Another night started out well. The busiest part of the shift was behind us. Every employee had received their break on time, and the registers and self-checkout machines were functioning without incident. Even the clock was ticking faster than usual. With one more round of breaks to give before the shift was over, freedom was in view.

A cashier waved me over to a checkstand. There was a tote bag zippered closed and sitting on the ground. "There's a loaded gun in this bag," he said. He explained that, a few minutes earlier, a customer had handed him the bag before heading into the aisles to shop. "I don't want to bring my loaded gun into the store. Can you keep an eye on it?" he had said. The cashier was freaked out. "I don't want to be responsible for a weapon," he explained.

I called for George.

"Did you check to see if there is really a gun in the bag?" he asked.

The cashier and I refused to open it. "We're not touching a bag that might have a loaded gun inside!"

The guard agreed that was probably the smart choice. "It doesn't really matter anyway," he said. "We can't bar people from bringing guns into the store." He was referring to Utah's "constitutional carry" law, which allowed people to carry weapons virtually anywhere without a permit.

"I know about the law," I retorted. "But most customers don't announce that they are carrying. It's a little weird."

The cashier said that there had been something suspicious about the shopper. "He *really* wanted me to know he had brought a gun into the store," he said.

The bag's owner reappeared. He was wearing a white button-up shirt, slacks, and a tie. "I've been watching your gun," George told him. "You should know that you scared employees by bringing it in here."

The customer became agitated. "I've been drinking," he said. "I was worried about dropping the weapon while I was shopping. It could have gone off and killed someone. Now you're telling me that I should have taken it into the aisles?"

Was there really a loaded gun in the bag, or was he trying to scare us? Why would someone want to frighten supermarket employees? The whole situation was unsettling. A cashier who overheard the conversation looked like she was preparing to sprint to the exit. "I'll walk you out," George said. The shopper picked up the tote and carried it along with his groceries.

Word about the customer whom everyone referred to as "Gun Man" went around the store. Aurelie told me that she was afraid every day of being shot at work. "If someone started shooting, we would be in the line of fire," she said. I agreed that the Front End was a good place to kill a lot of people. "We're sitting ducks," Aurelie went on. The same wide aisles and bright lights that made the store convenient for shoppers appeared menacing from another angle.

Workers killed on the job may seem like a vestige of the industrial era. We know that, in 1911 in New York City, the Triangle Shirtwaist Factory fire killed more than 140 workers—mostly women—because the exits were blocked to stop employees from stealing. And most of us have heard stories about mine accidents, from the 1900 Scofield disaster that killed 200 men to the explosion in Monongah, West Virginia, a few years later where more than 350 miners lost their lives. The service economy can seem safer by comparison. But other threats to workers' lives may be replacing fire and explosion. After years of decline, workplace violence is on the rise overall and is now a leading cause of death on the job. And most "active shooter" situations happen in stores.

While I was on the job, a man walked into a supermarket in Boulder, Colorado, and shot ten people to death, including employees. In 2019, a gunman fueled by racial hatred had killed twenty-three people at a Walmart in El Paso, Texas. And, in 2022, another white supremacist shot ten people at a supermarket in Buffalo, New York. Workers' vulnerability has prompted unions to demand silent alarms and training for active shooter attacks.

A few days after the Gun Man incident at TGS, George approached a group of cashiers. "If someone starts shooting, you need to know where the nearest exit is," he told them. One employee said that he had already thought about it. "The nearest exit is the emergency door next to the pharmacy," he said. "But that door doesn't open right away." He was right. The door didn't open for fifteen seconds after the handle was pushed. The delay was a theft deterrent. A shoplifter trying to flee out that exit would find himself trapped in the store long enough to be caught.

To workers, the delay looked like a death trap. "You can fire a lot of bullets in fifteen seconds," the cashier protested. "Try to get out that way, anyway," George said. "It's your best option." The guard's advice was correct. But an emergency exit that took fifteen seconds to open seemed like a metaphor for solidarity on the Front End. It made sense in theory but was a failure in practice. I couldn't protect anyone—or myself—from violence.

Signs of the limits of supermarket solidarity piled up like abandoned groceries in the gobacks cart. Employees' lack of access to affordable health care was a consistent theme at the store. Darth announced that he was dumping his company health insurance policy. He couldn't afford the thirty-dollar-per-week cost. "I could never pay the deductible anyway," he said.

I didn't try to talk Darth out of canceling his insurance. Though I was still paying for my plan, I doubted my decision too much to try to persuade anyone. Instead, I changed the subject and asked my colleague what he was doing after work. "I'll do what I always do," Darth said. "Drink a glass of wine, watch an episode of *Extreme Home Makeover*, and have a good cry."

The next day, I overheard Aurelie and another cashier discussing whether the company health plans were worth the cost. The cashier said, "I have my doubts. But I signed up for insurance in case I get cancer or if I'm in a bad car accident."

Aurelie had decided against enrolling. "I go to Planned Parenthood once a year for my women's exams. They have a sliding scale for low-income people."

The other cashier considered this argument. "But what if you get really sick? Don't you need some kind of protection?"

Aurelie answered without skipping a beat. "In that case, I would just kill myself," she said. "It wouldn't be worth living anymore."

It was not the first time I had heard a cashier mention death as a solution to economic precarity. One day, the phone rang on the Front End. Travis was on the line. I had not met him yet, but others had told me that he was a long-time cashier who had been at home recovering from a stroke. Travis was calling to report that he would be out a little while longer. "I feel well enough to work," he told me. But his doctor would not give him permission to return to the job. "Please write a note explaining that I still haven't been approved," Travis said. "Please say that I want to come back, but the doctor won't let me."

Two weeks later, Travis returned to the Front End. "What's it like to have a stroke?" I asked. He told me that the incident had happened at home. "I leaned down to feed my poodle, and it felt like someone stabbed me in the back of the head," he said. Travis drove to the emergency room where a receptionist gave him a form to fill out. He couldn't remember anything after that because he passed out in the waiting room. When he woke up five days later, the doctors said that his brain was bleeding, and he had fallen into a coma. Eight months after that, Travis was back behind a TGS checkstand.

Thin and frail from his ordeal, the sixty-year-old had trouble standing for an entire shift. I sometimes walked by his register and saw that his knuckles were white from gripping the counter. His uniform was usually soaked with sweat. One day, a call went out over the radio. "Travis has fallen down!" He had lost his balance walking to his checkstand. My coworker went back to the hospital to be treated for a fractured arm.

Later, I ran into Travis shopping at TGS with his arm in a sling. He was anxious about medical bills. Since he couldn't work, he didn't qualify for a company plan. Instead, the cashier was paying $800 a month for COBRA. The federal program allowed him to pay out of pocket for insurance until he could return to the store. But Travis would not be able to keep up those payments for long. He told me that he was despondent at his lack of options. "If I can't work, then I might as well be dead," he said.

Poverty has a profound effect on mental health. Studies have confirmed that income loss leads to depression and anxiety. So does the lack of a social safety net. One study from the University of Michigan showed that, in 2021, mental health problems increased along with the end of COVID economic stimulus programs, including an eviction moratorium, child tax credits, and expanded relief for the unemployed. Travis was caught between his desire to work, his illness, and a lack of public support for people in his situation.

By then, I had almost given up on workplace solidarity. Bonnie's death had blunted my motivation, and the effects of economic precarity felt insurmountable. Then TGS hired a new Front End supervisor. Traci had years of experience in the industry, including as a supervisor in a national chain. I assumed that anyone with that résumé would know more than I did about how to support employees in crisis. Maybe she would bring a new level of wisdom and practical experience to the Front End.

When I first met Traci, I couldn't believe she had survived the industry so long. About thirty years old and thin as a spaghetti noodle, she didn't look the part of a tough, experienced leader. She quivered in fear during the after-work rush, regularly left perishable gobacks out overnight, and didn't seem to know what to do when carts disappeared from the lobby. Before long, she developed a reputation as an authoritarian prone to outbursts.

Cindy pulled me aside one day to report that Traci had reprimanded her for chatting with a cashier instead of bagging an order. "Can you stop talking so much and focus on your work?" Traci had said. Cindy expected me to intervene. "*You* don't talk to me like that," she said. "Can't you teach Traci how to supervise?" The request put me in a bind. Cindy had a right to respectful treatment. But she did not have a right to avoid work. I worried that my acts of solidarity had given my colleagues a false sense of freedom.

One day, Darth sent a cashier on a break. Traci screamed at him in front of a customer. "I'm in charge of breaks!" My new colleague was not entirely wrong. Darth was challenging her authority, a form of hazing that I had also experienced in my first weeks on the job. But instead of enduring the hazing until it passed or calmly discussing the issue with a manager, Traci dug herself a deeper hole. She called a top boss on the radio, sobbing. "I can't work in these conditions!" The next day, I heard a group of employees making fun of the public meltdown. "Did you hear that the new supervisor cried *on the radio*?" one of them said.

Unlike when two colleagues made fun of the i-grocery manager, I didn't join in the laughter this time. Traci's problems directly impacted my department. If she couldn't pull it together, we would all suffer the consequences. I was grateful when she was demoted to cashier. "Traci is not emotionally stable enough to supervise the Front End," a manager told me.

In her new role, she continued to create chaos. She called out regularly for illness or for "personal reasons." One evening, she went to lunch. Thirty minutes later, she called the Front End from her car to say she wouldn't be back. She was sobbing. "I'm having some kind of panic attack."

I begged her not to go home. Her departure would leave us short-staffed. "Are you sure you want to do this?" I asked. "You can take a few extra minutes to collect yourself." Traci insisted that she was in no state to work.

The incident led to another round of condemnations from colleagues. "Traci needs to suck it up like the rest of us!"

I did not know what ailed Traci. But frustration with her behavior overwhelmed my capacity to sympathize. Everyone at TGS was struggling in one way or another, even if they kept their feelings to themselves. Staffers who worked harder in Traci's absence also deserved consideration. Still, I didn't want her to lose her job. It was possible that she would recover and find her psychological footing in time. In the meantime, I scrambled to keep the Front End operational. When she finally quit, I was relieved. I needed a break from the stress.

I didn't get it. One night, Emery was the last cashier on shift. I preferred to have at least two cashiers to close the store. But it was a slow night, so I was confident that the nineteen-year-old and I could make it work. My colleague was a math major. He had told me that he wanted to become an elementary school teacher to share his love of numbers with kids. Quick-witted and reliable, Emery was open about his family's mental health struggles. A few weeks earlier, a younger cousin had attempted suicide after social isolation during the pandemic led to a bout of depression. And an uncle who had recently lost a job had been hospitalized for depression.

Emery's situation was not unique. Several colleagues admitted they often felt down. Once, when a cashier didn't show up, Paula told me that it was common for the employee to be unreachable for days at a time. "She's probably in one of her funks again," she said. Another cashier warned me that he might need extra bathroom breaks. "Frequent urination is a side effect of the mood stabilizer that my doctor prescribed," he said.

While the pandemic may have explained some of the suffering at TGS, mental health crises have been on the rise since 2020, especially for the young. A 2025 report from the National Bureau of Economic Research cited declining workplace conditions as a major contributor to "young worker despair." Since jobs are a mark of social value, low-status roles communicate to employees their place in the social order.

About an hour before closing, Emery disappeared from his checkstand. I had turned around to answer the phone, and when I turned back, he was gone. Customers arrived to find the Front End unstaffed like a ghost ship whose crew had mysteriously disappeared. I directed shoppers to the self-checkout machines. Maybe Emery had gone to the bathroom and would be right back? A cart collector came inside. "Emery told me to tell you that he was having a mental breakdown and had to leave." *Not again.* I was going to have to cashier for the rest of the night. I wouldn't be able to close the registers, shut down the self-checkout machines, or run reports until the doors were locked and the last customers had left.

A manager of the stocking crew came by. "You're alone up here?" I explained what had happened. "A mental breakdown!" he said. "We all have mental breakdowns every day! If that kid can't work the last hour of his shift on a slow-ass night like this, then his hours should be cut!" The manager threatened to report the incident. A cart collector was listening to the rant. To the twenty-year-old, it probably sounded like I was conspiring with the manager to punish Emery.

After serving the last shoppers, I went straight to the lobby where two employees were deep in conversation. I was sure they were talking about Emery, his family's mental health struggles, and my betrayal. "I came out here to apologize for not defending Emery a few minutes ago," I said. "I should have told the manager that he left work because he was sick." I was trying to reclaim my status as the sympathetic supervisor who acted in solidarity with colleagues, even if it meant lying to the bosses.

"The manager just threatened to cut Emery's hours," one of the cart collectors said. "But if he is suffering from mental health issues, it isn't fair to do that to him. He needs help, not punishment." The employees weren't focused on my behavior but on their colleague's well-being. "TGS needs to be more understanding," the other employee added. "When workers are sick or depressed, they should be able to call out or go home early without fear of their hours being cut or losing their jobs." My colleagues were arguing that employees should be treated like human beings. Of course, I agreed in theory. But if every suffering worker was allowed to "call out or go home early" without consequence, who would run the Front End?

I had convinced myself that one person with some authority could improve working conditions for everyone. For most of the previous year, I had been a critic of a culture of individualism in the store. I had judged colleagues who believed that if our pay was poor, if we were tired, or if there was a staffing crisis, it was because one person had made a bad decision, or the wrong people were in charge. But my recent efforts had reinforced the idea that an individual could change everything, that a few strategic acts of resistance could improve the store for all of us.

But the small freedoms I offered were short-term fixes at best. Even worse, from taking labor away from other departments to involving colleagues in lies and deceptions, many attempts at solidarity benefited some while putting others at risk.

The next day, Emery came in for his shift. The long, brown hair that Whitney was always telling him to tie up was partially covering his face like a curtain. "I guess we need to talk about last night," he said. The cashier explained that he had had a panic attack. "My heart was racing. I couldn't breathe," he explained. "My mind couldn't focus."

I told him that I was sorry. "Do you feel better today?"

He nodded.

"You need to talk to someone about what happened, someone other than me, since I am in no position to help you," I advised. Then I said something I would not have said twenty-four hours earlier. "You left us without a closing cashier. That can't happen again. If it does, I'm going to have to report it."

Emery nodded.

"You're at number three today," I said.

When I started at the store, Kevin's photo was on the wall as part of a display celebrating TGS's longest-serving staffers. The stocker's bio said that he had been at the store for seven years and that, on his days off, he liked to spend time "outside with the trees." When I finally met Kevin in person, I didn't recognize him. He was in his sixties, but the photo had showed him at least thirty years younger. He explained that he wanted colleagues to see what he had looked like during his "glory days," when his favorite pastime was attending Rolling Stones concerts.

One day, Kevin arrived at TGS looking like he had not slept or showered in days. His red hair was stringier than usual, and his unbelted pants hung low on his hips. Colleagues warned him that customers could see his backside while he stood at the cooler stocking kombucha and iced tea. Gordon called out, "I'm going to publish a coffee table book of butt cracks, and yours will be the centerfold!" Kevin still didn't pull his pants up. He wasn't himself.

A few days later, he came in on his day off and stopped by the Front End to chat. "I'm not doing well in the head," he told me. “I’m going through some kind of depression.” Kevin had come to the store to talk to his boss about his mental state. “I’ve been at the supermarket too long,” he said. “I’m going crazy.” Kevin felt broken by repetition and routine. “All I do is the same thing over and over day in and day out,” he explained. “Nothing ever changes around here.” I tried to be encouraging. “You have a lot of experience and could get hired at a lot of places.” But I wasn’t as sure as I pretended to be about his prospects.

Kevin told me that quitting wasn’t a real option. He could not survive more than a couple of weeks without a paycheck, and he was afraid he could do no better than TGS. “Who will hire an aging, burned-out grocery employee with swollen feet?” he wondered. A top boss had offered to vary Kevin’s duties to try to cure his depression. I couldn’t imagine what variation might look like in a job that consisted of unloading trucks and stocking shelves and then doing it again the next day and the one after that.

A couple of weeks later, TGS hosted a “cheese festival,” offering shoppers free samples. I saw Kevin at one of the sample stations wearing a T-shirt that said SAY CHEEEEEESE! He was supposed to be delighting shoppers with slices of Grana Padano and Stilton. Instead, he ignored customers and stared off into space. Tricks to manipulate time and pause the repetition were short-term measures at best. Anyone who stayed long enough at the supermarket knew that the clock always won in the end.

Kevin never again seemed like the smiling colleague who had once neglected his own job to help me when there was no cashier scheduled to open the store.

A fifty-eight-year-old security guard also started calling out regularly. He would work one or two shifts and then miss the next two in a row. One day, he confessed to me that he was in pain. "My hip is so sore that I can barely walk," he explained. I mentioned that several Front End employees were in a similar situation. "Working on your feet your whole life takes a toll," he said. "I've never had a sit-down job." Days later, he put in his two weeks' notice. He told me that he planned to draw on his social security. "I'll figure out what to do next when it runs out."

Some forms of suffering implicated me more than others. One day, the worker assigned to do shopping cart runs was struggling to keep up. Customers complained that there were no carts in the lobby. I wished there was a Pause button that I could press to freeze activity in the store and give the employee time to catch up. Instead, I shifted people around like pieces on a chessboard. I closed one lane, moved the shoppers to a neighboring register, and sent the cashier to collect carts. Next, I roped off a second register. The cashier thought I was sending her to lunch. Instead, I performed a supervisor's sleight of hand. "Do a cart run first. Then clock out for your lunch."

The next cashier on shift would cover the self-checkout cashier's lunch. But thirty minutes later, I could send her on a cart run. When Lucia arrived an hour after that, I planned to close off Aurelie's lane so she could collect carts before taking her break. Charles was on the schedule as a bagger. But if I moved him into a checkstand, that would provide an additional open register. The chess game would lengthen checkout lines, reduce the number of baggers, and delay workers' breaks by at least fifteen minutes. But we might be able to keep the lobby stocked.

Everything went south an hour later when a bus stopped in front of TGS and dozens of people got out. Wearing lanyards and matching shirts, the shoppers were attending a conference at a nearby convention center. They lined up at checkstands to buy dinner boxes, beverages, and snacks to take back to their hotel rooms. With five people in her line, I could not close off Aurelie's lane. A manager said into the radio, "There are no carts in the lobby. Who's on duty?" I responded that we were backed up, and the only employee available for a cart run was Charles. The radio went silent. The manager knew that Charles's bad leg made him too slow to do the job. We were both evaluating people based on whether they were young, old, athletic, or disabled.

It wasn't the first time I had made the calculation. Another day, a teenager called to say he wasn't coming in for his cart shift. His brother, with whom he lived, had tested positive for the COVID virus. The employee had not been tested. "But I don't want to take any chances," he said.

I looked around the Front End and saw that no one was physically capable of getting carts. Gordon's bad back made him a poor candidate, and there was no question of sending Travis. Another cashier was wearing an orthopedic boot after suffering a broken foot. Her doctor had told her that standing for long periods had likely put pressure on her foot until a bone had snapped like a twig. My sympathy for my injured colleague existed alongside a less benevolent reaction. *There's one less person who can do cart runs.* Like the self-checkout stations, my coworkers glitched and broke down.

I called the i-grocery manager. "Remember when I let you take Christopher when you were short-staffed?"

The manager sighed. It was payback time. "I can send you someone for thirty minutes," she said.

"Make sure it's someone young and fit," I replied.

I had not felt this unnerved since my first days in the store. The anxiety of learning to cashier had abated as I had mastered the job. And I had been troubled to learn about workers' repetitive stress injuries. But since there was nothing that I could do to keep my colleagues safe, I did not feel implicated. Carts were a different story. I could avoid assigning the task to others by doing it myself.

The day when a bus full of conference attendees came into the store, I headed to the parking lot. Outside, some customers had returned carts to the holding pen, while others were scattered from one end of the space to the other. I collected the full-size carts, using a swinging gate at the top to push them inside one another and create a compact line.

Next, I tied the carts together by attaching a rope pulley to the first and last carts in a row of five, a total load of about 250 pounds. (I would have to come back to collect the smaller carts, which could be roped together in a row of ten.) To protect my back, I used my legs and arms to push the row to the elevator and maneuver it inside, the TGS version of parallel parking. I exited the elevator backward, pulling the carts behind me. The door kept closing, so I had to step back inside several times to hit Door Open while I edged the carts into the lobby.

I unhooked the carts and rolled them one by one into the stall where two customers were waiting to grab them. Then I returned to the Front End in search of water. A customer needed to return some items. A cashier needed help with a price check. A bottle of ketchup fell off a shelf and broke into a thousand pieces. "Cleanup on aisle five!" I said into the radio. "Bring the mop!" The lobby was already nearly empty again. I headed back to the garage. I smashed my middle finger between two carts as I was tying them together. By the time I got back to the Front End, the nail was purple. Days later, it fell off.

For weeks, during rushes, I assigned myself the role of

cart runner in chief. I spent shifts herding carts while listening for the radio so that I could rush back inside if necessary.

Carts got into my head. At night, while trying to fall sleep, I heard the clanging sound they made when they were pushed together. I stopped using carts to do my own grocery shopping. I couldn't stomach the idea that a store employee would have to collect my cart. Once, while walking to work before dawn, I saw a TGS cart tipped over on the sidewalk blocks from the store. Months earlier, my sympathy for an abandoned cart had made me question my sanity. Now all that mattered was that an extra one in the lobby might mean one less trip to the parking lot. I turned the cart upright and rolled it back to TGS.

My plan to be a one-woman solidarity machine had run into the barrier of my own exhaustion and pain. I toiled in a state of indecision, trying to reconcile two ideas. I knew that supermarket work was skilled and socially necessary. Sometimes it felt downright noble. At the same time, I wanted out.

I might have stayed a little longer at TGS except for two incidents that occurred around Halloween, nearly a year into my employment. One day, Kirsten was bagging for a cashier in training. I knew that if the employee needed help, Kirsten could step in, so I didn't linger near the register like I usually did for trainees. But when Kirsten went on break, the cashier was left alone. Minutes later, she waved me over to explain that her receipt tape dispenser had jammed in the middle of a transaction, and a customer had left without paying.

I understood what had happened. When the register spit out a receipt, it meant that a transaction was complete. Due to the mishap, neither the cashier nor the customer had realized that the order had not been paid for. "The man just left," my colleague said. "He's probably right outside." I rushed to the exit and saw the shopper. About eighty years old and slightly hunched over, he was moving so slowly that I could have easily caught up to him. But something held me back. I couldn't bring myself to chase after the customer. Instead, I lingered in the doorway and watched him walk away with his grocery bag.

Back on the Front End, Kirsten had returned from break and was showing the cashier how to fix her receipt tape dispenser. "Did you catch him?" Kirsten asked.

"No," I said. "I didn't see anyone." I didn't want to admit to my colleagues that I had lost my motivation to do the most basic part of my job: making sure customers paid for their groceries. Instead, I voided the order so that the cashier's till wouldn't be short.

A few days later, a cashier called me to self-checkout. "There's an angry customer," she warned. "He keeps saying that we've charged him incorrectly." The shopper had scanned and bagged his groceries and paid with a gift card. But before leaving, he saw an error on his receipt. "You charged me ten dollars extra," he said. *You* referred to me and to the machine. I was a cyborg: part-human, part-robot.

I looked at the receipt and tried to understand what the customer was talking about. He shoved his phone in my face. "Look at this!" He was showing me a screen that looked like a gift card transaction report. There was a discrepancy between the amount listed on the receipt and the amount on the screen. His gift card had been debited at a higher amount.

As far as I could tell, all his groceries had been scanned and priced correctly. There was no sign of an error. But the man kept pointing to his phone, as if the numbers on the screen were proof that he had been overcharged. Even if he was correct, I didn't know what I was supposed to do about it. "Sir," I said, "the company that issued the gift card may have overcharged you. Maybe there is a fee or something?" He stomped his foot. "A fee! A fee! There is no fee. I've used this card many times before. *You* overcharged me."

I should have walked away. I should have called a manager or a top boss. I should have done anything but what I did. I didn't call anyone. *How dare this shopper come into my supermarket and accuse me of overcharging him!* "I can't help you," I said calmly. "I can't just give you money back because you want me to. You'll have to take it up with the gift card company." I wished the customer a nice day as sarcastically as possible and turned around. He followed me to a checkstand and shoved his phone in my face again. "I'm taking your picture and calling your manager!"

The next week, Whitney told me that she had been called into a meeting to discuss a customer complaint. The man had not only contacted the TGS corporate office, he had written a letter to the commerce agency that licensed companies to do business in the state. He claimed that TGS had overcharged him and that an employee had refused to help. He included my name and photograph and demanded that I be fired. Emails were sent. Meetings were held. Whitney informed me that the top bosses had decided to keep me on. They instructed her to give me a written warning for "insubordination." One more of those, and I would be fired.

The top bosses also told Whitney to call the shopper and apologize for my rudeness. "This is not how we train cashiers to treat customers," she had said. When I told her how the man had been belligerent, she sympathized. "I know these situations can get out of hand quickly," she said. "But you should have called a manager." My boss was disappointed and confused about why I had not followed protocol. "I defended you this time," she explained. "But I hope I don't have to do it again." I was sorry that Whitney had been put in that situation. But the incident had happened so fast, and I had been exasperated. I wasn't sure I would act differently the next time.

In one way or another, TGS employees were all living and working in a version of Darth's favorite video game, where he hit raptors over the head with a rock to knock them out. Each morning, he updated us on how many raptors he had rendered unconscious the night before. "Why do you have to knock them out?" I asked one day. His expression suggested I had just asked the dumbest question he had ever heard. "If you don't, they eat you. Knocking them out makes them tame."

I still wasn't sure I understood. "They don't wake up mad?" I asked. "It seems like they would."

Darth was tired of explaining the game to a dunce like me. "If you don't hit them, they kill you. It's them or you," he said. "You have to choose."

CONCLUSION

Dignity

The incident that I think about the most from TGS happened a few months after I had left the job. I was in the store one morning doing my grocery shopping when an ambulance pulled up outside. I didn't know who was working on the Front End that day or if I would recognize anyone. Since returning to the status of shopper, I had come back several times. But there had been fewer and fewer employees left whom I knew. After a while, it was as if I had never worked at the supermarket.

I headed toward the Front End and saw two paramedics leaning over someone who was on the ground behind number one. Even though I couldn't see her face, I knew it was Cindy. Number one had been the bagger's favorite checkstand, the place where she had chatted up her regular customers and stored her bottle of lukewarm Diet Coke.

Near the end of my year on the job, Cindy had become frailer and more unsteady on her feet. She often seemed out of it. One day, she hit her head on a defibrillator hanging on the wall. A few minutes later, she went into the bathroom and vomited. The next day, she came to work with a purple goose egg that she had tried unsuccessfully to cover with makeup. "You should be at home," I said. She told me that she couldn't afford to take the day off.

A few minutes later, I saw her standing at the end of a checkstand staring off into space while groceries piled up on the counter. She started talking about her husband, who had been killed in an accident three decades earlier. "I like the idea that you go to heaven and meet the person again," she said. "But what if you don't?" Later that afternoon, Cindy vomited again. "I guess I will go home," she said.

She called the store the next day to say she was taking some time off. Since I had already put in my two weeks' notice at that point, I never worked with her again.

The day that paramedics were treating Cindy on the Front End, I asked an employee what had happened. "She was bagging an order and just collapsed," he said. "She's been struggling with health problems for a while." The employee didn't know that I had worked side by side with Cindy and had witnessed her decline.

Days later, Cindy died in the hospital. She was eighty years old. Employees posted memorials on an online message board that I was still a member of. One said they couldn't imagine their workplace without "our Front End matriarch" who "worked hard and never complained." The comment got to me. Cindy loved her job and her customers. But that didn't make it right that she needed an hourly wage to make ends meet into her ninth decade.

A regular customer who saw her being put into an ambulance may have assumed that they were witnessing an unfortunate situation involving a single worker. I knew that Cindy's struggles told a broader story about economic precarity in the retail industry. Advocates and unions have for years proposed policies that would benefit workers everywhere. For Cindy, the dozens of supermarket employees I knew, and the millions that I will never meet, I add my voice to the call for change.

Supermarket workers should earn living wages. Cashiers and other grocery employees perform labor that society cannot do without. Their contributions were briefly acknowledged during the COVID pandemic, when some employers offered "hero pay" of up to two dollars more per hour. But the paltry premium was scrapped a few months later. We should reclaim the idea that grocery workers are heroes—and not just during a crisis. When work is underpaid, the people doing it become devalued. Large retailers have seen record profits in recent years. They can well afford to pay workers what they deserve.

Living wages would benefit people on both sides of the checkstand, and not only because we want to live in a society where workers can afford to take care of their families. Employees who are hungry, sick, or anxious about their futures are less likely to be friendly and polite. As shoppers, we must learn to see the connection between our experience in stores and employees' working conditions. Gratitude is not a substitute for material improvements to people's lives. These days, grocery workers' economic challenges are particularly stark. Since 2024, their wages have declined 15 percent when adjusted for inflation.

As customers, it can feel like injustice at the supermarket is out of our hands. After all, employers pay what the market allows. The truth is that pay scales in the industry are a product of what one scholar called a "shift from high-wage manufacturing jobs to lower-paid service-sector work." After trade deals such as the North American Free Trade Agreement led to the offshoring of manufacturing jobs, former factory employees found themselves working in retail stores for lower wages. Pay in the service industry is a direct result of public policy, not free markets.

The levers of government power can reverse the worst aspects of the service economy. One place to start is raising the federal minimum wage, which has been stuck at a shameful $7.25 for more than fifteen years. We may think that the figure is irrelevant since grocery workers already earn more per hour on average. But the wage sets a floor that influences pay rates across the economy. Raising the federal minimum would pressure employers of all kinds to raise pay, benefiting all low-income workers and their families.

Another barrier to higher pay is the false idea that grocery workers are unskilled. The truth is that supermarket jobs require a variety of technical knowledge as well as focus, concentration, communication skills, and the ability to think on one's feet. The "unskilled" insult also suggests that retail employees are fundamentally different from those in the white-collar professions. But store workers have the same talents and capacities as anyone else. The main difference is that they earn too little to live on. I urge my college-educated peers to abandon the idea that our degrees entitle us to live lives of dignity denied to others.

My experience at TGS rebuts the "unskilled" myth in another way. As the holder of a graduate degree, I should have been rewarded with a significantly higher wage than colleagues who held the same position. But I was paid at the same rate as others. TGS had relatively fixed pay rates for workers in different categories regardless of educational attainment. While my education may have explained why I was hired directly into a supervisor role, there was no "college premium" at TGS. Retail workers' wages are not a reflection of employees' education or skills. They are a social crime that should shock the conscience and demand redress.

Supermarket jobs should also be securer. If we do not live in a food desert, grocery stores can seem like pillars of our communities. They are always there for us. But workers live in a different reality where store closures and lost jobs are common. In what some called a "retail apocalypse," store closures spiked in 2025 due in part to private equity buyouts. When a factory offshores jobs or lays off workers, the news understandably provokes alarm. But there is less public outcry when a supermarket closes its doors. We should see unemployed cashiers and shuttered stores as signs of a social crisis on par with the loss of a manufacturing plant.

Beyond boosting pay and job security, we must address working conditions. Take unpredictable scheduling. Some cities have passed "fair workweek" laws to eliminate the most exploitative practices. In New York City, San Francisco, Seattle, and Chicago, employers can be penalized for unpredictable scheduling. Laws requiring that employees receive advance notice of their schedules are a bare minimum reform that would give workers more autonomy over their lives. If implemented industry-wide, such laws would also improve employees' mental health.

Perhaps the most disturbing lesson from TGS was the near-universal experience of pain and injury. For long-term employees or older workers, the suffering came with the added burden of knowing that they would soon be unable to perform. The crisis is so severe and has been neglected for so long that it requires an urgent response, such as a union-led commission charged with redesigning the supermarket. Areas of focus could include rebuilding checkout areas with lower counters and more space so that cashiers can stand or sit depending on their preference. Hard floors must be replaced with padding to protect feet and ankles.

Even with these reforms, injury would still be unavoidable in jobs where workers scan, bag, lift, and move groceries. For that reason, changes to supermarket architecture must come with social reforms. Employees should have access to paid time off for rest and injury recovery. And like workers everywhere, they need quality health care and retirement benefits so that they can leave jobs with their health and dignity intact.

At TGS, employees were surveilled, sometimes without their knowledge. Some retail unions have called for banning the use of information collected from electronic systems in employment decisions. Like predictable scheduling, privacy is a question of autonomy and dignity. In the short term, workers should know how they are being monitored and sign off on how the information will be used. In a just world, employees would have broad authority over their workplace, including electronic systems.

At TGS, self-checkout machines added to workers' labor while deskilling their jobs. One immediate solution is a limit on how many machines a single employee is required to monitor. Another is assuring that workers are trained to operate and repair the machines. They should receive additional pay for developing this expertise and for participating in the design of policies that spell out their rights and responsibilities with regard to shoplifters and abusive customers. Employers must not be allowed to sidestep the social costs of reducing human contact at checkout.

The broken promise of self-checkout has broader implications for automation in the retail industry. For example, several large retailers, including Walmart and Kroger, have announced plans to replace price tags on shelves with electronic labels, or "ESLs." Critics have warned that, in combination with facial recognition software, ESLs could permit retailers to adjust prices for individual customers according to local conditions. The price of water might go up in a drought, or the last package of toilet paper might come with a higher price tag.

Stores have rejected those concerns. They argue that ESLs will improve customer service by allowing workers to spend more time helping shoppers. Sound familiar? Companies made similar "convenience" claims about self-checkout. One lesson of my experience at TGS is that shoppers should never take retailers' promises about automation at face value. No technology can magically improve customer service. When retailers say that an innovation is in shoppers' best interest, they are most likely prioritizing the bottom line.

The main lesson of my year at TGS is that, as a society, we must take up larger questions about how capitalism leads to bad outcomes for everyone. Our economy consigns millions of us to low-wage jobs and financial hardship, while others benefit from our labor and a few lead lives of unimaginable luxury and privilege. The anthropologist David Graeber introduced the concept of "bullshit jobs" whose sole purpose is "keeping us all working." Employers, he wrote, have convinced us that "anyone not willing to submit themselves to some kind of intense work discipline for most of their waking hours deserves nothing." Graeber's proposal was that we get rid of the useless jobs so that everyone is free to work less and enjoy their lives.

Doing essential (not bullshit) work at TGS gave me a

slightly different view. Maybe a key to ensuring that all jobs are less horrible and better paid is not so much in separating the pointless from the essential but in making sure that everyone has to spend some time doing the ones that count. Until more shoppers see the supermarket from the other side of the checkstand, employees like Cindy will work until they die. And we will see more ambulances outside supermarkets.

It would be hard to overstate the importance of unions in improving supermarket jobs. Invariably, organized grocery employees earn more than those who do not belong to a union. Boosting workers' bargaining power is the best way to improve lives.

But we can't expect the employees who need unions the most to bear the burden of organizing them, especially in hostile places. The work of improving retail jobs must start outside stores. Shoppers must take a leading role in lowering the risks to workers and in creating the conditions for successful organizing.

A shoppers' movement should seek to shift the balance of power from employers to workers and communities. To start, customers should urge Congress to pass the Protecting the Right to Organize Act of 2021. The PRO Act includes measures that would eliminate "right to work" laws and make it easier for employees to organize.

A lack of enforcement of anti-monopoly laws has led to a wave of corporate consolidation and private equity buyouts, including the 2015 acquisition of Safeway by Albertsons and Amazon's purchase of Whole Foods two years later. The floodgates opened in 2019, with more than three hundred grocery industry mergers occurring in that year alone. Such deals lead to suppressed wages, higher prices, and the elimination of jobs. Shoppers should demand the enforcement of laws against retail industry mergers that harm workers.

Shoppers must also build alternative grocery models that prioritize community over profits. We would not be starting from scratch. In the 1930s, consumer cooperatives were a popular way to bypass corporate chains. Customers joined with their neighbors to buy in bulk and get better prices from wholesalers. After the stock market crash of 1929, shoppers opened cooperative retail outlets. The stores were run by local people whose labor earned points toward the purchase of goods. The stores operated according to the mantra "Food for people, not profit."

Black shoppers were key to a thriving cooperative movement. Racial discrimination taught them the importance of what the scholar Jessica Gordon Nembhard called a "solidarity economy." Organizations like the Young Negroes Cooperative League and the Brotherhood of Sleeping Car Porters saw community stores as a part of a project of racial liberation.

More recently, cities and towns have tapped into the history of shopper activism to create public supermarkets. From Florida to Kansas, municipalities have opened stores in areas where corporations are reluctant to invest. City-owned stores use public funds to subsidize the purchase of food so that stores can sell for less. The model allows the shops to focus on accessibility and affordability. Officials in Atlanta have announced plans to establish outlets, while the Minneapolis city council is considering a similar proposal. In New York City, in 2025, Mayor-Elect Zohran Mamdani proposed opening city-owned outlets to address food insecurity in the five boroughs.

Municipal stores have an uphill climb in a country where small outlets lack the market power of Kroger or Albertsons. Corporations can afford to lobby Congress and launch public relations campaigns to convince shoppers that public stores are a threat. We should not give in to fearmongering. Instead, we should see alternatives to corporate stores as part of a long tradition of reform rooted in the idea that food is a human right and that workers deserve a living wage.

Big retailers want us to believe that people on opposite sides of the checkstand have opposing needs. They want us to assume that we can only have affordable groceries if the people selling them are underpaid, injured, or in pain. This is false. Corporate power is our mutual enemy. Fair prices and living wages are a package deal. If shoppers want a better world, joining forces with workers to remake the supermarket is a good place to start.

Days before his murder, Martin Luther King Jr. gave a speech in Memphis in support of striking sanitation workers. He said that employees who picked up trash were serving humanity, no less than the doctor who cured disease. We should apply that thinking to workers of all kinds. The motto King offered that day doubles as a mission statement for the supermarket: "All labor has dignity."

Acknowledgments

This book originated in an article that I published in 2021 in *The New Republic* with the support of the Economic Hardship Reporting Project. *Cleanup on Aisle Five* exists in large part because Alissa Quart and the EHRP team believed in me. I am grateful to my agent, Ayla Zuraw-Friedland, who steered this book through choppy waters and kept the faith. Sarah Feld provided fact-checking. Researchers and field experts Brianna Bagley and William Knight kept me honest. Thanks to the librarians at the Salt Lake City Library who always found what I was looking for, even during the pandemic. It has been a professional and personal pleasure to work with Alessandra Bastagli and the team at One Signal.

I wouldn't be a writer without the support of my parents, Kent and Lynne Larson, and my brothers, Brett and Beau. Barbara Katz, Joel Owen, and the Sohn clan supported me in big and small ways. Friends and intellectual collaborators offered advice and support. Gratitude to Astra Taylor, Aaron Bornstein, Luke Herrine, and especially to Dawn Lueck. *Un grand merci à* Patrick Saurin, Marie-Claire Guidotti, Emilie Neyme, Danielle Balouka, and Marseille Michael for the conversation, hospitality, and delicious meals. I wrote the first draft of this book in the home of François Monseu–Van Cleemput, Emmanuelle Azria, and Louise and Alma.

Most of all, thank you to the long-suffering Michael Sohn. I promise to stop obsessing about the supermarket now. Maybe.

Notes

Introduction: Welcome to Your Neighborhood Supermarket!

4 *legal barriers made worker organizing difficult*: "Chapter 34 of Utah Right to Work Law," Utah State Legislature, https://le.utah.gov/xcode/Title34/Chapter34/C34-34_1800010118000101.pdf.

5 *virtually no chance of a future*: Andrew Kay, "Academe's Extinction Event: Failure, Whiskey, and Professional Collapse at the MLA," *Chronicle of Higher Education*, May 10, 2019, https://www.chronicle.com/article/academes-extinction-event-failure-whiskey-and-professional-collapse-at-the-mla/.

5 *winning billions in loan relief*: Ann Larson, "Why Canceling Student Debt Should Be a Universal Benefit," *The Nation*, June 17, 2022, https://www.thenation.com/article/society/biden-student-debt-corinithian/.

7 *one of the most common jobs in the country*: Rex Nutting, "No, 'Truck Driver' Isn't the Most Common Job in Your State," MarketWatch, February 12, 2015, https://www.marketwatch.com/story/no-truck-driver-isnt-the-most-common-job-in-your-state-2015-02-12.

7 *offered advice for how to shop for groceries safely*: Tara Parker-Pope, "How Do I Make Thanksgiving Shopping Safer?," *New York Times*, November 19, 2020.

9 *lead to a higher state of consciousness*: Don DeLillo, *White Noise* (Penguin, 1984), 22.

9 *"human bodies and human needs"*: Rhian Sasseen, "Lost in the Supermarket," *The Baffler*, May 4, 2022, https://thebaffler.com/latest/lost-in-the-supermarket-sasseen.

11 *"It is next to impossible not to become"*: Simone Weil, "Factory Work," *Politics*, December 1946, 372.

Chapter 1: Customer Service

20 *earned under $15 on average*: Errol Schweizer, "Why Economic Justice Begins in the Food Industry," *Forbes*, April 20,

2022, https://www.forbes.com/sites/errolschweizer/2022/04/20/why-economic-justice-begins-in-the-food-industry/.

20 *not kept up with rising prices*: Pavithra Mohan, "Kroger and Albertsons Cut Worker Hours: A New Report Looks at the Impact to Workers," *Fast Company*, May 9, 2025, https://www.fastcompany.com/91330323/kroger-and-albertsons-cut-worker-hours-a-new-report-looks-at-the-impact-to-workers.

20 *unionized employees earned middle-class wages*: Sapna Maheshwari and Michael Corkery, "Business Booms at Kroger-Owned Grocery Stores, but Workers Are Left Behind," *New York Times*, February 12, 2022.

20 *pay fell off a cliff along with unionization rates*: Seth Kershner, "Breaking the Chains: Can Labor Unions Organize Retail Workers?," *In These Times*, January 6, 2017, https://inthesetimes.com/article/breaking-the-chains-can-labor-unions-organize-retail-workers.

20 *only about 4 percent of retail workers*: "Union Members—2024," News Release, US Bureau of Labor Statistics, January 28, 2025.

20 *did not pass the benefits to workers*: Maheshwari and Corkery, "Business Booms."

20 *lowest wages in the retail industry*: Catherine Ruetschlin and Dedrick Asante-Muhammad, "The Retail Race Divide: How the Retail Industry Is Perpetuating Racial Inequality in the 21st Century," Demos, June 2, 2015, https://www.demos.org/research/retail-race-divide-how-retail-industry-perpetuating-racial-inequality-21st-century.

20 *more likely to be assigned customer service roles*: Arlie Russell Hochschild, *The Managed Heart: Commercialization of Human Feeling* (University of California Press, 2012), 20.

22 *Many grocery workers are food insecure*: Errol Schweizer, "Feeding Wall Street While Starving Stores," *The Checkout*, May 2025, https://grocerynerd.substack.com/p/grocery-update-special-feature-the?open=false#%C2%A7feeding-wall-street-while-starving-stores.

22 *three-quarters of workers at Kroger*: "Hungry at the Table: White Paper on Grocery Workers at the Kroger Company," Economic Roundtable, January 11, 2022, https://economicrt.org/publication/hungry-at-the-table/.

22 *hundreds of thousands of its employees relied*: Schweizer, "Feeding Wall Street."

22 *Walmart, for example, took in more than $26 billion*: Jarod

Facundo, "War in the Aisles," *American Prospect*, June 12, 2024, https: //prospect.org/2024/06/12/2024-06-12-war-in-the-aisles/.

22 *provides limited food aid to low-income people*: Christopher Boss, *Why SNAP Works: A Political History and Defense of the Food Stamp Program* (University of California Press, 2023), 13.

22 *Forty percent of beneficiaries were children*: Meghan McCarron, "Experts Say SNAP's Food Budget Doesn't Match How People Actually Eat," *New York Times*, November 13, 2025.

22 *Ronald Reagan demanded reductions*: Boss, 113.

22 *welfare reform policies led to significant cuts*: Boss, 133.

22 *slashed the program*: Talia Wexler, "Trump's 'Big Beautiful' Bill Will Cut $186 Billion from SNAP Through 2035," CNBC, August 8, 2025, https://www.cnbc.com/2025/08/08/trumps-spending-bill-cuts-billions-in-snap-benefits.html.

22 *woman who cooks for a family after coming home*: Boss, *Why SNAP Works*, 13.

22 *23 percent of cashiers rely on SNAP*: Scarlet Reznickova, "How Big Food Corporations Take Advantage of SNAP," Union of Concerned Scientists, March 2023.

23 *tenants didn't pay more than 30 percent*: Sonya Acosta and Erik Gartland, "Families Wait Years for Housing Vouchers Due to Inadequate Funding," Center on Budget and Policy Priorities, July 22, 2021, https://www.cbpp.org/research/housing/families-wait-years-for-housing-vouchers-due-to-inadequate-funding.

23 *waiting list could be years long*: Acosta and Gartland.

25 *premiums had outpaced inflation*: Sam Hughes, Emily Gee, and Nicole Rapfogel, "Health Insurance Costs Are Squeezing Workers and Employers: As Premiums Rise Faster Than Wages, Workers Face Greater Cost Sharing, Leaving Some Underinsured," Center for American Progress, November 2022, https://www.americanprogress.org/article/health-insurance-costs-are-squeezing-workers-and-employers/.

25 *to buy steak*: Jeremy Lybarger, "The Price You Pay," *The Nation*, July 2, 2010.

25 *kicked poor mothers off assistance*: Janine Fitzgerald, "The Disciplinary Apparatus of Welfare Reform," *Monthly Review*, November 2004, https://monthlyreview.org/articles/the-disciplinary-apparatus-of-welfare-reform/.

26 *suffer from tooth pain and related symptoms*: Hannah Mac-

Dougall, "Dental Disparities Among Low-Income American Adults: A Social Work Perspective," *Health and Social Work* 41, no. 3 (2016): 208–10.

26 *from the moment they open their mouth*: "Poor People 'Have Fewer Teeth' Than the Rich, Study Suggests," BBC, November 18, 2014.

26 *age of sixty-five are missing all of their teeth*: Greg Kaufmann, "Taking on the Dental Crisis: A Q&A with Bernie Sanders: Students Miss 50 Million Hours of School Each Year Because of Dental Problems. A Hearing Wednesday Confronts the Crisis," *The Nation*, February 2012.

26 *highest rates of toothlessness in the world*: Hawazin W. Elani, Sam Harper, et al., "Social Inequalities in Tooth Loss: A Multinational Comparison," *Community Dentistry and Oral Epidemiology*, February 10, 2017.

26 *tooth pain is a common cause of absences*: Jessica Glenza, "'Crisis in Dental Care': Bernie Sanders on His Fight for Better Teeth for Americans," *The Guardian*, May 24, 2024, https://www.theguardian.com/us-news/article/2024/may/24/bernie-sanders-dental-health-care-bill.

26 *associated with economic hardship*: Susan D. Emmett and Howard W. Francis, "The Socioeconomic Impact of Hearing Loss in US Adults," *Otology and Neurotology*, March 2015.

26 *social isolation and even dementia*: Kouki Tomida, Takahiro Shimoda, et al., "Risk of Dementia with Hearing Impairment and Social Isolation," Alzheimer's Association, May 16, 2024.

28 *this kind of retaliation is illegal*: "Your Rights During Union Organizing," National Labor Relations Board, https://www.nlrb.gov/about-nlrb/rights-we-protect/the-law/employees/your-rights-during-union-organizing.

29 *questioned the relationship between serotonin and depression*: Joanna Moncrieff, Ruth E. Cooper, et al., "The Serotonin Theory of Depression: A Systematic Umbrella Review of the Evidence," *Molecular Psychiatry* 28, July 2022.

29 *"the exploitation inherent in wage labor"*: Seth J. Prins, Sarah McKetta, et al., "The Serpent of Their Agonies: Exploitation as Structural Determinant of Mental Illness," *Epidemiology* 32, no. 2 (2021): 308.

31 *socially awkward, even humiliating, experience*: Tracey Deutsch, *Building a Housewife's Paradise: Gender, Politics, and American Grocery Stores in the Twentieth Century* (University of North Carolina Press, 2010), 15.

31 *day-old goods, or nothing at all*: Deutsch, 14.
31 *judged by how well they performed*: Deutsch, 18.
31 *cared about what their families ate*: Deutsch, 20.
31 *much like their Southern counterparts*: Deutsch, 23.
31 *attach a piece of gum*: Lucius C. Harper, "Following Your Dollar to a Job," *Chicago Defender*, April 16, 1938.
32 *"chickens dying from various diseases"*: Harper.
33 *permitted easier swiveling and pivoting*: Philippe Askenazy, Jean-Baptiste Berry, et al., "Working in Large Food Retailers in France and the USA: The Key Role of Institutions," *Work, Employment and Society* 26, no. 4 (2012).
33 *customers bag their own groceries*: Talib Visram, "Why Don't Cashiers in the U.S. Get to Sit Like the Ones in Europe?," *Fast Company*, January 19, 2023, https://www.fastcompany.com/90836431/why-dont-cashiers-in-the-u-s-get-to-sit-like-the-ones-in-europe.
34 *as many as one thousand items per hour*: Fahad Algarni, "Literature Review of Musculoskeletal Disorders and their Risk Factors Among Supermarket Cashiers," *Rehabilitation Science*, May 2021: 21; Camilo A. Vargas, *Universal Design of a Future Grocery Retail Checkstand* (VDM, 2009), 536.
34 *common among cashiers*: Jonathan Karmel, *Dying to Work: Death and Injury in the American Workplace* (Cornell University Press, 2017), 52.
34 "*an invisible but intensely heated finger*": H. G. Wells, *War of the Worlds* (William Heinemann, 1898), 36.
35 *develop the technology as a battlefield weapon*: Jeff Hecht, "A Short History of Laser Development," *Optical Engineering*, 2010, F104.
35 *"the biggest breakthrough in the weapons area"*: Robert W. Seidel, "From Glow to Flow: A History of Military Laser Research and Development," *Historical Studies in the Physical and Biological Sciences* 18, no. 1 (1987): 114.
35 *Lasers flopped*: Brian Resnick and *National Journal*, "A Brief History of Militarized Lasers," *The Atlantic*, December 12, 2014, https://www.theatlantic.com/politics/archive/2014/12/a-brief-history-of-militarized-lasers/453453/.
35 *collaborated with the Radio Corporation of America*: "Pack of Chewing Gum Becomes First-Ever Item Scanned with UPC Bar Code," History, May 27, 2025, https://www.history.com/this-day-in-history/june-26/barcode-scanner-invention-first-use.

35 *lasers could read barcodes*: "Pack of Chewing Gum."
35 *sixty-seven cents*: Judy Deeter, "50th Anniversary: A History of the First UPC Barcode Scan," Miami County Visitors and Convention Bureau, June 20, 2024, https://www.homegrowngreat.com/upc-barcode-anniversary/.
35 *displayed in the Smithsonian Museum*: Gavin Weightman, "The History of the Bar Code," *Smithsonian Magazine*, September 23, 2015, https://www.smithsonianmag.com/innovation/history-bar-code-180956704/.
35 *an "epidemic" of upper body injuries*: Karmel, *Dying to Work*, 49.
36 *keep American workers safe*: Karmel, 33.
36 *attacked the agency*: Karmel, 34.
36 *it virtually stopped enforcing safety standards*: Karmel, 35.
36 *was to push employees to work faster*: Shane Hamilton, *Supermarket USA: Food and Power in the Cold War Farms Race* (Yale University Press, 2018), 199.
37 *scanned at the breakneck pace*: Nelson Lichtenstein, *The Retail Revolution: How Wal-Mart Created a Brave New World of Business* (Macmillan, 2009), 54.
37 *"thrill at the till"*: Xan Rice, "The Aldi Effect: How One Discount Transformed the Way Britain Shops," *The Guardian*, March 5, 2019, https://www.theguardian.com/business/2019/mar/05/long-read-aldi-discount-supermarket-changed-britain-shopping.

Chapter 2: Community

45 *our "neglected desires" to be part of a society*: Rebecca Solnit, "How to Survive a Disaster," Literary Hub, November 15, 2016, https://lithub.com/rebecca-solnit-how-to-survive-a-disaster/.
47 *"rudeness, disrespect, or insensitive behavior"*: Christine Porath, "Frontline Work When Everyone Is Angry," *Harvard Business Review*, November 9, 2022, https://hbr.org/2022/11/frontline-work-when-everyone-is-angry.
47 *a jump of about 15 percent*: Porath.
47 *blamed the phenomenon partly on overwork*: Porath.
50 *tens of thousands of the stores*: Cory Lewis Sparks, "Locally Owned and Operated: Opposition to Chain Stores, 1925–1940" (PhD diss., Louisiana State University, 2000).
50 *Housewives' Advisory Service corresponded with customers*: Charles F. Phillips, "A History of the Kroger Grocery

and Baking Company," *National Marketing Review* 1, no. 3 (1936): 210.

50 *notoriously dirty*: Marc Levinson, *The Great A&P and the Struggle for Small Business in America* (Hill and Wang, 2012), 49.

50 *cleaned up stores and added ventilation*: Phillips, "A History of the Kroger," 210.

50 *soft, pleasing colors and adding "kiddie corrals"*: James M. Mayo, *The American Grocery Store Book: The Business Evolution of an Architectural Space* (Praeger Press, 1993), 175.

51 *set by executives and posted*: Tracey Deutsch, *Building a Housewife's Paradise: Gender, Politics, and American Grocery Stores in the Twentieth Century* (University of North Carolina Press, 2012), 52.

51 *"changed this condition overnight"*: Robert E. Weems, *Desegregating the Dollar: African American Consumerism in the Twentieth Century* (NYU Press, 1998), 18.

51 *might never set foot in them*: Sparks, "Locally Owned and Operated," 334.

51 *Mom and pops even allowed shoppers*: Deutsch, *Building a Housewife's Paradise*, 36.

51 *chains ended credit sales*: Deutsch, 52.

51 *see corporate stores as a threat*: Deutsch, 79.

51 *anti–chain store movement*: Daniel Scroop, "The Anti–Chain Store Movement and the Politics of Consumption," *American Quarterly* 60, no. 6 (2008): 925.

51 *260 anti–chain groups in thirty-five states*: John Harper Frederick, "The Anti-Chain Store Movement in the United States, 1927–1940" (PhD diss., University of Warwick, 1981), 103.

51 *founded the Colored Merchants Association*: Weems, *Desegregating the Dollar*, 19.

52 *"rather have thieves and gangsters"*: Matt Stoller, *Goliath: The 100-Year War Between Monopoly Power and Democracy* (Simon & Schuster, 2019), 161.

52 *HUGE CORPORATIONS . . . ARE DISPLACING THE NEIGHBORHOOD STORE*: Clark Evans, "Big Business Now Sweeps Retail Trade," *New York Times*, July 1928.

52 *steep taxes on chains*: Scroop, "The Anti–Chain Store Movement."

52 *Chains beat back the opposition*: Deutsch, *Building a Housewife's Paradise*, 52.

52 *not tax-deductible for stores*: Ali Swenson, "Stores Can't Write

Off Customer Donations at Checkout," AP, November 30, 2021, https://apnews.com/article/fact-checking-000329849244.

52 *"glean benefits associated with being viewed"*: Casey E. Newmeyer, Katie Kelting, et al., "Would You Like to Donate Today? Why Charity at Checkout May Backfire," ResearchGate, November 2019, doi: 10.13140/RG.2.2.24801.04962.

52 *only covered food that had to be prepared*: "Retailer Eligibility—Prepared and Heated Foods," US Department of Agriculture, https://www.fns.usda.gov/snap/retailer-eligibility-prepared-foods-and-heated-foods.

53 *"bad" foods*: Christopher Boss, *Why SNAP Works: A Political History and Defense of the Food Stamp Program* (University of California Press, 2023), 154.

55 *determined by policymakers and elected officials*: Boss, 178.

55 *TGS could lose its license to sell*: "SNAP Fraud Prevention," USDA Food and Nutrition Service, https://www.fns.usda.gov/snap/fraud.

61 *"tale of two retirements"*: Teresa Ghilarducci, *Work, Retire, Repeat: The Uncertainty of Retirement in the New Economy* (University of Chicago Press, 2024), 4.

61 *Since almost half of families have no retirement*: Ghilarducci, 6.

61 *punching clocks in warehouses or toiling*: Ghilarducci, 4.

62 *baby boomers lost their homes*: Ghilarducci, 190–91.

62 *offer all workers access to a publicly funded pension*: Ghilarducci, 182.

62 *their life experience makes them good candidates*: Abha Bhattarai, "Retail Workers in Their 60s and 70s and 80s Say They Are Worried About Their Health—but Need Money," *Washington Post*, March 2020.

62 *an employee looked exhausted and miserable*: Jack Hobbs, "I Raised $170K for an Elderly Worker—but My Good Deed Got Me in Trouble," *New York Post*, November 10, 2022.

62 *raised tens of thousands of dollars*: Deep Das Barman, "An Elderly Kroger Cashier Was Living in a Homeless Shelter. A Stranger's Kindness Turned It Around," *Market Realist*, November 20, 2024, https://marketrealist.com/who-is-charlie-kroger-the-one-who-helped-out-a-homeless-cashier-at-kroger/.

63 *working people prefer* predistributive *policies*: Erica Etelson, "Working-Class Americans Prefer a 'Hand-Up' to a 'Hand-out,'" *The Nation*, July 23, 2024, https://www.thenation.com

/article/politics/working-class-democrats-predistribu tion-welfare/.

63 *people across the political spectrum favor a federal jobs guarantee*: Etelson.

63 *inflationary effects would be "insignificant"*: Scott Fulwiler, Stephanie Kelton, et al., *The Macroeconomic Effects of Student Debt Cancellation* (Levy Institute, 2018), 6.

63 *giving families more money to spend*: Fulwiler, Kelton, et al., 7.

64 *"Large corporations . . . have used supply problems"*: Isabella Weber, "Could Strategic Price Controls Help Fight Inflation?," *The Guardian*, December 29, 2021, https://www.theguardian.com/business/commentisfree/2021/dec/29/infla tion-price-controls-time-we-use-it.

64 *attributing 50 percent of the increases*: Andrew Gover, José Mustre-del-Rio, and Alice von Ende-Becker, "How Much Have Record Corporate Profits Contributed to Recent Inflation?," Federal Reserve Bank of Kansas City, January 2023.

70 *legacy of the industrial era*: Aiha Nguyen, *The Constant Boss: Labor Under Digital Surveillance* (Data & Society, 2021), https://datasociety.net/wp-content/uploads/2021/05/The_Constant_Boss.pdf.

71 *accept Big Brother's gaze*: Nguyen.

Chapter 3: Convenience

75 *opened in Memphis in 1916*: Mike Freeman, *Clarence Saunders and the Founding of Piggly Wiggly: The Rise and Fall of a Memphis Maverick* (History Press, 2011), 34.

75 *fought in the Civil War*: Freeman, 9.

75 *By age nineteen, he was working*: Freeman, 11.

75 *"dispense with the employment"*: Shane Hamilton, *Supermarket USA: Food and Power in the Cold War Farms Race* (Yale University Press, 2018), 12.

75 *"not with a silver spoon"*: Freeman, *Clarence Saunders*, 24.

75 *"Every customer will be her own clerk"*: Freeman, 27.

75 *she turned and left*: Freeman, 34.

76 *where a clerk handed her the butter*: Freeman, 34.

76 *"every forty-eight seconds"*: Freeman, 34.

76 "*She pays the cashier and away she goes!"*: Freeman, 29.

76 *two more Piggly Wiggly outlets*: Freeman, 35.

80 *tripled the number of cars*: Rhonda F. Levine, *Class Struggle and the New Deal* (University Press of Kansas, 1988), 26.

80 *they quit in droves, forcing Ford*: Levine, 52.

80 *Sylvan Goldman noticed that customers*: Ratha Tep, "How the Shopping Cart Went From Failure to Fixture," History, July 29, 2025, https://www.history.com/articles/shopping-cart-inventor-sylvan-goldman-supermarkets.

80 *"folding basket carriages"*: "Goldman's Folding Basket Carriage," National Museum of American History, https://americanhistory.si.edu/collections/object/nmah_1216280.

80 *tired of pushing babies around*: Lawrence Van Gelder, "Shopping Carts: Carrying the Load Across the U.S.," *New York Times*, October 4, 1975.

81 *"why not you?"*: Mac Macfadyen, "The Rise of the Supermarket," *American Heritage*, October–November 1985.

81 *helped to reduce grocers' overall costs*: Marc Levinson, *The Great A&P and the Struggle for Small Business in America* (Hill and Wang, 2012), 169–170.

82 *workers citing poor treatment and overwork*: David Fuller, Bryan Logan, et al., "How Retailers Can Attract and Retain Frontline Talent amid the Great Attrition," McKinsey and Co., August 17, 2022, https://www.mckinsey.com/industries/retail/our-insights/how-retailers-can-build-and-retain-a-strong-frontline-workforce-in-2024.

86 *no evidence that the machines are faster*: Andrews, *The Overworked Consumer*, 136.

95 *giving up on cashierless systems*: Sam Becker, "It Hasn't Delivered: The Spectacular Failure of Self-Checkout Technology," BBC, January 15, 2024.

95 *attributing as much as 23 percent of losses*: Adrian Beck, "Global Study on Self-Checkout in Retail," ECR Retail Loss, 2022, https://www.ecrloss.com/research/global-study-on-self-checkout-in-retail.

95 *limiting or replacing cashierless checkout*: Christian Oliver, "Walmart Is Replacing Self-Checkout in These States," *Newsweek*, April 19, 2024, https://www.newsweek.com/walmart-replacing-self-checkout-states-1892323.

95 *mandate that stores adequately staff self-checkout*: "Self-Service Checkout Staffing Requirements Ordinance," Long Beach Economic Development," August 12, 2025, https://www.longbeach.gov/edo/self-service-checkout-staffing-requirements-ordinance/.

95 *putting workers in the position of stopping thieves*: "Workers, Community, Applaud Long Beach City Council Action

on Regulating Self-Checkout," UFCW324, June 18, 2025, https://ufcw324.org/workers-community-applaud-long-beach-city-council-action-on-regulating-self-checkout/.

97 *introduced a cashierless supermarket*: Hallie Golden, "'Just Walk Out': Amazon Debuts Its First Supermarket with No Checkout Lines," *The Guardian*, February 27, 2020, https://www.theguardian.com/us-news/2020/feb/25/amazon-go-grocery-supermarket-seattle-technology.

97 *installed in about twenty Amazon stores*: Alina Selyukh, "No More 'Just Walk Out' at Amazon Grocery Stores," NPR, April 3, 2024, https://www.npr.org/2024/04/03/1242508931/no-more-just-walk-out-at-amazon-grocery-stores-the-new-bet-is-smart-shopping-car.

98 *closing physical stores*: Kate King, "Amazon, King of Online Retail, Can't Seem to Make Its Physical Stores Work," *Wall Street Journal*, February 4, 2025.

98 *sensors and cameras that followed their every move*: Selyukh, "No More 'Just Walk Out.'"

98 *other tasks once done by employees*: Ramishah Maruf, "Amazon's Cashier-Less Technology Was Supposed to Revolutionize Grocery Shopping. It's Been a Flop," CNN Business, April 3, 2024, https://www.cnn.com/2024/04/03/business/amazons-self-checkout-technology-grocery-flop.

98 *inserting a key into the display*: Freeman, *Clarence Saunders*, 131.

98 *He called his new shop Keedoozle*: Freeman, 135.

98 *"robot grocery store"*: Freeman, 131.

98 *clean up the mess*: Freeman, 146.

98 *increasing the grocer's labor costs*: Freeman, 140.

98 *decided not to buy at the counter*: Freeman, 140.

98 *he declared bankruptcy*: Freeman, 124.

98 *government seized his assets for unpaid taxes*: Freeman, 147.

99 *"was too much for the average mind to comprehend"*: Freeman, 154.

99 *social nightmare that we are just waking up from*: Daniel Schneider and Kristen Harknett, *Please Wait, Help Is on the Way: Self-Checkout, Understaffing, and Customer Incivility in the Service Sector* (Harvard Kennedy School, 2024), 5.

100 *remained stable over time*: Andrews, *The Overworked Consumer*, 93.

100 *especially serious in stores with self-checkout:* Schneider and Harknett, *Please Wait*, 5.

100 *bad for everyone*: "Self-Checkout Machines Cause Retail Theft and Put Workers in Danger," UFCW Western States Council, August 14, 2024, https://www.ufcwwest.org/self-checkout-machines-cause-retail-theft-and-put-workers-in-danger/.

101 *than on housework, cooking, cleaning, or answering email*: Andrews, *The Overworked Consumer*, 73.

101 *grocery delivery to customers who pay a monthly fee*: Anne D'Innocenzio, "Amazon Expands Same-Day Perishable Grocery Delivery," *Fast Company*, August 13, 2025, https://www.fastcompany.com/91385691/amazon-expands-same-day-perishable-grocery-delivery.

101 *for paying members of its Prime program*: D'Innocenzio.

103 *"life and limb"*: Michael Burawoy, *Manufacturing Consent: Changes in the Labor Process Under Monopoly Capitalism* (University of Chicago Press), 1979, xi.

103 *"face one another in conflict and competition"*: Burawoy, 81.

Chapter 4: Abundance

107 *sales of snacks are through the roof*: Michael Browne, "Super Bowl Is a Boon to Supermarkets," *Supermarket News*, January 23, 2019, https://www.supermarketnews.com/consumer-trends/super-bowl-is-boon-to-supermarkets.

109 *employs more people than any other*: *Food Chain Workers in 2025: Labor and Exploitation in the Food System* (Food Chain Workers Alliance, 2025), 1.

109 *food staffers earn low wages*: *Food Chain Workers in 2025*, 1.

109 *second-highest rate of employee amputations*: *Food Chain Workers in 2025*, 8.

109 *a major producer of the global supply*: Benjamin Lorr, *The Secret Life of Groceries* (Penguin Random House, 2020), 217.

109 *up to 60 percent of Thai shrimp production*: Lorr, 215.

109 *threatened with death*: Lorr, 215.

109 *slept together in a crawl space*: Lorr, 215.

110 *up to 40 percent of food produced*: "Food Waste FAQs," US Department of Agriculture, https://www.usda.gov/about-food/food-safety/food-loss-and-waste/food-waste-faqs.

110 *hundreds of millions around the world go hungry*: "8 Facts to Know About Food Waste and Hunger," World Food Program USA, March 22, 2022, https://wfpusa.org/news/8-facts-to-know-about-food-waste-and-hunger/.

110 *The largest contributor to landfills*: Sengupta, "Inside the Global Effort."

110 *up to 10 percent of greenhouse gas emissions*: Sengupta.

110 *contact with rodents or insects*: "Food Waste FAQs," USDA.

110 *31 percent of waste—or 133 billion pounds*: "The Estimated Amount, Value, and Calories of Postharvest Food Losses at the Retail and Consumer Levels in the United States," USDA, February 2014, https://www.ers.usda.gov/publications/pub-details?pubid=43836.

110 *over-order to create the appearance*: "Food Waste FAQs," USDA.

110 *grown in the global south and then shipped*: Margaret Renkl, "Please Don't Buy Flowers for Valentine's Day," *New York Times*, February 14, 2024.

111 *"environmental crime"*: Renkl.

111 *more damage to the planet than an eight-ounce steak*: Amanda Shendruk, "Why Giving Roses on Valentine's Day—or Any Day—Is a Bad Idea," *Washington Post*, February 12, 2024.

111 *stores advertise pledges to sustainability*: "10 Most Sustainable Grocers of 2025," Progressive Grocer, April 10, 2025, https://progressivegrocer.com/10-most-sustainable-grocers-2025.

112 *a greater environmental impact than other foods*: Graham Readfearn, "Climate Impact of Food Miles Three Times Greater Than Previously Believed," *The Guardian*, June 20, 2022, https://www.theguardian.com/environment/2022/jun/21/climate-impact-of-food-miles-three-times-greater-than-previously-believed-study-finds.

113 *an urban neighborhood with no grocery store*: Michele Ver Ploeg, David Nulph, and Ryan Williams, "Mapping Food Deserts in the United States," USDA, December 1, 2011, https://www.ers.usda.gov/amber-waves/2011/december/data-feature-mapping-food-deserts-in-the-u-s.

113 *In New York City, three million people*: "Can Government Owned Grocery Stores Help Solve America's Food Desert Problem?," Food and Environment Reporting Network, March 24, 2025.

113 *One in four Atlanta residents*: Shannon Jerry, "From Food Deserts to Supermarket Redlining: Making Sense of Food Access in Atlanta," *Atlanta Studies*, August 14, 2018, https://doi.org/10.18737/atls20180814.

113 *half of North Dakota residents*: Stacy Mitchell, "The Great

Grocery Squeeze," *The Atlantic*, December 1, 2024, https://www.theatlantic.com/ideas/archive/2024/12/food-deserts-robinson-patman/680765/.

113 *no store and no car*: Jeremy Ney, "Food Deserts and Inequality," Social Policy Data Lab, January 24, 2022, https://www.socialpolicylab.org/post/grow-your-blog-community.

113 *Black customers are twice as likely*: Ney.

113 *"food apartheid"*: Anna Brones, "Karen Washington: It's Not a Food Desert, It's Food Apartheid," *Guernica Magazine*, May 7, 2018, https://www.guernicamag.com/karen-washington-its-not-a-food-desert-its-food-apartheid/.

113 *paying higher prices for basic goods*: Ney, "Food Deserts and Inequality."

113 *by banning large retailers from cutting prices*: Mitchell, "The Great Grocery Squeeze."

113 *independent grocers flourished across the country*: Mitchell.

113 *Reagan stopped enforcing antitrust laws*: Mitchell.

114 *dismissed the higher-profile case*: "FTC Dismisses Lawsuit Against PepsiCo," Federal Trade Commission, May 22, 2025.

114 *leaving shoppers without a store*: Mitchell.

115 *bags must be used at least three times*: "Paper, Plastic, or Reusable?," *Stanford Magazine*, September 2017, https://stanfordmag.org/contents/paper-plastic-or-reusable.

117 *a machinist named Margaret E. Knight*: "Margaret Knight Invented a Machine That Shapes the Way We Shop," Smithsonian, March 5, 2024, https://womenshistory.si.edu/blog/margaret-knight-invented-machine-shapes-way-we-shop.

117 *worked in a cotton mill*: "Margaret E. Knight: Machine for Making Flat-Bottom Bags," National Inventors Hall of Fame, https://www.invent.org/inductees/margaret-e-knight.

117 *safety mechanism to prevent workplace injuries*: "Margaret E. Knight."

117 *designed the machine that mechanized*: "Margaret Knight Invented a Machine."

117 *Scottish immigrant named Robert Gair*: Matthew Shaer, "Where Does All the Cardboard Come From? I Had to Know," *New York Times*, November 28, 2022.

117 *automate the production of easily foldable boxes*: Shaer.

117 *Individual packages of cereal, crackers*: Lorr, *The Secret Life*, 26.

118 *three-quarters of baggers reported a work-related injury*: Ma Janice J. Gumasing, Yogi Tri Prasetyo, et al., "The Effects of

Biomechanical Risk Factors on Musculoskeletal Disorders Among Baggers in the Supermarket Industry," *Work: A Journal of Prevention, Assessment, and Rehabilitation* 75, no. 1 (2023).

118 *repeat movements at a higher velocity*: Cheryl Fairfield Estill, "Evaluation of Supermarket Bagging Using a Wrist Motion Monitor," *Human Factors: The Journal of the Human Factors and Ergonomics Society* 40, no. 4 (1998): 631.

121 *saw its sales jump 500 percent*: Kellen Browning and Erin Griffith, "Instacart Searches for a Direction as Its Pandemic Boom Fades," *New York Times*, April 29, 2022.

125 *earn less than men even when they do the same jobs*: "Sexism in the Retail Industry," United for Respect, 2024, https://united4respect.org/sexism-retail/.

127 *"by an infinite accumulation"*: Louis, Edouard, *Change* (Farrar, Straus and Giroux, 2024), 269.

Chapter 5: Autonomy

133 *only pay workers when they are absolutely necessary*: Karen Levy and Solon Barocas, "Refractive Surveillance: Monitoring Customers to Manage Workers," *International Journal of Communication* 12 (2018): 8.

133 *sometimes less*: Daniel Schneider and Kristen Harknett, "Hard Times: Routine Schedule Unpredictability and Material Hardship Among Service Workers," *Social Forces*, August 2022, https://pmc.ncbi.nlm.nih.gov/articles/PMC9366729.

133 *with no guarantee of hours*: Schneider and Harknett.

133 *when business picks up again*: Levy, "Refractive Surveillance."

133 *asking for additional shifts from colleagues*: Madison Van Oort, "Wearing Out: Digital Precarity in Just-in-Time Retail" (PhD diss., University of Minnesota, 2018), 89.

133 *Facebook pages to find extra hours*: Esther Kaplan, "The Spy Who Fired Me," *Harper's*, March 2015, https://harpers.org/archive/2015/03/the-spy-who-fired-me/.

133 *assigned to serve shoppers*: Schneider and Harknett, "Hard Times."

133 *creates burdens beyond low pay*: Schneider and Harknett.

133 *falling in and out of eligibility*: Schneider and Harknett.

133 *high-interest financial products*: Schneider and Harknett.

133 *"aren't predictable enough to plan"*: Adelle Waldman, "It's Not Just Wages. Retailers are Mistreating Workers in a More Insidious Way," *New York Times*, February 19, 2024.

134 *childhood depression, sleep disorders, and obesity*: Lynn M. Glynn, "Predictability Can Reduce the Burden of Adverse Childhood Experiences: Policies to Promote It," *Policy Insights from the Behavioral and Brain Sciences* 12, no. 1 (2025): 70.

135 *a phenomenon the media referred*: Ann Larson, "'The Great Resignation' Is a Great Exaggeration," *The Nation*, April 18, 2022, https://www.thenation.com/article/economy/great-resignation-workers/.

136 *reported sleep problems and unhappiness*: Daniel Schneider and Kristen Harknett, "Consequences of Routine Work Instability for Worker Health and Wellbeing," *American Social Review*, February 2019, https://pubmed.ncbi.nlm.nih.gov/33311716/.

136 *"what you're actually selling is your life"*: Barbara Ehrenreich, *Nickel and Dimed: On (Not) Getting by in America* (Picador, 2011), 187.

137 *housecleaning jobs that didn't pay her enough*: Stephanie Land, *Maid: Hard Work, Low Pay, and a Mother's Will to Survive* (Hachette Books, 2019).

140 "*perceptual illusions*": Dan Zakay, "Psychological Time as Information: The Case of Boredom," *Frontiers in Psychology*, August 2014, https://www.frontiersin.org/journals/psychology/articles/10.3389/fpsyg.2014.00917/full.

141 *fight-or-flight reaction to a hazardous situation*: Virginie Van Wassenhove, Marc Wittman, et al., "Psychological and Neural Mechanisms of Subjective Time Dilation," *Frontiers in Neuroscience*, April 25, 2011, https://pmc.ncbi.nlm.nih.gov/articles/PMC3085178/.

141 *experiences that deprive us of stimulation*: Andra Geana, Robert C. Wilson, et al., "Boredom, Information-Seeking and Exploration," *Proceedings of the Annual Meeting of the Cognitive Science Society*, 2016: 1754.

141 *"buddy punching"*: Van Oort, "Wearing Out," 106.

142 *how long call center staffers are on the phone*: Kaplan, "The Spy."

142 *rash of back and shoulder surgeries at UPS*: Kaplan.

142 *track warehouse workers' exact location*: "Amazon Warehouse Workers to Get State of the Art Augmented Reality Equipment. Now They Might Get More Bathroom Breaks," Patent Yogi, 2018, https://patentyogi.com/latest-patents

/amazon/amazon-warehouse-workers-to-get-state-of-the-art-augmented-reality-equipment-now-they-might-get-more-bathroom-breaks/.

143 *Identimation (now called G4S)*: Van Oort, "Wearing Out," 91.

143 *protected the Dakota Access Pipeline*: Van Oort, 91–92.

143 *since 2003, it has provided security*: "Contract to G4S Secure Solutions," USAspending.gov, https://www.usaspending.gov/award/CONT_AWD_ACD00200303DACD3C0008_7012_-NONE-_-NONE-.

143 *monitored their movements*: Karen Levy, *Data Driven: Truckers, Technology, and the New Workplace Surveillance* (Princeton University Press, 2022), 95.

143 *covering the transmitter with tinfoil*: Levy, 98.

143 *manually entering their time*: Van Oort, "Wearing Out," 130.

145 *up to thirty days per year along with paid holidays*: Adewale Maye, "No-Vacation Nation, Revised," Center for Economic and Policy Research, May 22, 2019, https://cepr.net/publications/no-vacation-nation-revised/.

145 *on the economy's bottom rungs*: Adewale.

145 *the less likely they are to get paid time off*: Adewale.

148 *"infantilized dependency"*: Philip Hancock, "Employee Recognition Programs: An Immanent Critique," *Organization* 31, no. 2 (March 2022).

148 *see themselves as failures*: Hancock.

149 *"their own desires and ambitions"*: Hancock.

152 *those that are rare or strange*: William J. Matthews and Ana I. Gheorghiu, "Repetition, Expectation, and the Perception of Time," *Current Opinion in Behavioral Sciences* 8, April 2016: 110–16.

153 *the kid offers Tom an apple*: "Tom Sawyer Whitewashing the Fence," chapter 2 in *The Adventures of Tom Sawyer* (Dover Thrift, 1998).

153 *"the slaughter of innocents"*: "Tom Sawyer Whitewashing."

Chapter 6: Choice

160 *feelings of regret and inadequacy and even depression*: Barry Schwartz, *The Paradox of Choice: Why Less Is More* (Ecco, 2016), 5.

160 *promise to help bewildered consumers decide*: Margaret Sanger-Katz, "It's Not Just You: Picking a Health Insurance Plan Is Really Hard," *New York Times*, December 11, 2020.

163 *"feel crazy"*: Madison Van Oort, *How Retailers Surveil and Exploit Workers in the Digital Age and How Workers are Fighting Back* (MIT Press, 2023), 93.

164 *participating in an elaborate illusion*: *The Economic Cost of Food Monopolies: The Grocery Cartels* (Food and Water Watch, 2021), 5.

164 *almost 80 percent of all pasta products*: Nina Lakhani, Aliya Uteuova, and Alvin Chang, "Revealed: The True Extent of America's Food Monopolies, and Who Pays the Price," *The Guardian*, July 2021, https://www.theguardian.com/environment/ng-interactive/2021/jul/14/food-monopoly-meals-profits-data-investigation.

164 *control two-thirds of the market*: *Economic Cost of Food Monopolies*, 17.

164 *about three-quarters of yogurt sold*: *Economic Cost of Food Monopolies*, 5.

164 *70 percent of beer sold*: Patrick Woodall and Tyler L. Shannon, "Monopoly Power Corrodes Choice and Resiliency in the Food System," *Antitrust Bulletin* 63, no. 2 (2018): 11.

164 *seventeen craft beer makers*: Lakhani, Uteuova, and Chang, "Revealed."

164 *same company that distributes Budweiser*: Woodall and Shannon, "Monopoly Power," 11.

164 *Ninety-three percent of the soda*: Lakhani, Uteuova, and Chang, "Revealed."

164 *Dasani, Smartwater, Vitaminwater, Minute Maid, and Simply*: *Economic Cost of Food Monopolies*, 11.

164 *PepsiCo owns Tropicana and Aquafina*: *Economic Cost of Food Monopolies*, 10–11.

165 *Fritos, Lay's, and Tostitos*: *Economic Cost of Food Monopolies*, 5.

165 *Whiskas, Pedigree, Sheba, and Cesar*: Luisa Beltran, "Candy Maker Mars Is the Biggest Vet Provider in the Country: Inside Its Sprawling Operation," *Fortune*, June 10, 2024, https://fortune.com/2024/06/10/mars-candy-snickers-pet-care-vet-clinics-petsmart-private-equity/.

165 *operated sixteen thousand grocery stores*: Marc Levinson, *The Great A&P and the Struggle for Small Business in America* (Hill and Wang, 2012), 109.

165 *"grandma"*: Levinson, 2.

165 *John Updike needed a name*: Levinson, 2.

165 *the largest retailer in the world*: Levinson, 1.
165 *opened a coffee-importing business*: Levinson, 91.
165 *became a bestseller*: Levinson, 92.
165 *in competition with other milk suppliers*: Levinson, 92.
165 *precision bread-delivery system*: Levinson, 92.
165 *salmon, producing peanut butter, and more*: Levinson, 93.
166 *asked a judge to order its breakup*: Levinson, 242.
166 *pressure food manufacturers to give it*: Levinson, 229.
166 *declined to sell its products*: Levinson, 229.
166 *put manufacturers out of business*: Levinson, 243.
166 *laws against the bullying tactics*: Stacy Mitchell, "The Policy Shift That Decimated Local Grocery Stores," Institute for Local Self-Reliance, November 26, 2024, https://ilsr.org/article/independent-business/policy-shift-local-grocery/.
166 *a chain or a locally owned competitor*: Woodall and Shannon, "Monopoly Power," 5.
166 *around two-thirds of all grocery sales*: *Economic Cost of Food Monopolies*, 1.
166 *we are patronizing Kroger*: "Kroger Family of Companies," Kroger, https://www.kroger.com/i/kroger-family-of-companies.
166 *all owned by Albertsons*: "About ACI," Albertsons Companies, https://www.albertsonscompanies.com/about-aci/overview/default.aspx.
166 *Californians who flock to Foods Co.*: "Kroger Family of Companies."
166 *they are shopping at Kroger*: "Kroger and Murray's Cheese Announce Merger," Kroger, https://ir.kroger.com/news/news-details/2017/Kroger-and-Murrays-Cheese-Announce-Merger/default.aspx.
166 *about 13 percent more for groceries*: Errol Schweizer, "How Profit Inflation Made Your Groceries So Damn Expensive," *Forbes*, September 12, 2022, https://www.forbes.com/sites/errolschweizer/2022/09/12/how-profit-inflation-made-your-groceries-so-damn-expensive/.
166 *simply passing on their increased costs*: Catherine Rampell, "An Inflation Conspiracy Theory That Is Infecting the Democratic Party," *Washington Post*, May 12, 2022.
167 *raised prices by up to 30 percent*: Veronica Riccobene, "Big Food, Big Profits, Big Lies," *The Lever*, June 3, 2024, https://www.levernews.com/big-food-big-profits-big-lies/.
167 *profits explode more than 700 percent*: Chris Isidore, "High

Egg Prices Send Profits at Largest Producer Soaring More Than 700%," CNN, March 29, 2023, https://edition.cnn.com/2023/03/29/business/egg-profits-cal-maine.

167 *Retailers' profits also spiked*: Errol Schweizer, "How Profit Inflation Made Your Groceries."

167 *Kroger offered buybacks to shareholders*: Schweizer.

170 *racial discrimination in job assignment and pay*: Martha Ross and Nicole Bateman, *Meet the Low-Wage Workforce* (Brookings Institute, 2019), 42.

171 *"turn alienation into connection" and "oppression into strength"*: Astra Taylor and Leah-Hunt Hendrix, "Solidarity and Strategy: The Forgotten Lessons of Truly Effective Protest," *The Guardian*, March 14, 2024, https://www.theguardian.com/world/2024/mar/14/solidarity-and-strategy-the-forgotten-lessons-of-truly-effective-protest.

171 *"You have a responsibility to live"*: Eve L. Ewing, "Mariame Kaba, Everything Worthwhile Is Done with Other People," *ADI Magazine*, Fall 2019, https://adimagazine.com/articles/mariame-kaba-everything-worthwhile-is-done-with-other-people/.

173 *if a worker cut themselves while sawing up a side of beef*: According to OSHA, in 2013, at least four thousand workers were injured in incidents involving meat and food slicers. See the report: "Preventing Cuts and Amputations from Food Slicers and Meet Grinders," OSHA, Fact Sheet, https://www.osha.gov/sites/default/files/publications/OSHA3794.pdf.

179 *entrepreneur behind Piggly Wiggly*: Mike Freeman, *Clarence Saunders and the Founding of Piggly Wiggly* (History Press, 2019), 21–22.

179 *walkable aisles presented a theft risk*: Freeman, 33.

179 *separate entrances and exits and gates*: Freeman, 40.

184 *misclassify hourly workers as managers*: Lauren Cohen, Umit Gurun, et al., "Too Many Managers: The Strategic Use of Titles to Avoid Overtime Payments," NBER Working Paper, May 25, 2025.

184 *employers steal billions each year*: David Cooper and Teresa Kroeger, "Employers Steal Billions from Workers' Paychecks Each Year," Economic Policy Institute, May 10, 2027, https://www.epi.org/publication/employers-steal-billions-from-workers-paychecks-each-year/.

184 *robbery or other street crimes*: "Wage Theft Costs American Workers as Much as $50 Billion a Year," Economic Policy

Institute, September 11, 2014, https://www.epi.org/press/wage-theft-costs-american-workers-50-billion/.

184 *rolled back efforts to protect workers from the crime*: "President Trump's Policies Are Hurting American Workers," Center for American Progress, January 26, 2018, https://www.americanprogress.org/article/president-trumps-policies-hurting-american-workers/.

184 *twenty-three companies they accused of wage theft*: "Warren, Brown Open Investigation into 23 Companies' Overtime Avoidance Practices and Possible Wage Theft," Elizabeth Warren Senate website, June 28, 2023, https://www.warren.senate.gov/oversight/letters/warren-brown-open-investigation-into-23-companies-overtime-avoidance-practices-and-possible-wage-theft.

184 *enable the Department of Labor to enforce the law*: "Trump's Department of Labor Continues its Onslaught Against Workers," Century Foundation, July 22, 2025, https://tcf.org/content/commentary/trumps-department-of-labor-continues-its-onslaught-against-workers/.

Chapter 7: Solidarity

197 *desperate for affordable food*: Andrew F. Smith, *Eating History: Turning Points in the Making of American Cuisine* (Columbia University Press, 2009), 175.

197 *as many as one thousand products*: Smith, 178.

197 *Jamaica Estates, Queens*: Smith, 175.

197 *top employee at A&P*: Smith, 177.

197 *"Pile it high and sell it cheap"*: Sylvie Rosen, "The World's Greatest Price Wreckers: The Rise of American Supermarkets in the 1930s" (thesis, Columbia University, April 2019), 33.

197 *"15,000 housewives"*: Rosen, 32.

197 *bare-bones space with fewer employees*: Dominick Luis Fortugno, "Wal-mart vs. the Supermarket Chains and the Fight for the American Retail Food Industry" (thesis, Empire State College Thesis, 2006), 13.

197 *Cullen owned fifteen outlets*: Smith, *Eating History*, 178.

198 *if it meant saving money*: Max Mandell Zimmerman, *The Supermarket: A Revolution in Distribution* (McGraw Hill, 1955), 52.

198 *a fad that would not last*: Zimmerman, 45.

198 *transitioned to the one-stop-shop model*: Smith, *Eating History*, 178.

198 *1,200 supermarkets across the country*: Zimmerman, *The Supermarket*, 69.

198 *mom and pops closed their doors*: Smith, *Eating History*, 178.

198 *clashed with police*: Rhonda F. Levine, *Class Struggle and the New Deal: Industrial Labor, Industrial Capital, and the State* (University of Kansas Press, 1988), 53.

198 *raided food warehouses, looted supermarkets, and declared hunger strikes*: Levine, 52.

198 *pressured President Franklin Delano Roosevelt*: Levine, 52–53.

199 *carry weapons virtually anywhere*: Utah Code Section 102.2, "Open and Concealed Carry of a Firearm Outside of an Individual's Residence," May 7, 2025.

200 *exits were blocked to stop employees*: "The Triangle Shirtwaist Factory Fire," OSHA, US Department of Labor, March 2011, https://www.osha.gov/aboutosha/40-years/trianglefactoryfire.

201 *workplace violence is on the rise overall*: Scott A. Hendricks, Kitty J. Hendricks, et al., "Trends in Workplace Homicides in the U.S., 1994–2021: An End to Years of Decline," *American Journal of Industrial Medicine*, December 8, 2023, 563.

201 *leading cause of death on the job*: Emma Cohn and Nina Mast, *Workplace Health and Safety Standards: State Solutions to the US Worker Rights Crisis* (Economic Policy Institute, 2025), 7.

201 *most "active shooter" situations happen in stores*: *Active Shooter Incidents in the United States in 2021* (Federal Bureau of Investigation, 2022), 13.

201 *shot ten people to death*: Andi Babineau and Zoe Sottile, "Gunman Who Killed Ten at Colorado Grocery Store Sentenced to Life Without Parole," CNN, September 23, 2024, https://www.cnn.com/2024/09/23/us/king-soopers-boulder-shooting-trial-verdict.

201 *killed twenty-three people at a Walmart*: Morgan Lee and Jamie Stengle, "Gunman in Racist Attack at a Texas Walmart Pleads Guilty and Families Confront Him in Court," AP, April 24, 2025, https://www.ap.org/news-highlights/spotlights/2025/gunman-in-racist-attack-at-a-texas-walmart-pleads-guilty-and-families-confront-him-in-court/.

201 *white supremacist shot ten people*: "Gunman Who Killed Ten Black People in N.Y. Supermarket Wants Federal Charges Dropped, Says Grand Jury Was Too White," NBC News, August 14, 2025, https://www.nbcnews.com/news/us-news/gunman-killed-10-black-people-ny-supermarket-wants-charges-dropped-say-rcna225134.

201 *silent alarms and training for active shooter attacks*: "Retail Worker Safety Act Signed into Law by Governor Hochul," RWDSU, September 4, 2024, https://www.rwdsu.org/news/retail-worker-safety-act-signed-into-law.

204 *income loss leads to depression and anxiety*: Daniel Kim, "Financial Hardship and Social Assistance as Determinants of Mental Health and Food and Housing Insecurity During the COVID-19 Pandemic in the United States," *SSM Population Health*, 2021: 5.

204 *eviction moratorium, child tax credits, and expanded relief*: Patrick Cooney and Luke H. Shaefer, *Material Hardship and Mental Health Following the Covid-19 Relief Bill* (University of Michigan Poverty Solutions, 2021), 2.

206 *mental health crises have been on the rise since 2020*: Lindsey Culli, "Nearly 1 in 10 Adults in the US Experienced a Mental Health Crisis Last Year," Johns Hopkins School of Public Health, August 19, 2025.

206 *"young worker":* David G. Blanchflower and Alex Bryson, "Rising Young Worker Despair in the United States," NBER Working Paper Series, July 2025.

Conclusion: Dignity

221 *scrapped a few months later*: Michael Corkery, "'Hero' Pay Raises Disappear for Many Workers," *New York Times*, July 14, 2020.

221 *Large retailers have seen record profits*: Isabella Simonetti and Julie Creswell, "Food Prices Soar, and So Do Companies' Profits," *New York Times*, November 1, 2022.

221 *since 2024, their wages have declined 15 percent*: Pavithra Mohan, "Kroger and Albertsons Cut Worker Hours: A New Report Looks at the Impact to Workers," *Fast Company*, May 9, 2025, https://www.fastcompany.com/91330323/kroger-and-albertsons-cut-worker-hours-a-new-report-looks-at-the-impact-to-workers.

221 *"shift from high-wage manufacturing jobs"*: Nelson Lichtenstein, *A Fabulous Failure: The Clinton Presidency and the Transformation of American Capitalism* (Princeton University Press, 2023).

222 *direct result of public policy*: Jeff Faux, "NAFTA, Twenty Years After," Economic Policy Institute, January 3, 2014, https://www.epi.org/blog/nafta-twenty-years-disaster/.

222 *shameful $7.25 for more than fifteen years*: Sebastian Mar-

tinez Hickey and Ismael Cid-Martinez, "The Federal Minimum Wage is Officially a Poverty Wage," Economic Policy Institute, April 28, 2025, https://www.epi.org/blog/the-federal-minimum-wage-is-officially-a-poverty-wage-in-2025/.

222 *benefiting all low-income workers*: "Why the US Needs At Least a $17 Minimum Wage," National Employment Law Project, July 31, 2023, https://www.nelp.org/insights-research/why-the-us-needs-at-least-a-17-minimum-wage/.

223 *closures spiked in 2025*: Hugh Cameron, "Store Closures on Track to Far Exceed 2024 Levels," *Newsweek*, July 11, 2025, https://www.newsweek.com/store-closures-exceed-2024-levels-2096509.

223 "*retail apocalypse*": Bethany Biron, "The Last Decade was Devastating for the Retail Industry. Here's How the Retail Apocalypse Played Out," *Business Insider*, December 23, 2019, https://www.businessinsider.com/retail-apocalypse-last-decade-timeline-2019-12.

223 *employers can be penalized for unpredictable scheduling*: George Morrison, "The High Stakes of Fair Workweek Compliance for Grocers," Progressive Grocer, April 22, 2024, https://progressivegrocer.com/high-stakes-fair-workweek-compliance-grocers.

223 *also improve employees' mental health*: Morrison.

224 *banning the use of information collected from electronic systems*: Aiha Nguyen, *The Constant Boss: Labor Under Digital Surveillance* (Data & Society, 2021), 54, https://datasociety.net/wp-content/uploads/2021/05/The_Constant_Boss.pdf.

225 *plans to replace price tags on shelves with electronic labels*: Jenn McMillen, "Walmart, Kroger and Whole Foods Use Digital Pricing. What Customers Should Know," *Forbes*, September 9, 2024, https://www.forbes.com/sites/jennmcmillen/2024/09/09/walmart-kroger-and-whole-foods-use-digital-pricing-what-customers-should-know/.

225 *price of water might go up in a drought*: "Warren, Casey Investigate Kroger's Use of Digital Price Tags, Warn of Grocery Giant's 'Surge Pricing' Causing Price Gouging and Hurting Customers," Elizabeth Warren Senate website, August 7, 2024, https://www.warren.senate.gov/newsroom/press-releases/warren-casey-investigate-krogers-use-of-digital-price-tags-warn-of-grocery-giants-surge-pricing-causing-price-gouging-and-hurting-consumers.

225 *Stores have rejected those concerns*: Sara Ruberg, "Kroger and

Walmart Deny 'Surge Pricing' After Adopting Digital Price Tags," *New York Times*, October 23, 2024.

225 *"keeping us all working"*: David Graeber, "On the Phenomenon of Bullshit Jobs: A Work Rant," *Strike!*, August 2013.

226 *those who do not belong to a union*: Richa Naidu, "Insight: Retail Workers in Unions Reap Higher Wages Even as U.S. Organizers Suffer Setbacks," Reuters, July 9, 2021, https://www.reuters.com/business/retail-workers-unions-reap-higher-wages-even-us-organizers-suffer-setbacks-2021-07-09/.

226 *make it easier for employees to organize*: "The PRO Act and Right to Work," AFL-CIO, https://proact.aflcio.org/the-pro-act-and-right-to-work/.

226 *2015 acquisition of Safeway by Albertsons*: "Albertsons and Safeway Complete Merger Transaction," PR Newswire, January 2015, https://www.prnewswire.com/news-releases/albertsons-and-safeway-complete-merger-transaction-300028412.html.

226 *Amazon's purchase of Whole Foods two years later*: Nick Wingfield and Michael J. de la Merced, "Amazon to Buy Whole Foods for $13.4 Billion," *New York Times*, June 2017.

226 *three hundred grocery industry mergers*: *The Economic Cost of Food Monopolies: The Grocery Cartels* (Food and Water Watch, 2021), 2.

226 *suppressed wages, higher prices, and the elimination*: Brendan Ballou, "Private Equity Is Gutting America and Getting Away with It," *New York Times*, April 28, 2023; Cara Brumfield et al., *Concentrated Power, Concentrated Harm: Market Power's Role in Creating and Amplifying Racial and Economic Inequality* (Georgetown Center on Poverty and Inequality, 2022).

227 *Customers joined with their neighbors*: Lynn Pitman, *History of Cooperatives in the United States* (Center for Cooperatives, 2018), 2.

227 *earned points toward the purchase of goods*: Jonathan Rowe, "Cooperative Economy in the Great Depression," *Yes! Magazine*, May 8, 2006, https://jonathanrowe.org/money-cooperative-economy-in-the-great-depression.

227 *the mantra "Food for people, not profit"*: Jon Steinman, "Grocery Story: How Food Co-ops Transformed an Industry," PCC Community Markets, July 2020, https://www.pccmarkets.com/sound-consumer/2020-07/grocery-story-how-food-co-ops-transformed-an-industry/.

227 *"solidarity economy"*: Anca Voinea, "Jessica Gordon-Nembhard on Past Lessons for Economic Empowerment," NCBA, July2020,https://ncbaclusa.coop/blog/jessica-gordon-nembhard-on-past-lessons-for-economic-empowerment/.

227 *saw community stores as part of a project of racial liberation*: Steven Dubb and Jessica Gordon Nembhard, "The Past and Future of Black Co-ops," *Nonprofit Quarterly*, December 2024, https://nonprofitquarterly.org/the-past-and-future-of-black-co-ops-a-conversation-with-jessica-gordon-nembhard/.

227 *From Florida to Kansas*: Steve Dubb, "Socialism American-Style Hits Baldwin, Florida," *Nonprofit Quarterly*, November 2019, https://nonprofitquarterly.org/socialism-american-style-hits-baldwin-fl/.

227 *municipalities have opened stores*: Omar Ocampo and Maya Khadr, "How City-Owned Grocery Stores Can Tackle Food Insecurity," Inequality.org, August 5, 2025, https://inequality.org/article/how-city-owned-grocery-stores-can-tackle-food-insecurity/.

227 *focus on accessibility and affordability*: Ocampo and Khadr.

227 *Officials in Atlanta*: "City of Atlanta Partners with Invest Atlanta Board to Approve $8.1 Million To Help Establish Two Grocery Stores with Fresh Food Options in Food Deserts," InvestAtlanta, December 19, 2024, https://www.investatlanta.com/about-us/news-press/city-of-atlanta-partners-with-invest-atlanta-board-to-approve-81-million-to-help-establish-two-grocery-stores-with-fresh-food-options-in-food-deserts.

227 *Minneapolis city council is considering*: Babs Santos, "Minneapolis Leaders Explore City-Owned Grocery Store," Fox 9, July 14, 2025, https://www.fox9.com/news/minneapolis-city-council-explores-city-owned-grocery-store.

227 *city-owned outlets to address food insecurity*: Bryce Covert, "One Way to Fight Rising Food Prices: Public Grocery Stores," *The New Republic*, March 24, 2025.

227 *lack the market power of Kroger or Albertsons*: Stacy Mitchell, "The Policy Shift That Decimated Local Grocery Stores," Institute for Local Self Reliance, November 26, 2024, https://ilsr.org/article/independent-business/policy-shift-local-grocery/.

228 *"All labor has dignity"*: "The 50th Anniversary of Martin Luther King Jr's 'All Labor Has Dignity,'" *Beacon Broadside*, March 2018.

About the Author

Ann Larson is a writer and activist focused on economic justice. Her writing has appeared in *The Nation*, *The New Republic*, *The Chronicle of Higher Education*, and *Fast Company*, among other publications. She is the author of *Cleanup on Aisle Five* and the coauthor of *Can't Pay, Won't Pay: The Case for Economic Disobedience and Debt Abolition*. She is a cofounder of the Debt Collective and a Fellow with the Economic Hardship Reporting Project.